THE USE AND ABUSE OF THE BIBLE

THE USE AND ABUSE OF THE BIBLE

A BRIEF HISTORY OF BIBLICAL INTERPRETATION

HENRY WANSBROUGH

t&t clark

Published by T&T Clark International
A Continuum Imprint
The Tower Building,   80 Maiden Lane,
11 York Road,   Suite 704,
London SE1 7NX   New York, NY 10038

www.continuumbooks.com

Henry Wansbrough has asserted his right under the Copyright, Designs and Patents
Act, 1988, to be identified as the Author of this work.

British Library Cataloguing-in-Publication Data
A catalogue record for this book is available from the British Library

ISBN: 978-0-567-56933-2 (Hardback)
            978-0-567-09057-7 (Paperback)

Typeset by Pindar NZ, Auckland, New Zealand
Printed and bound in Great Britain by CPI Antony Rowe Ltd,
Chippenham, Wiltshire

Contents

Foreword

Some years ago I was much struck by Frances Young's *The Art of Performance*. In a series of illuminating lectures the author likens the Scripture to a musical score which can be faithfully performed in a variety of ways. What is an authentic performance of a great classic? Should Handel's *Messiah* be performed with baroque instruments and techniques that were in use in 1742? Handel himself made changes to the oratorio in the decade after its first performance. Should the version thus changed be considered the authentic version, or should Handel's reasons for making the changes (for instance, to satisfy the disgruntled author of the libretto) be first assessed? Frances Young writes of a 1986 performance of *Romeo and Juliet* in modern dress, with Montagues and Capulets as rival street gangs. What would be the criteria for deciding whether this was an authentic performance? Is Jean Anouilh's reading of the Antigone myth more authentic than that of Sophocles, or is each of them equally valid?

Which Bible?

In recent decades interest in the continuing life, or reception history, of biblical texts has increased. It is no longer sufficient to search out the original meaning of texts. Awareness has increased that biblical texts were read and re-read, and that as they were read and re-read the texts themselves developed and their application changed. Prophecies originally uttered with application to the threat of the Assyrian advance in the eighth century BC were adjusted to apply to the Babylonian threat in the seventh. The prophet Amos has nine chapters of sheer threat of doom and disaster, without any ray of light. To these were later added five verses of hope and promise, which quite change the outlook of the prophecy as a whole.

A 'canonical reading' – that is, a reading of a biblical passage in the light of the whole canon of Scripture – may give a biblical passage a sense different to that intended by its first human author. In which

sense should it be read? In either or both? If the New Testament
gives a passage a sense different from that in which it was originally
pronounced (for instance, the famous prophecy of Isa. 7.14, used by
Mt. 1.23 to interpret the virgin birth of Jesus), is that the 'real' meaning? Handel's *Messiah* is again relevant here, for the texts were chosen
by the librettist, Charles Jennens, to underline the stubbornness of
the Jews in not accepting the obvious sense of their own scriptures. Is
this messianic meaning really so obvious and so compelling? Is it the
authentic sense?

Further problems arise through the development of septuagintal
studies. For many centuries – basically since St Jerome was bullied by
the mockery of Jewish rabbis into preference for the Hebrew Bible, but
certainly since the Protestant Reformation – it has often been held that
the authentic text of the Old Testament was the Hebrew Bible, and that
this was older and generally more reliable than the Greek translation
known as the Septuagint. However, the Septuagint was valued for many
instances of development in revelation and theology over and above the
'original' Hebrew text. A position now more common among scholars is
that variations from the Hebrew text in the Septuagint may represent a
textual tradition parallel to and perhaps older than the Hebrew text as
we have it now. The oldest extant full text of the Hebrew Bible is, after
all, the Aleppo Codex dating from the tenth century AD.

What is the Bible?

One of the outstanding achievements of the Second Vatican Council
was its teaching on Scripture. Two points may be stressed. *Dei Verbum*
(one of the principal documents of the Council, which focuses on
Scripture) brought firmly to the forefront the purpose of revelation: it
was God's loving self-gift, an offer of friendship and a gift that demanded
a response in love and friendship. The purpose of the whole Bible is to
show, in myriad different ways, a rich and varied interrelationship: the
ways of God to his human creatures, and the ways – sometimes fervent,
sometimes grateful, sometimes reluctant, sometimes errant – of human
creatures to their God. The purpose of the Bible is not to teach history
or science or politics; on these topics it is often inaccurate. Its purpose
is to help us understand the God-given and God-sustained position of
human beings in the world. At the same time Vatican II put an end,
once and for all, to the debate about the two sources of revelation, a
debate which pointed up a fundamental divergence between Roman
Catholics and Protestants. There were not to be two sources of revelation, as in Judaism, where the two sources consist in the written and oral
Torah (*torah she katub* and *torah she be al-pe*), both claiming descent from
Moses. For Catholic Christians there was but one source, the Scripture

as seen through the eyes of the Church and taught by the Church. The knowledge and understanding of how Scripture has been read in the Church is therefore an important factor in coming to an appreciation of divine revelation.

The official teachers of the Church are held to be the successors of the Apostles. This does not mean they are the only teachers; it is their function to guide and encourage others in their search for the truth. The whole priestly people of God share in the prophetic function of preserving and deepening the understanding of revelation. 'The Holy Spirit distributes special graces among the faithful of every rank, ena- bling them to undertake various tasks or offices for the renewal of the Church.'[1] This includes scholars and students of every hue. Nor does the Catholic Church hold that these 'special graces' are distributed by the Holy Spirit only to those who are within the visible bounds of the Catholic Church. Insights into the divine revelation can be, and are, gleaned from everywhere, but especially from those of the three great Abrahamic faiths, including Judaism and Islam.

There have been many ways in which the Scriptures have been interpreted in Christianity and on its fringes. It is the purpose of this book to capture some of these. No claim to complete coverage can be made; I have simply selected authors or moments that are either my favourites or seem to me to have special interest or importance. Not all of them have contributed to the true understanding of divine revela- tion, for sometimes the Scriptures have been used as a stick to beat a hobby-horse or – worse – a drum. On the whole, the words of the lover to his beloved in Song 4.3 may be applied:

> Yours lips are a scarlet thread
> And your words enchanting.

The scarlet thread does not always run straight. No more did Ariadne's, but it eventually guided Theseus out of the labyrinth.

Working eclectically, but chronologically, we first study the use of the Old Testament in the New. Most of the authors of the books of the New Testament were Jewish, and it was to be expected that they would use the Scriptures according to the current practices of argument and proof within Judaism, practising the same methods as we find in other first-century Jewish writing. The same is, of course, true of Jesus's own use of Scripture. The second chapter leaps over the important Apostolic Fathers and the apologists, choosing for the second century two highly dissimilar writers. One of these is Melito of Sardis, chosen for his lyric exegesis of the text of the Passion. The other is Irenaeus of Lyons, with whom, at the end of a century of chaotic experimentation, the concept of orthodoxy begins to be formed, and who shows at least pockets of steady, scientific exegesis. Then comes another pair (but in separate chapters); first the great Origen, often acclaimed as the greatest Scripture scholar of the ancient Church, but eclipsed because after his death he was unjustifiably accused of heresy. Origen handed the baton to the irascible and contentious figure of Jerome, that great classicist who gave the Western Church much of its Latin Bible. No survey in English (and certainly none from the north of England) could omit the learning and humour of the beloved Venerable Bede, often regarded as the last of the Fathers. For the high Middle Ages two contrasting figures have been chosen; Bernard of Clairvaux may be regarded as the climax of monastic formation through the Bible, and Thomas Aquinas – more often celebrated as a systematic theologian, but in reality a thoughtful exponent of the Bible – as the initiator of modern biblical study. The equal share of women in the Church must never be forgotten, and the discussion of the Bible in the Middle Ages concludes with the central-ity of the Bible in the mysticism of two remarkable and very different women from Norfolk, Julian of Norwich and Margery Kempe.

This brings us to the Reformation and the brilliant but sometimes maverick exegesis of Martin Luther in his spirited struggle against the unyielding forces of Rome. Still in the era of the Reformation, and after an interlude for the political use of the Bible in early seventeenth-century England and the genesis of the great King James Version, the brothers John and Charles Wesley are seen using the Bible in their enthusiastic revival of religion in the early days of the Industrial Revolution. Finally come two modern studies, on the manipulation of the Bible in support of the modern State of Israel and on the develop-ment of biblical prayer in *lectio divina*.

I am grateful for the support of many friends during this project, and especially Dominic Mattos, Senior Editor for Biblical Studies at T&T Clark/Continuum, not least for his insistence that *Balaam's Ass* would not be a suitable title for the book.

CHAPTER 1

The Interpretation of the Old Testament in the New

Introduction

In order to understand the use and interpretation of the Bible in the New Testament, the best starting point is the use of the Bible within Judaism. The Bible[1] was the only authoritative work within Judaism. The Bible itself did not, of course, yet exist, for no decision had been made about a 'canon' of Scripture, nor about which books among the sacred writings were normative and which were not. The expression within Judaism was books that 'soil the hands', since the sacred books (or rather the sacred scrolls) were so sacred that it was necessary to wash before and after touching them. There were sacred books in circulation other than those that were eventually settled as being those that 'soil the hands'. For instance, the New Testament Letter of Jude quotes and makes use of the *Book of Henoch* and the *Assumption of Moses*, books that were highly revered, but which were not eventually included in either the Jewish or the Christian canon of Scripture. By far, the most authoritative books were the Pentateuch, the first five books of the Bible or the Torah. In his copious works explaining Judaism to the Graeco-Roman world, the first-century Jewish philosopher Philo quotes overwhelmingly from the Torah. An index of his references gives 65 pages of references to the Pentateuch and 5 pages to the rest of the Bible. The proportion of references in the New Testament to the Old Testament is similar, with significant differences: a 40-column index gives 12 columns of references to the Pentateuch, but the Psalms (5 columns) and Isaiah (6 columns) have gained a significantly more important position in the Christian use of the Old Testament. This will remain important in Christianity.

Within Judaism, the technique of understanding the Bible may best be described as *midrash*, a noun derived from the Hebrew verb *darash* (to seek). It is therefore understood as an investigation, seeking out the meaning of the biblical text. There are two sorts of *midrash*:

1

midrash halakhah and *midrash haggadah.* These correspond roughly to
the imperative and the indicative, respectively: the former tells us what
to do, the latter describes how things are. The former is derived from
the verb *halakh* (to walk), and consists of formulating rules of conduct
or legal rulings; the latter, derived from the verb meaning 'to tell, to
narrate', elaborates on the stories of the Bible in order to bring out
the points the teller considers important for the understanding of the
text and of life.

Two further factors in the current Jewish interpretation of the Bible
must also hold an important place. These are the interpretation of the
Bible in the writings of Qumran, the so-called Dead Sea Scrolls, and in
the use of the Bible in the apocalyptic writings circulating in Judaism
in the first century. Both of these are especially important to us, for
both they and the Christian writings stem from eschatological communities. Both the Qumran and the Christian community were strongly
eschatological in that both were centred upon the conviction that God
was about to bring history to its climax by a decisive intervention. The
Qumran community were waiting for this to occur and the Christian
community were convinced that it had already occurred in the ministry,
death and resurrection of Jesus. Jesus's whole teaching was centred
upon the kingship, reign or sovereignty of God. He came to proclaim
and effect its renewal. This was the decisive moment of history, the
climax of God's preparation of Israel. No time was to be lost, for the
kingdom was pressing. A personal response could not be delayed.

We may distinguish four separate focal points in the use of the Bible
in the New Testament.

- **The teaching of Jesus**: Jesus's thinking is, of course, founded on
  biblical teaching, principally about the kingship of God. He explicitly
  uses the Bible principally for *halakoth* (rules of conduct), but also for
  haggadah (how things are, how to regard the world).
- **Paul's use of Scripture**: Paul was a highly trained Jewish teacher,
  using traditional scriptural arguments in a variety of sophisticated
  ways.
- **Apocalyptic language**: Some passages in the Gospels, and especially
  the book of Revelation, use the Scriptures in a way characteristic of
  the Jewish apocalyptic writings of the time.
- **Actualization of Scripture in the description of events**: Both the
  Gospels and Paul narrate and reflect on the life of Jesus in the light
  of the Scriptures, displaying the same attitude to the eschatological
  actualization of the Scriptures as that known from the interpretation
  of Scripture at Qumran.

The Teaching of Jesus

The importance of the Bible in the teaching of Jesus may be illustrated from Mark 12, a chapter in which Mark assembles a group of controversies with the Jewish authorities as a climax to his ministry immediately preceding his arrest. First Jesus tells the story of the wicked vinedressers (Mk 12.1-12). The prophet Isaiah (Isa. 5.1-8) had used the image of the vineyard of the Lord as a parable for Israel, decrying its infidelity. Jesus now develops this parable in the haggadic manner, directing the blame on to the leaders, as the tenants of the vineyard. The leaders recognise that Jesus is aiming at themselves, and determine to arrest him. The use of this figure is pointed enough to provoke a lethal reaction.

Then (I miss out the political trap about a tribute to Caesar set by the Pharisees, Mk 12.13-17) the Sadducees set Jesus a riddle based on another biblical passage, a legal ruling of Deut. 25.5-10. Their objective is to show that the more recent teaching on life after death would make nonsense of the levirate law, which obliged a brother to marry a childless widow of his brother. Jesus answers in the classic manner, opposing their argument from the Torah with a phrase drawn also from the Torah (Exod. 3.6). This may be regarded as a *haggadah*, for it undercuts their question, showing that the question is based on a false understanding of life after death and of the relationship of God to those who have died. So again the whole issue is about the interpretation of the Old Testament.

Next, the lawyer sets a question of *halakah*: Which is the first, the most important, commandment (Mk 12.28-34)? This is a question which was frequently asked at the time and is attested in the Jewish literature. There is a famous story about the gentile who posed a similar question of the two most illustrious Jewish rabbis of the first century. He asked first R. Shammai, then R. Hillel, to teach him the whole law while he stood on one leg. Shammai sent him away brusquely; Hillel quoted him the golden rule (as in Mt. 7.12). Jesus, for his part, replies to the lawyer's question by quoting two passages from the law: Deut. 6.4-5 and Lev. 19.18. Again he goes beyond the lawyer's standard question by bracketing the second commandment with the first.

Finally, Jesus himself sets a puzzle from the Psalms, to show that the popular conception of the messiah as a royal son of David is too limited (Mk 12.35-37). This again is a question of interpreting Scripture, and of interpreting the psalm which, of all the psalms, is the most frequently cited in the New Testament to show the exaltation of the risen Christ to the right hand of God. For this reason the interchange is often held to be the product of the primitive Christian community.[2] Jesus was indeed hesitant about accepting the messianic title of 'son of David', perhaps because of its political implications. Here he is showing the difficulty of this title.

This collection of incidents shows the importance of the interpretation of Scripture in Jesus's ministry. One of the principal questions, which arises again and again in the course of his ministry, is the interpretation of the law and its observance. In a religion for which observance was so important, different principles could be brought into play, and indeed on many subjects the settling of such questions was the reason for the prominence of the 'scribes' (the Greek term really means 'lawyers'). Different solutions to such questions could be and were put forward by different schools, quoting different authorities. It was the job of the scribes/lawyers to present these and reach a solution. Jesus argues perfectly correctly according to rabbinic principles, though often reaching different solutions to those currently accepted. His arguments were not, however, outrageous, and it has been held that the reason the scribes and Pharisees appear nowhere in the account of Jesus's arrest and trial is that they were at least moderately favourable towards him, and that there was no bitter hostility between them and Jesus. The hostility towards the Pharisees arose only later. Paul, writing in the 50s, has nothing hostile to say about the Pharisees, and with pride proclaims that he himself was a Pharisee (Phil. 3.5). It was only in the 70s, with the writing of the Gospels, that hostility between Christians and Pharisees comes to be seen. Jesus himself argues like a Pharisee, and his confrontations with the scribes and Pharisees can be seen as originally being discussions between Pharisees! Though his consistent line of interpretation would have been unpalatable, it is expounded with good rabbinic reasoning.

The rules for interpretation of Scripture – how Scripture should be used in argument, especially in establishing rules for conduct – are said to have been originally codified by the great first-century rabbi, Hillel. They constitute the seven *middoth* or rules of R. Hillel.[3] One of the most obvious of these is precedent, which we see Jesus quoting in the Markan story of plucking corn on the Sabbath (Mk 2.23-28). There Jesus quotes the precedent of David purloining the sacred showbread as justification for breaking a sacred rule in a case of dire need. Matthew, the most Jewish of the Gospels, is not satisfied with this precedent, finding it not sufficiently close to the matter in hand (breaking the Sabbath). Matthew adds (Mt. 12.5-6) a closer precedent: priests breaking the Sabbath to offer sacrifice (which would normally be classified as work). Matthew adds a third justification for Jesus's action, following another of Hillel's principles: to interpret the Scripture by the Scripture. As the guiding principle he quotes the prophet Hosea (Hos. 6.6 in Mt. 12.7): 'what I want is love, not sacrifice'. This could be seen as the cardinal principle for the Matthean Jesus in interpreting the law; it is quoted twice more in Matthew (Mt. 9.13; 23.23). Putting love in pole position underlies all Jesus's moral teaching.

In the following story, Matthew (Mt. 12.11-12) again adds to Mark's version (Mk 3.1-6) a tighter legal precedent for breaking the Sabbath to heal: Jesus points out that it is legitimate to haul a sheep out of a pit on the Sabbath,[4] so how much more is it legitimate to heal a human being on the Sabbath? This ('how much more?') uses another of Hillel's rules of interpretation, commonly known by the Latin tag *a fortiori* (all the more so).

Again and again in the Gospels Jesus is seen engaging in legal argument about the law by exactly the methods practised by the rabbis; namely, pitting one text against another. The principal difference in Jesus's treatment consists in the weight given to a particular text over another, which betrays a whole different emphasis and cast of mind. Thus in the controversy over divorce (Mk 10.1-12), Jesus pits one text against another, giving precedence to the creation story in Gen. 1.27 and 2.24 over the Mosaic legislation of Deut. 24.1. So in effect he appeals to human nature as it was created by God, overruling the provisions of the law. Similarly, in the controversy over Corban (Mk 7.9-13), Jesus cites the command to honour and support parents (Exod. 20.12) as binding, in preference to a traditional rabbinic interpretation of the importance of a vow – again an appeal to the natural order of things and natural human interrelationships against imposed traditions.[5]

The same is true for Jesus's wider treatment of the Sabbath. He does not negate the Sabbath, one of the principal provisions of the law, but he does relativize it – and that in two ways. First, he subordinates its observance to human perfection: 'The Sabbath was made for man, not man for the Sabbath' (Mk 2.27). This again has far-reaching implications in the same direction of valuing the human nature created by God above the ritual law. Second, in a Christological statement of shattering consequences for his own status with regard to the law, he proclaims his own sovereign mastery over the provisions of the law: 'The son of man is master even of the Sabbath' (Mk 2.28). In this Jesus does go beyond any ruling within normal rabbinic argumentation, as also in his disregard of the normal cultic arrangements for forgiveness of sin (Mk 2.5). Normally a sacrifice would be required, but Jesus short-circuits this. However, the controversy remains entirely about the application of scriptural norms.

Paul's Use of Scripture

As might be expected from someone who had studied at Jerusalem under Gamaliel II, one of the most distinguished rabbinical teachers of his day, in the generation after Jesus (Acts 22.3), Paul's use of

Scripture is highly sophisticated, showing both an impressive degree of skill and an effectively honed argument. He uses these rabbinical skills to argue his own Christian case. He does, of course, use Scripture in a straightforward way, just as Jesus did, to prescribe ways and principles of behaving. Thus he grounds the right of missionaries to receive a wage on the analogous case of an ox treading out the corn (1 Cor. 9.9): the ox must be allowed to munch the corn (Deut 25.4). So although Paul maintains stoutly that there is no obligation on Christians to obey the Jewish law, he is somewhat selective in this, prepared to adduce the provisions of the law as a precedent for Christian practice. He also establishes the priority of men over women by reference to their temporal and genetic priority in the Creation story (1 Cor. 11.8) – a doubtful argument, as he virtually admits in the following verses!

Paul's method of argument based on the Scripture is also strongly influenced by the rules codified by Hillel. Thus in Romans 5 his argument for the universal effect of Christ's saving work as the second Adam is based on the *a fortiori* argument 'if death came to many through the offence of one man, *how much greater* an effect the grace of God has had . . . through the one man Jesus Christ' (Rom. 5.15). Similarly, in Second Corinthians, if the ministry of Moses was glorious, *how much more* glorious the saving ministry in the Spirit: 'if it is glorious to administer condemnation, to administer saving justice is *far richer* in glory' (2 Cor. 3.9).

Another argument used by Paul is a more specialist rabbinical one, and the more interesting in that it would nowadays seem less persuasive and less cogent. This is the principle known to Hillel and the rabbis as *gezera shawah*, an analogical argument based on equating two matters mentioned in Scripture because the two passages use the same word. Thus in Rom. 4.2-8 Paul argues that Psalm 32 supports Genesis 15 because both use the word 'impute':

> Abraham put his faith in God and this was *imputed* to him as uprightness. (Gen. 15.6)

> Blessed are those to whom the Lord *imputes* no guilt. (Ps. 32.2)

To a modern mind these two passages do not say the same thing: the first speaks of Abraham's faith, the second of divine forgiveness for sin. The use of the same word 'impute', however, allows the two passages to be brought into relationship.

Another instance of this argument (in Gal. 3.10-14) is even more subtle, revolving round the expression 'everyone is accursed who . . .,' associating the two texts:

Everyone is accursed who does not observe this Law. (Deut. 27.26)

Everyone is accursed who is hanged. (Deut. 21.23)

The original context of these two passages is entirely different, yet Paul uses the merely verbal coincidence to prove that 'Christ [hanged on a tree] redeemed us from the curse of the Law by being cursed for our sake' (Gal. 4.13).[6]

Paul's skill in rabbinic argument is seen perhaps at its most brilliant in the way he takes traditional Jewish positions and turns them on their head for his own purposes. He does this frequently, in a way that must have infuriated his opponents. Particularly in Galatians, where he is arguing against those who claim the continued validity of Jewish legal observance, he twice uses this move. Paul's opponents must have argued the dignity of the law from the fact that the angels were its mediators. Paul replies mockingly that if the law were mediated by angels it was not directly from God (Gal. 3.19). Again, Jews commonly held that Isaac, son of the free woman Sarah, was the ancestor of the Jews, while the slave-girl Hagar was mother of the gentiles through Ishmael. Paul replies mischievously that Jerusalem (the mother city of Judaism) is an enslaved city, while the mother city of Christians, the heavenly Jerusalem, is free (Gal. 3.21-31). Christians, therefore, are the free children of the free mother, while the Jews are the enslaved children of the slave-girl – exactly the opposite position to that held by the Jews as their birthright.[7]

It is, however, not only in controversy that Paul uses the Scriptures. It is striking that the vast majority of his quotations and allusions to the Bible are contained in the letters to the Galatians, the Corinthians and the Romans. There were large Jewish communities in Galatia, Corinth and Rome who would appreciate these Jewish arguments, but perhaps Paul reckoned that such communities as Philippians, Thessalonians and Colossians (all in north Greece) were not sufficiently Jewish to pick up and be swayed by such use of the Bible. However, even in Philippians it is clear that Paul's view of Christ cannot be fully grasped without a knowledge of the Bible. The lovely hymn to Christ – quite possibly not composed by Paul but adopted by him and included in his letter – concludes with the exaltation of Christ (Phil. 2.9-11):

And for this God raised him high,
And gave him the name which is above all other names

So that *all beings* in the heavens, on earth and in the underworld
Should bend the knee at the name of Jesus

And that *every tongue should acknowledge* Jesus Christ as Lord
To the glory of God the Father.

The staggering boldness of this confession can be appreciated only if it
is realized that the words I have put in italics are a quotation from Isa.
45.23. In its original context of Deutero-Isaiah, which is repeatedly at
grips with Babylonian polytheism and idolatry, this is a strong affirmation of monotheism: no other gods can stand beside the Lord of the
whole world. To apply this to Jesus, and to assert that the homage due
to the Lord is due also to the risen Christ, is an almost blasphemously
strong assertion of the divinity of Christ. In addition, Jesus is attributed
'the name which is above all other names', viz. *kyrios*, the Greek translation of the unspeakable name YHWH, the Lord. Furthermore, this
claim is asserted not to detract from the glory of God but actually to
contribute 'to the glory of God the Father'.

Apocalyptic Language

A particular way in which the New Testament interprets the Bible, or
rather makes use of the conventions of biblical writing, is in the use of
apocalyptic conventions. There were in Jewish circles of the first century
a number of works in circulation which professed to reveal (*apocalypto*
in Greek) what would take place soon at the end of time, for there
was abroad a vivid expectation that the end of time would not be long
delayed, that the world was in its last age, and God would soon deliver
his chosen ones. The most important of these is the post-biblical *First
Book of Henoch*, a collection of apocalyptic writings from the second
and first centuries.[8] It was widely diffused and influential at the time
of the New Testament, existing in multiple copies at Qumran.[9] The
New Testament Letter of Jude 14-15 quotes it as prophecy: 'It was with
them in mind that Enoch, the seventh patriarch from Adam, made his
prophecy when he said . . .'.

These writings normally involved a heavenly messenger descending
from heaven to reveal the manner of this ending. In the *Book of Henoch*,
the messenger is Henoch of Gen. 5.24, whose mysterious removal to
heaven ('Enoch walked with God, then was no more, because God took
him') makes him a suitable revealer of the secrets of heaven. He speaks
in coded biblical language, using biblical images of animals, numbers,
lurid cosmic disturbances, passage between earth and heaven and the
reverse. Such cosmic imagery had first been used by the prophets to
describe the disastrous divine interventions to punish unfaithful Israel
by the hand of the Assyrian and Babylonian invaders, and then later to
describe the saving divine interventions by which Israel was brought
back from exile and re-established in Jerusalem. This becomes the

classic language and imagery of divine intervention.

Apocalyptic writing in the New Testament makes use of these conventions drawn from prophetic writings in the later parts of the Old Testament. One early such writing is 'The Apocalypse of Isaiah' (Isaiah 24–27, one of the latest portions of the book of Isaiah[10]). Though lacking many features that will become commonplace in later apocalyptic writing, these chapters use the cosmic imagery of total destruction of the world (24.3-6, 19-21; 27.1). The daring imagery of the earth lurching and jolting, the moon confused and the sun ashamed (24.20, 23), prepares for later apocalyptic writing. God's judgement will extend beyond Israel to embrace all nations (25.7; 26.11). The oppressor will be destroyed and the oppressed lifted up (27.6-11). Also included in the Book of Isaiah is 'The Little Apocalypse of Isaiah' (Isaiah 34–35). Here the imagery, though not yet as bizarre as such imagery will later become, is already rich: the heavens rolled up like a scroll, streams turning to pitch. Again, creation as a whole is involved both in the destruction (34.1-2, 5) and in the restoration (35.1-2).

Perhaps most important for understanding the use of such conventions in the Gospels is Daniel's vision of the Son of Man (Dan. 7.1-28), which provides the background for the prophecies of the coming of the Son of Man in the 'Synoptic Apocalypse' (Mk 13.24-27; Mt. 24.30; Lk. 21.25-28). Without an understanding of this mode of writing, these accounts seem to be simply imaginative and poetic ravings. The crux of Daniel's vision is the grant of power by the Ancient of Days to the one like a human being, or Son of Man. He, a human as opposed to the brute beasts who have already been described, represents 'the holy ones of the Most High' (Dan. 7.27), who will be restored after persecution. This vision of the Son of Man is used in Mark with all the imagery of cosmic turmoil: 'The sun will be darkened, the moon will not give its light, the stars will come falling out of the sky and the powers in the heavens will be shaken. And then they will see the Son of Man coming in the clouds with great power and glory. And then he will send the angels to gather his elect from the four winds, from the ends of the world to the ends of the sky' (Mk 13.25-27).

This same vision of Daniel is also the presupposition of Jesus's reply at the Jewish interrogation in the synoptic Passion narrative, when Jesus declares, 'You will see the Son of Man seated at the right hand of the Power and coming on the clouds of heaven' (Mk 14.62).

The important point, however, is that the words and images derive their meaning from previous prophecies. In the same way, at the baptism of Jesus, the revelation of the word of the divine voice in Mk 1.10 is shown by the heavens 'split open', as in Isa. 63.19; 64.1. This is slightly, but significantly, different from Mt. 3.16 and Lk. 3.21, where the heaven(s) are 'opened', the verb that mirrors the heavenly vision of

Ezek. 1.1. There the same verb is used: 'heaven *opened* and I saw visions from God', the vision being the awesome chariot-throne of God.

Similarly, in the final vision of the New Jerusalem in the book of Revelation, each detail derives its sense from an allusion: the 12 gates and 12 foundation-stones indicate the 12 Apostles, representing the new 12 tribes of Israel, as well as being perfectly solid and balanced by their number. Every number in the book of Revelation has its symbolic value: seven (the highest primary digit) is the number of perfection, six (lacking one) the number of imperfection, etc. The open gates (Rev. 21.25) indicate the entry of all nations as in Isa. 60.11; the river of life (Rev. 22.1) alludes to the stream life of Ezekiel's vision in Ezek. 47.1-12; the divine light (Rev. 21.23) to Isa. 60.1, 19-20. For the modern reader such imagery needs to be laboriously unpicked and documented; for the ancient reader these familiar images would fall into place automatically.

Actualization of Scripture in the Description of Events

The part played in the New Testament by allusion to the Old Testament can scarcely be exaggerated. To the original hearers, familiar with the Bible and with no other book, such allusions would immediately recall well-known scenes, enriching the meaning of the words on a different plane, in just the way a catch-phrase from a popular TV serial or football theme song would conjure up a whole world for a modern audience. A few examples must suffice from the Gospels, in which the scriptural allusion shows the meaning of the events described.

At the Annunciation, the phrases 'The Lord God will give him the throne of his ancestor David; he will rule over the House of Jacob for ever and his rule will have no end' would recall the whole scene of Nathan's promises to David in 1 Sam. 7.8-16. It implies the fulfilment of these promises in Jesus, thus giving the force of a context and explanation of these words.

When Jesus replies to the messengers of John the Baptist, 'Tell John what you hear and see; the blind see again and the deaf hear,' etc., he is in fact telling John that he is fulfilling the prophecies of the eschatological healings of the last days, as foretold by Isa. 35.5-6. John had himself, as he shows in Mt. 3.7-12 and Lk. 3.7-9, been expecting a messiah of judgement, cutting down the rotten tree, separating the wheat from the chaff. He sends from prison to ask Jesus what he means by acting as he did, puzzled that Jesus was not executing judgement, but instead was forgiving and healing. The allusion to Isaiah puts the mission of Jesus in a different context: healing instead of punishment.

The way in which the narrative of the feeding of the five thousand is structured contains unmistakable allusion to a miracle by Elisha, showing that Jesus is in the line of the prophets, but working a far greater miracle. Instead of Elisha's proportion of 20:100, Jesus's is 5:5,000; not five people to a loaf (more like a pitta-bread), but a thousand. The elements, however, are the same:

		Elisha	Jesus
1)	Command to give them food	2 Kgs 4.42	Mk 6.37a
2)	Reply: 'This is absurd'	4.43a	6.37b
3)	Repetition of command	4.43b	6.39
4)	Feeding	4.44a	6.41
5)	They eat and have some left over	4.44b	6.42-44.

More particularly, the New Testament authors regard the events of the life of Jesus as in some way fulfilling the meaning of the Scriptures, completing the meaning the original authors envisaged. In so doing, they were treating the Scriptures in a way attested by other writings of the first century. The only direct evidence we have for the understanding of Scripture at the time of Jesus comes from the Qumran scrolls. A number of the scrolls are biblical commentaries, called *pesharim* (interpretations). The *pesharim* show that the members of this eschatological community believed that the texts of Scripture had a hidden or secret eschatological meaning, which would be made clear at the end of time.

Typical of this type of understanding of the Scriptures is the Qumran *Commentary on Habakkuk*, which sees the prophecies of Habakkuk fulfilled in the history of their own community. I quote one example: '*Because of the blood of men and the violence done to the land, to the city, and to all its inhabitants* (Hab. 2.8). Interpreted, this concerns the wicked priest whom God delivered into the hands of his enemies because of the iniquity committed against the teacher of righteousness' (1 QpHab. 9.9-10).

The wicked priest and the teacher of righteousness were two key figures in the early history of the Qumran community. It is characteristic of the Qumran understanding of the Scriptures that they should see Habakkuk as fulfilled in their own history. Just as the earliest Christians were an eschatological community, so the community of the Qumran scrolls were waiting for the Messiah and the fulfilment of the Scriptures. They quote the Scriptures in the same way and with the same formulas as the New Testament. This is particularly clear in 1 Cor. 15.3-5. There Paul gives a short passage, which represents the earliest tradition we have, proclaiming the death and resurrection of Jesus. It is the earliest creedal statement of the central events of the Christian faith, seemingly learnt by heart by the Disciples.[11] Twice in this short passage occurs the formula 'in accordance with the Scriptures'. This formula also occurs frequently in the documents of Qumran,[12] showing that the understanding of the Scriptures among the authors of the Dead Sea Scrolls coincided with this attitude. The most obvious difference between the process in the scriptural commentaries at Qumran and in the New Testament is that they work in opposite directions: the Qumran documents (being commentaries on Scripture) take the scriptural passage as their point of departure and apply that to current events, whereas the New Testament writers take the life of Jesus as their point of departure and apply the Scripture to that. The Qumran commentaries explain the Scriptures in the light of events of the community's life, whereas the New Testament explains events in the life of Jesus in the light of the Scriptures.

The text or texts to which the resurrection 'according to the Scriptures' refers is probably Hos. 6.2:

> He has struck us and he will bind up our wounds
> After two days we will be raised up
> And we shall live in his presence.

The original sense of this verse in Hosea does not necessarily imply resurrection from the dead. 'After two days' is a phrase meaning 'after a short time'. When the resurrection of Jesus occurred, however, this was seen to be the veiled meaning of the prophetic text. The verb used for 'raised up' is the word constantly used of the resurrection of Christ in the New Testament, which suggests that this is the passage the first Christians had in mind. The passage is also interpreted by first-century Jewish exegesis (as shown in the Aramaic targum[13]) in the sense of resurrection from the dead: 'He who has smitten us will heal us. On the day of the revivification of the dead he will raise us up and we shall be brought back to life before him.'

Another scriptural text whose 'veiled meaning' is seen to be fulfilled in the resurrection is Ps. 16.10, as interpreted in Peter's speech at Pentecost: 'You will not abandon me to Hades or allow your holy one to see corruption.' The obvious meaning of this prayer in its original context is a prayer of confidence about the psalmist's own preservation. Peter's speech, however, takes the hidden meaning to be that David was speaking about Christ: 'He spoke with foreknowledge about the resurrection of the Christ: he is the one who was *not abandoned to Hades* and whose body did not *see corruption*' (Acts 2.31). The same interpretation is given in Paul's speech at Antioch in Acts 13.35-37.

One might well expect this use of Scripture to be most prominent in Matthew, the most Jewish of the Gospels and written for a community of Christians sprung from Judaism. So he sees in Isa. 7.14[14] an indication of the virgin birth and – a theme important in Matthew – of the divine presence of Christ in his community. This latter theme brackets the gospel of Matthew (also 28.20 and 18.19); in order to read this in the text Matthew makes the slight change from '*you* will call his name Emmanuel' to '*they* will call . . .', the sort of slight verbal adjustment that is typical of midrashic interpretations.

Similarly, the text of Isa. 40.3 is used in Mt. 3.3 with a different meaning from the original. In the original it foretold the return of Israel from exile, and 'the Lord' referred to God, returning with his people (paralleled in the second half of the verse by 'make straight the paths of our God'). Matthew – or the tradition before him – sees it to refer to the coming of Jesus at the opening of his ministry. 'The Lord' now hints already at the divinity of Jesus, and 'paths of our God' has become 'his paths', by another slight verbal adjustment: 'A voice of one that cries in the desert, "Prepare a way for the Lord, make his paths straight"' (Mt. 3.3).

The same sort of process of interpretation or application of a text occurs in the prayer of the apostolic community in Acts 4.25-27. Psalm 2 is seen to be minutely fulfilled in the events of the Passion, again with one of those slight but significant Christological adjustments, 'the Lord and his anointed' becoming 'your holy servant Jesus whom you anointed':

'Why this uproar among the nations
this impotent muttering of the peoples?
Kings on earth take up position, princes plot together
against the Lord and his anointed.'

This is what has come true: in this very city Herod and Pontius Pilate *plotted together* with the gentile *nations* and the *peoples* of Israel, against your holy servant Jesus whom you *anointed*. (Acts 4.25-27)

The pursuit of this understanding of the Scriptures, uncovering their hidden meaning, was not a casual activity. At Qumran it was a principal study: 'Where there are ten, there shall never lack a man among them who shall study the law continually, day and night' (1QS 6.6) – no doubt each of the ten in shifts, rather than one man 24/7! 'Blessed is the man who makes the Law his care day and night', says Psalm 1. Such prolonged and careful study of the law is still characteristic of Hasidic circles in Judaism. It is remarkable that Luke especially stresses that a guide is needed for understanding the Scriptures: Jesus himself expounds the Scriptures at Nazareth (Lk. 4.21), to Martha and Mary (10.41), to the Disciples on the road to Emmaus (24.27); similarly Philip expounds the Scriptures to the Ethiopian (Acts 8.35). When the Apostles proceed to the appointment of the seven, they say, 'It is not right for us to desert the Word of God and serve tables. . . . We will concentrate on prayer and the service of the Word' (Acts 6.2-4). This concentration on the service of the Word is presumably the development of doctrine and the correlation of the life of Jesus with the ancient Scriptures, whose fruit we see in the use of the Bible in the New Testament.[15]

Perhaps the most striking of all the series of allusions occurs in the Passion narratives. It has been maintained that the early Disciples of Jesus 'knew nothing more about the passion than the fact of the crucifixion',[16] and that all the details are deduced from what, in view of Scripture, *must have* happened, rather than from memory of what *did* happen. I consider this an exaggeration, but agree that there is difficulty in attributing many of the details to eyewitness testimony. In the eyes of the evangelists, the explanation provided by the scriptural allusions is far more important than the bare facts. The accounts of the Passion should therefore be regarded as an interpretation of the events rather than as a chronicle or narrative.

Four instances of the many such allusions that permeate the synoptic Passion narratives may be given.

- The stress on the silence of Jesus before his judges, both at the Sanhedrin investigation (Mk 14.61) and before Pilate (Mk 15.5),[17] is an allusion to the song of the suffering servant: 'Ill-treated and afflicted he never opened his mouth, like a lamb before its shearer he was dumb and did not open his mouth' (Isa. 53.7).
- 'At noon there was darkness over the whole earth' (Mk 15.33) is in fact an allusion to the darkness at noon prophesied by Amos 8.9 for the Day of the Lord, the dread day of reversal and retribution. So it does not describe an interesting meteorological phenomenon but indicates that the Crucifixion is this Day of the Lord.
- The mockery of the crucified Jesus by the chief priests – 'He put his trust in God, now let God rescue him if he wants him, for he did say, "I am God's son"' (Mt. 27.43) – uses the actual words put in the mouth of the godless in mocking the just in Wis. 2.18-20. Rather than a remembered record of what they said, this is an indication that the chief priests are the godless and that the crucified Jesus is undergoing the fate of the just. Whatever their actual words, this is in fact what they were saying.
- Strongest of all are the use and reminiscences of Psalm 22 (21). This psalm of hope begins with the cry of distress, 'My God, my God, why have you forsaken me?', continues through the suffering of the just man, and finally issues in the triumph of God and the vindication of the sufferer. This is the whole thrust of the Passion narrative, which ends in the triumphant vindication of Jesus at the resurrection.

The psalm is seen as aptly giving the clue to this interpretation. Numerous other details of the psalm are reflected in details of the Passion narrative:

vv. 7-8	They sneer and wag their heads	Mt. 27.39
	He trusted in the Lord, let the Lord save him	Mt. 27.43
v. 18	They divide my garments among them	Mt. 27.35
	and cast lots for my clothing	Jn 19.24

By contrast with these last words of Jesus as given by Mark and Matthew, Luke gives Jesus's last words in another psalm verse: 'Into your hands, Lord, I commend my spirit' (Ps. 31 [30].5, in Lk. 23.46). This is more accommodated to the theology of Luke's Passion account, in which the human distress of Jesus is less evident, and Jesus's control of events is more prominent. So in Luke, Jesus ends not by being killed but by yielding up his own spirit into the Lord's hands.

The Johannine Passion narrative is similarly shot through with quotations from Scripture, each with John's favourite formula, 'that the scripture should be fulfilled'. These too must be considered the actualization of a 'hidden' or 'secret' meaning of the Scripture, for each in its original context means something very different:

- 13.18 'that the scripture should be fulfilled "He who shared my food has lifted his heel against me"' (Ps. 41 [40].9)
- 15.25 'that the word written in their Law should be fulfilled, "They hated me without cause"' (Ps. 35 [34].19)
- 17.12 'Not one of them was lost except the son of perdition, that the scripture should be fulfilled', perhaps referring to Ps. 109 (108).8-9
- 19.24 'that the scripture should be fulfilled, "They divided my clothing among them and for my raiment they cast lots"' (Ps. 22 [21].18)
- 19.28 'Jesus, knowing that all was fulfilled, that the scripture should be fulfilled said, "I thirst"' (Ps. 22 [21].18)
- 19.36-37 'These things happened that the scripture should be fulfilled, "No bone of his will be broken" (Ps. 34 [33].20), and again another scripture says, "They will look on him whom they pierced"' (Zech. 12.10).

These details must all be the product of an intensive study of Scripture to discover those passages whose 'secret' meaning could be seen as 'fulfilled' in the Passion narrative. The thought process behind this use of Scripture is not easy to understand. In what sense are these passages fulfilled? In what sense were they left unfulfilled beforehand?

Most statements are not fulfilled or unfulfilled, but only true or false, unless they are predictions, which at first sight none of the first four of these quotations used in John is. They are statements about the past. Only the last two (19.36-37) are statements about the future, and in their original form they were intended as statements about the immediate future of the speaker at the time, to be fulfilled long before the Passion of Jesus.

The answer to this puzzle seems to be twofold. First, we are dealing with God's word, and the New Testament authors (in this case John) understand the words to have been spoken not only about their immediate situation but also with relevance to the wider future. The message of God is addressed not only to the situation of the original author but also to all time. Second, we must ask just how the words and actions are relevant to the wider future. The thought behind this is the consistency of God's dealings, of God's shaping of history. The earlier events and the earlier words create a pattern into which the later events fit. This gives rise to what is often known as the 'typological sense'. The typological sense means that a mould is created into which a later event fits, just as molten metal is poured into a clay mould. This was certainly greatly used in the later understanding of Scripture, as we shall see in the section on Melito of Sardis (p. 18). So Abraham's willingness to sacrifice his son was seen as the mould and pattern for God the Father's offering of his Son on the Cross, and the crossing of the Red Sea was seen as the mould and pattern for the Christian passing through the water of baptism.

In this way, Paul sees the failures of the people in the desert during the exodus despite drinking from the rock – 'and that rock was Christ' (1 Cor. 10.4) – to be a type or mould for the failure of the Corinthians despite their receiving the Eucharist. He can say, 'These things happened to them type-wise [*typikos*] and were written down for our instruction'. In other words, the failures in the desert created the pattern that would make clear what was happening when the Corinthians fell into the same mould.[18] In the same way, Luke can present the Risen Christ explaining to the disciples on the way to Emmaus, 'starting with Moses and going through all the prophets, he explained to them the passages throughout the scriptures that were about himself' (Lk. 24.27), no doubt explaining the patterns, which, from Moses onwards, were being prepared for Jesus to fulfil.

In Matthew a whole series of these patterns is seen, which Jesus surpasses: great as is the Temple, Jesus, in the same mould, is greater than the Temple (Mt. 12.6). Jonah's three days in the whale are a mould for Jesus's three days in the tomb (12.40). The repentance of Nineveh at Jonah's preaching is a countersign to the failure to repent at the preaching of the one 'greater than Jonah' (12.41). The Queen of the

South admiring the wisdom of Solomon is a countersign of the members of this generation not recognizing the one 'greater than Solomon' (12.42). Perhaps the most condensed and close-packed instances of all uses of the Old Testament in the New occur in the Matthean account of the death of Judas (Mt. 27.3-10), featuring the price of a prophet (Zech. 11.12-13, 30 pieces of silver), Jeremiah's purchase of a field as a guarantee of salvation (Jer. 32.6), the suicide of David's traitor (2 Sam. 17.23), and the Valley of Slaughter (Jer. 19.6). All of these suggest overtones that come to rest, or are fulfilled, in the betrayal of Jesus and its consequences. They all supply a mould or pattern that makes deeper sense of these events and helps to explain their meaning.

Conclusion

It is impossible in one short, introductory chapter to give more than a rough sketch of the way the Bible is used and interpreted in the New Testament.[19] It would be possible and desirable to enter into much more detail about the way individual passages of the Bible were interpreted by New Testament authors to express their theological views. In this investigation, however, it has become clear that in this matter, as in so many others, the discovery of the Dead Sea Scrolls has importantly widened and deepened our understanding of the New Testament. Like the authors of the Qumran commentaries, Jesus was acutely aware that his mission was an eschatological one. In his activity he sees the fulfilment of Scripture, and even his moral teaching, the lessons for life and legal decisions that he draws from Scripture, indicate a firmly eschatological stance. His followers, also, though to a gradually decreasing extent, formed an eschatological community. They scrutinized the Scriptures to see how they were fulfilled in the life and actions of Jesus; the life of Jesus fulfilled the prophecies. Furthermore, at least some of the New Testament writers express themselves in a way that shows that they saw the true – or at least the hidden – meaning of the words of Scripture in Jesus's actions. Had Matthew been writing a Qumran-type *pesher* (explanation) of Isaiah, he might well have written an explanation of 'a virgin shall conceive' (Isa. 7.14): 'Interpreted, this concerns the conception of Jesus in the womb of Mary'. The virginal conception mentioned in the Greek text of Isaiah provides the pattern or mould that is to be fulfilled in the conception of Jesus.

Further Reading

Dunn, J., *Jesus Remembered* (Grand Rapids, MI: Eerdmans, 2003).
Moyise, S., *Evoking Scripture* (Edinburgh: T&T Clark, 2008).
Moyise, S., *The Old Testament in the New* (Edinburgh: T&T Clark, 2004).

CHAPTER 2

The Second Century

Melito of Sardis

The Peri Pascha

Melito of Sardis is a fascinating character, but from external sources we know almost nothing about him. He is mentioned in sources some two centuries after his death as having been Bishop of Sardis in Asia Minor. Eusebius (c. 260–c. 340), in his *Ecclesiastical History*,[1] says that he wrote two books on the Pascha. There is also a letter, quoted by Eusebius,[2] from Polycrates, the leader of the bishops of Asia, to Victor, presbyter in Rome, mentioning 'Melito the eunuch, who governed all things in the Holy Spirit, and who lies at Sardis awaiting the visitation from heaven when he will be raised from the dead'. 'The eunuch' probably means that he was celibate, alluding to Mt. 19.12 'eunuchs for the Kingdom of Heaven'.

A number of short fragments from various works of Melito have long been known from quotations in Eusebius. However, from 1940 onwards various manuscripts have been discovered, eventually published in 1960, giving the full text of his *Peri Pascha*, a title which may be translated 'About the Pasch', though there is also a pun on the word, mistakenly linking 'pasch' to 'passion', so that it could be regarded as meaning 'About the Passion'. This pun is central to the work, for the central theme is to contemplate or celebrate the Passion of Jesus in the light of the Jewish Passover or Pasch. From the work itself we can discover a great deal.

Melito was a Quartodeciman, a 'fourteenther'; that is, one among the large fragment of the early Church who celebrated Easter not with separate commemorations of the Passion and (three days later) of the Resurrection, but in a single feast held on the 14th day of the month, the first spring month of the year, so the first month after the spring equinox (21 March). This is always – and Melito's work is

18

conspicuously marked by this – associated with a Johannine spirituality. In the Gospel of John, the 'hour' of Jesus, to which he looks forward from the marriage feast at Cana onwards, is the hour of Jesus's glorification, consisting in his raising up onto the Cross, which is at the same time his exaltation to the Father. This whole scenario is regarded by John, and is celebrated by the Quartodecimans, as one single 'hour' or moment.

The work is shot through with a flowery style, principally associated with the sophisticated Greek-speaking cities of Asia Minor (roughly the western part of modern Turkey), known as Asian rhetoric. Training in rhetoric was an essential part of schooling, and the rules were strict and definite. We know most about them from the work of Quintilian (c. AD 35–100), whose brilliant work *Institutio Oratorica*, written at the end of the first century, remained a school book and model for the whole classical world for some centuries. Thus the *Peri Pascha* divides crisply into the classic sections of a Roman law-court speech:

- *propositio*: the matter to be proved
- *narratio*: a narrative account of the events at issue
- *probatio*: an analysis of the events to show that they prove the point
- *peroratio*: final summing up.

Each of these sections ends with a doxology, a little hymn of praise,[3] which serves conveniently as a dividing line. The division thus outlined gives the piece a classic clarity. In addition, we find a whole series of rhetorical traits, such as paradox;[4] frequent rhetorical questions;[5] a certain amount of dramatic staging and exaggeration;[6] exclamations ('O mystifying murder!');[7] *prosopopoiea* (addressing absent persons, qualities or other things; the destroying angel;[8] Israel)[9] poetic lists without any connecting particle ('by adultery, by lust, by licence' [eight elements])[10] and 'I am your life, I am your light, I am your salvation' (nine elements).[11] The rich poetic imagery is also enhanced by two processes known as *homoioarcton* and *homoioteleuton*: words 'rhyming' by similar-sounding beginnings or endings.[12] These elements give the piece a remarkable brightness and sparkle.

All this gives rise to the intriguing question: What sort of work is it? Its elevated style and its imagery would certainly justify calling it a poetic work, though some sections of the *probatio*[13] are naturally more argumentative than celebratory. It is not sufficiently instructional or hortatory to be called a sermon. Is it therefore a sort of prolonged eucharistic prayer? There is no narrative of the institution of the Eucharist, but then neither is there such in the Johannine account of the Last Supper. It could certainly be used as a meditative prayer at the centre of the celebration of the Passion and Resurrection of the Lord.

Even the communities so strongly influenced by Johannine theology can hardly have celebrated the Eucharist without reciting the 'warrant' for it, the scriptural account of the institution, already traditional in Paul's day (1 Cor. 11.23-25), but could the celebration of the Pasch have occurred without a eucharistic celebration?

A fascinating feature of the work is its primitive theology. Certain features of the Christology would not be acceptable in the light of later definitions. A lot of water had to pass under the bridge before a formulation was reached that would be ultimately satisfactory. These features and their Trinitarian consequences are obviously still to be thought through. So in section 9 about Christ it is said, 'He is father in that he begets; he is son in that he is begotten'. To express the Incarnation as he 'wraps himself in the suffering one'[14] would later seem dangerously docetic. Such a formula as 'God has been murdered'[15] is at least questionable. Similarly, in the final doxology, 'he bears the Father and is borne by him' would later seem to carry insufficient distinction between the persons of the Trinity. It is also characteristic of a less-developed theology of the Trinity that none of the doxologies mention the Spirit.

Perhaps the most interesting feature of all in this document – and certainly the most relevant for us – is its relationship to Judaism. There is an amazing combination of reliance on and hostility towards Judaism. It must be remembered that the great city of Sardis (once the capital of Croesus of Lydia's magnificent kingdom) had a major Jewish colony. In later years the largest Jewish synagogue yet found in the ancient world was to be built there. It is disputed whether Melito himself was a Jew. Undoubtedly he moves with ease throughout the Old Testament, for the work is full not only of explicit biblical history but of neat allusion (in section 82 'You were not Israel, you did not see God' alludes to the meaning of the Hebrew word 'Israel' as 'man seeing God'). Melito is also thoroughly familiar with the Jewish traditions about the Passover (compare section 68 and the Mishnah tractate *Pesahim* 10.5), and the whole section contrasting the fate of the Hebrews at the Exodus and of their Egyptian masters is reminiscent of the book of Wisdom 11–19, a Greek book of the Bible. In sharp contrast to this is the virulent and merciless blame heaped on the Jews for the sufferings inflicted on Jesus,[16] which make uncomfortable reading in a more eirenic age, although some of the material[17] has formed the model for chants so powerful that they are still used in the liturgy of Holy Week. The violence of this section is typical of a domestic quarrel, suggesting opposition within a close community.

After this preliminary sketch of the stance of the work and its author, we are in a position to consider its exegetical approach to the biblical text.

Melito's Use of the Bible

Melito is influenced by the Johannine tradition not only in the Quartodeciman dating of the celebration, but in many other ways also. For a start, John sees the Passion and Resurrection as a single 'hour', the hour of Christ's exaltation. So, too, does Melito:

> This is the one made flesh in a virgin,
> Hung on a tree
> Buried in the earth,
> Raised from the dead,
> Taken up to the heights of heaven.[18]

The Johannine hostility to the Jews is also very evident. The term 'the Jews' in John is notoriously difficult to interpret. John seems sometimes to use it of the inhabitants of Judaea, or the Jewish people in general, but more often it is used of those Jews hostile to Jesus. This may well be the effect of the uneasy relationship between Christians and Jews at the end of the first century, as seen in the underlying threat that any who confess Jesus as Lord will be put out of the synagogue. Similarly, the background to Melito's hostility to the Jews may well be the result of opposition from the powerful Jewish community of Sardis. Almost the whole of the final section of his work[19] is a bitter reproach to Israel, putting all the blame for the death of Jesus onto Israel:

> This is the one who has been murdered,
> And where murdered?
> In the middle of Jerusalem.
> By whom? By Israel.
> Why? Because he healed their lame, cleansed their lepers, etc.[20]

The most important of all the Johannine traits is the supersession of the law in the Gospel. There is, however, an important difference here between Melito and John. For John the law comes through Moses; grace and truth through Jesus Christ (Jn 1.14). The law itself is a treasure and Moses is revered. John's attitude is that the great values and religious institutions of Judaism are not abolished but reach their fulfilment in Jesus, are subsumed into him. So for John, Jesus is the good shepherd, the true vine, the true manna, the paschal lamb. The fullness of each of these figures is found in Christ. By contrast, for Melito, when the truth comes, the provisional ceases to have value:

> The Law is antique but the Word is fresh,
> The type is temporary but grace is eternal,

> The sheep is perishable but the Lord is imperishable,
> Slaughtered as a lamb, risen as God . . .
> A type occurred but the truth has been found.

The basic image of a 'type' comes from metalwork: as we have seen, the type is the mould prepared beforehand, into which the molten metal is poured in order to make the finished product. Melito's basic attitude to the old law is to see it as an artist's model, a preliminary sketch, which has no further value once the final work is complete. This is most fully explained in the *narratio* section of his work:

> Nothing, beloved, is said or made
> without a model or a sketch.[21]
> Is not the intended product seen through the likeness struck?
> That is why a sketch is made in wax or clay or wood
> So that the intended product,
> Greater in size, stronger in power,
> More beautiful in shape, richer in fabrication
> May be seen in the small and perishable sketch.
> When that to which the type was directed comes into being
> The type itself is dissolved as useless
> Yielding up its likeness to the truth itself.
> What was once valuable becomes valueless
> Since what is in reality valuable has appeared.[22]

This schema is basic to the whole treatise. The two meanings given by Melito to 'Pascha', namely Passover and Passion, are throughout contrasted as perishable model and authentic, real or 'true' product (again here a Johannine influence, seen already in John's use of the Greek word *alethes, aletheia* as authentic, real, true bread from heaven, true shepherd, true light of the world). When the reality has been achieved, the sketch serves no further purpose and is ready to be destroyed. The Jewish Passover, at the Exodus and in its repeated celebration, was temporary and has no further value when the reality, the Passion of Jesus, has been achieved:

> The type was valuable before the reality,
> And the model wonderful before the interpretation.
> That is, the people was valuable before the Church arose
> And the Law wonderful before the gospel shone out.
> But when the Church arose and the gospel was put forward
> The type was made vain, handing over its power to the reality
> And the Law was fulfilled, handing over its power to the Church.
> Once the slaughter of the sheep was costly,

Now valueless through the life of the Lord.
Costly the death of the sheep,
Now valueless through the Lord's salvation.
Costly the blood of the sheep,
Now valueless through the Lord's spirit.
Costly the voiceless lamb
Now valueless through the blameless Son.
Costly the Temple below
Now valueless through the Christ above.
Costly Jerusalem below
Now valueless through Jerusalem above.
Costly the narrow heritage
Now valueless through the breadth of grace.[23]

Set as he is on the contrast between the old and the new, Melito then proceeds (in the *probatio,* the section on proof) to give an interpretation of the story of the Bible. It is a catalogue of disasters. Adam left an inheritance to his children:

Not purity but fornication
Not incorruption but corruption
Not honour but dishonour
Not freedom but slavery
Not kingship but tyranny
Not life but death
Not salvation but destruction.[24]

There follows a record of crime more reminiscent of Paul's catalogue of the sins of the gentiles in the first chapter of Romans than anything else. The only bright spots in his account of biblical history[25] are the prophecies of the Passion, from Moses, David, Jeremiah, Isaiah and the other prophets.

The final, most moving, section of the work confirms this view that the point of biblical history is to prepare for and foreshadow the Passion of Christ. It consists of a series of reproaches to Israel, bitterly blaming Israel for the sufferings of Christ. Melito contrasts the simultaneous joys of the celebration of the *pascha* (Passover) with the agonies of the *pascha* (Passion):

You were revelling, he was hungry
You were drinking wine and eating bread, he was drinking vinegar and
    gall
Your face was bright, his was grim
You were rejoicing, he was being tortured

You were singing, he was being judged
You were beating time, he was bring nailed
You were dancing, he was being buried
You were stretched on a soft couch, he in a coffin and the grave.[26]

In a passage which – despite its literary beauty – makes painful reading
from many points of view, Melito also contrasts the beneficence of God
in Israel's history, especially at the Exodus and in the ministry of Jesus,
with Israel's deliberate blindness and rejection of Jesus:

He it was who chose you and guided you on the way
From Adam to Noah
From Noah to Abraham
From Abraham to Isaac and Jacob and the 12 patriarchs.
He it was who guided you to Egypt
And guided you there and nourished you.
He it was who lit your way in a pillar
And sheltered you in a cloud,
Who cut the Red Sea and led you through
Scattering your enemies . . .

Ungrateful Israel, come to me and be judged about your ingratitude!
What price did you put on being led by him?
What price did you put on the discovery of your ancestors?
What price did you put on the guidance down to Egypt
And the nourishment there through noble Joseph?
What price did you put on the ten plagues?
What price did you put on the pillar by night and the cloud by day
And the crossing of the Red Sea?[27]

Melito's attitude is, then, that the sole purpose of the Old Testament
and the history of Israel was to provide a model for the work of Jesus.
It had a value in preparing the way for Christ, but only in terms of its
fulfilment. In the *Peri Pascha* he does not put forward any considera-
tions about the people of God being formed, guided and prepared to
be a suitable conceptual and moral basis for Christ himself. There is
no aspect of *praeparatio evangelica* through the long history of Israel, for
Judaism ceases to have any value or meaning once the reality of Christ
has arrived. This uncompromising and narrow stance must have been at
least partly dictated by the atmosphere of controversy with, and hostility
towards, the Jewish community of Sardis. It does much to negate the
beautiful poetic imagery and sparkling language of the work.

Irenaeus

Irenaeus and the Gnostic Background

At the other end of the second century – and at the other end of Christendom – comes Irenaeus of Lyons. A link with Melito is that he was brought up at Smyrna, only a few kilometres from Sardis. He writes with enthusiasm about Polycarp, the great Bishop of Smyrna, martyred in extreme old age in AD 160, and of Polycarp's mission to Rome in an attempt to solve the Quartodeciman disagreement.[28] He tells us that he knew Polycarp, whom he regards as his link to the age of the Apostles. Greek was his native language and he writes in Greek, though resident in a Latin-speaking Roman province at Lyons in southern Gaul. He apologizes (conventionally) at the end of the preface to his major work, commonly known as *Adversus Haereses*: 'for us who live among the Celts and are accustomed to transact practically everything in a barbarous tongue, you cannot expect rhetorical art'. (In the Roman Empire and to the Greeks, all those who did not speak Greek or Latin were 'barbarians'.) It is hard to see Irenaeus's apology as more than conventional. Although he did not use the sophisticated 'Asian' style which we saw in Melito, he was fully educated in the classics of Greek literature and quotes them with ease and wit. Nor was the area in which he lived all that uncivilized. He is a paradigm case of the interchange between East and West in the Roman Empire. The two cities associated with Irenaeus, Lyons and Vienne, were important cities of Roman Gaul, which had been incorporated in the Empire for some centuries. They would not have considered themselves uncivilized. Even if Celtic was their first language, Latin was perfectly current in the region. The number of Latin inscriptions from the area and the massive Roman buildings of Provence – theatres, amphitheatres, aqueducts – show that the area was thoroughly romanized. However, it was a commonplace in the Roman world that the intellectuals, teachers, doctors and the sharp-witted in general were Greeks. Perhaps Irenaeus – not without reason – considered that to the Romans drainage was more important than philosophy: he does not quote Roman literature!

Eusebius tells us that Irenaeus was a 'presbyter',[29] though he is usually considered to have been Bishop of Lyons. Possibly at this date there was in Gaul still no formal distinction between *presbyter* and *episcopos*, 'priest' and 'bishop'. Possibly the *episcopos* was one chosen from the body of *presbyteroi*. He wrote the five books of *Adversus Haereses* over a considerable period, sending the earlier books off before he had written (or even planned) the later ones. A fairly precise date may be gleaned from his list of Bishops of Rome,[30] which ends with Eleutherus, who was bishop AD 174–189. The Christians of Lyons underwent a fierce and heroic persecution in 177, making it unlikely that Irenaeus was engaged on this extended writing project at that time. So the work was probably written in the 180s, followed by his shorter *Demonstration of the Apostolic Preaching*, which refers to the earlier work.

The importance of Irenaeus's work is that here we have a writing which may be considered the beginning of orthodoxy after the doctrinal chaos of the previous half-century. He gives us a lucid and detailed statement of the basic truths of faith, God, Christ and salvation. From the earlier period the fullest post-apostolic exposition of the Christian faith we possess is Justin Martyr's writing, particularly his *Dialogue with Trypho the Jew* (c. AD 135). Obviously the dialogue with a Jew is more restricted, directed to one particular matter, the incarnation and messiahship of Jesus. Irenaeus knew and admired this work, written half a century earlier, and clearly made use of it; on occasion his arguments run on lines parallel to it. Justin is a philosopher, and I think Irenaeus also has a philosophical turn of mind, enjoying the same sort of philosophical argumentation and logic, though he can also burst into prayer on occasion.[31] But Irenaeus faces a different problematic. In the second century a new situation had arisen: the influx into Christianity of gentiles of a classical background. They attempted to understand Christ and Christianity in terms of their own background, losing touch to an extraordinary extent with the Jewish background of Christianity.[32]

For Irenaeus himself this blindness to the Jewish background has important consequences, both negative and positive. Negatively, he shows striking ignorance of Hebrew, hence an extraordinary passage[33] in which he gives etymologies of the divine names Sabaoth, Elohim, Adonai and the sacred Tetragrammaton, which show total ignorance of Hebrew. He also dizzily thinks (*Demonstration*, 43) that the two first words of the book of Genesis, *breshith bara* ('In the beginning he created'), include the word 'son'. In 3.8.1 he carefully, but quite incorrectly, insists that *mamuel* (which he thinks is the Hebrew for the Aramaic *mammon* in Lk 16.13) means 'glutton'; there is no such word in biblical Hebrew.

On the positive side, ignorance of the Hebrew Bible is a considerable help to Irenaeus in his proof of the divinity of Jesus, which he argues uniquely on the basis of the Greek text of the Bible. He exclusively uses the Greek Septuagint translation, which he argues with persuasive competence to be inspired.[34] From the earliest days this translation, stemming from the Greek-speaking Jews of Alexandria, had been the Bible of the Christian Church. It is the text of the Old Testament used consistently in quotation of the Old Testament in the New. It was not until two centuries later – and not without considerable opposition – that St Jerome hit on the idea of using the Hebrew as the basic text. Hence for Irenaeus wherever the Greek *kyrios* occurs it refers to the

LORD God. In fact it sometimes translates the sacred Tetragrammaton (YHWH, 'the LORD'), but sometimes means far less: 'the lord', a title merely of respect, not of worship. In the vocative it can mean merely 'Sir'! The use of *kyrios* for Jesus is an important element in his strong Christology: Jesus is the LORD God *tout court.* The later subtleties made possible by the distinction of the terms 'person' and 'nature' have not yet evolved and were therefore unavailable to Irenaeus. They are, of course, a feature of the controversies of the fourth century that led to clarification of the philosophy implied by the doctrine of the Trinity. These philosophical discussions had not yet developed in the Church. Without these subtleties, Irenaeus reads Lk 2.11 ('Today is born to you a saviour who is Christ the Lord') as 'Christ the LORD', an unambiguous affirmation of the human birth of God.

Irenaeus's Opponents

The background of Irenaeus's thought is formed by several schools or groups of people who posit a whole succession of emanations from God, called 'aeons'. It is not easy to discern the basic thrust of these theories – and of course Irenaeus has no interest in making them seem logical, persuasive or well founded – but three factors seem to combine to produce them.

1. **The pagan acceptance of many gods and demi-gods.** In the same way the various second-century groups whom Irenaeus discusses, under the general name of 'Gnostics', believe in a whole range of divine beings, or 'aeons'.[35] The ancients, Roman and Greek, had a god for every activity (e.g., Mars was god of war, Ceres goddess of crops, Minerva goddess of the household, Cupid god of love). So it is possible that these aeons are modelled on them. They have a variety of names, such as Silence, Mind, Truth, Praise, Union, Hope,[36] and many others. They emanate from the first principle,[37] or first father, in various ways and in various combinations. Are those who accept these aeons in fact searching for personifications of basic and important qualities, rather like the gods of Roman mythology? Are they intended as a way of describing the qualities of God, or the origin in God of all good things? All the aeons except the evil demiurge are contained within the pleroma (or fullness) of God, but Irenaeus objects that God is simple and not composite.[38]

2. **Some form of Neoplatonism.** Plato was sometimes understood by his Neoplatonic followers to hold that all material things are bad and corrupt. The only good things are the celestial ideas or concepts behind these material things. The mind (or the soul) that grasps these concepts is noble, but is entombed in a debased material body from which it needs to release itself. All the Gnostic systems

share the conviction that the material world was created not by the first principle but by a depraved force, the demiurge, which has emanated at some distance and considerable corruption from the first principle, and is cut off from the pleroma of God. The basic problem, which all this emanation theory was set up to solve, is the existence of evil in our experience, and the impossibility that a good God created an evil world. Salvation is only by intellectual knowledge, which provides an escape from the material world. Irenaeus gives the opinion of his opponents: 'Those who have knowledge about God and are initiated into the mysteries of Achamoth [one of the aeons – a meaningless name in a sort of Hebrew shape] are perfect, and cannot be defiled by being plunged into mud, any more than gold can'.[39] Putting the aeons between God and an evil world saves God from getting his fingers dirty.

3. **Some complicated form of number symbolism.** The importance of numbers recurs again and again, especially fours, eights and twelves. A particular example: Irenaeus tells us that one leader, Marcus, held:[40] 'Uniqueness and Unity existed together and produced two offspring, Single and One. Doubled, these made four. Two and four together gave the number six, and these six quadrupled conceived twenty-four entities. The names of this Tetrad may not be spoken and are known only to the Son. But the Father knows what they are, and Marcus pronounces their names with reverence and faith: Inexpressible, Silence, Father and Truth.'

In Greek these four words have 24 letters. A vestigial connection with Christianity is established by names (1.8.4 finds the aeon 'Sophia' or 'Wisdom' in Lk. 7.35 and in the search for the lost drachma), and also by the symbolism of numbers: 30 aeons are reflected in the 30 years of Jesus's hidden life (Lk. 3.23); the hours of hiring the workers in the vineyard (Mt. 20.1-6) also total 30.[41] Irenaeus himself occasionally uses numbers in a similar way; he calculates the end of the world after 6,000 years by combining the six days of Creation with 2 Pet. 3.8: 'For the Lord a day is like a thousand years'.[42]

At one stage Irenaeus suggests that these theories are attempting to do what the earliest Greek Presocratic natural philosophers such as Thales (fl. 585 BC) or Anaximander (fl. 546 BC) attempted: to explain the ultimate origin of things in fire, air, earth or water.[43] Whatever this theory was designed to express or explain, the outcome as presented by Irenaeus seems random nonsense, and Irenaeus wittily makes fun of it.[44] On one occasion he compares it to changing the stones of a mosaic portrait of a king so that the picture looks like a fox[45] (perhaps the ancient equivalent of drawing a moustache on a female portrait); or to the composition of a nonsense rhyme by randomly putting together lines drawn from different places in Homer.[46] On another occasion[47] he caricatures it: the original Powers, Gourd and Emptiness, produce a fruit called Cucumber, paired with Melon, and between them they produce "all the rest of Valentinus' idiot Melons" (in Greek 'melon' has the same slightly mocking, affectionate colloquial use as 'old fruit'). Perhaps his most wounding – but not unfair – criticism is that Valentinus is doing no more than return to the theories of the ancient Greek poet Hesiod, so delightfully mocked by the comic poet Aristophanes (2.14.1, referring to Aristophanes's *Birds*, 685–722). Typical also of Irenaeus's wit is the comparison of his opponents to an unskilled wrestler, who grabs his opponent, only to be thrown by that very hand-hold.[48] A similarly pleasing comparison to false teaching is the offer of water laced with gypsum under the pretence that it is milk.

Irenaeus's Positive Stance

1. The Rule of Faith

Much more interesting, however, and valuable than Irenaeus's arguments against these somewhat crazy theories,[49] is the positive contribution he makes in his interpretation of Scripture and doctrine. The first element of this, and perhaps Irenaeus's most important contribution to the whole theological scene, is the insistence on tradition as the basis of interpretation. From the beginning he contrasts the variety of these myths with the consistency and harmony of the Church's teaching: 'although scattered throughout the world, the Church carefully guards the kerygma as though she were living in one house, believes it as though having one soul and the same heart, and proclaims and teaches it as though having one mouth'.[50]

Irenaeus returns to this theme in the important passage at the beginning of his most significant positive teaching. He begins with the preliminary insistence that the interpretation of Scripture must always be within the tradition of the Church, citing first the solidity of the tradition of the Roman Church: 'Since it would be too long, in a work like this, to list the successions in all the Churches, we shall take only one of them, the Church that is greatest, most ancient, and known to all, founded and set up by the two most glorious apostles Peter and Paul at Rome, while showing that the tradition and the faith it proclaims comes down through the succession of bishops even to us. . . . For it is necessary for every Church – that is, believers from everywhere – to agree with this Church, in which the tradition from the apostles has always been preserved by those who are from everywhere, because of its more excellent origin.'[51]

Debate still continues whether Irenaeus here envisages the specifi-
cally Roman Church as the norm of teaching, or whether he envisages
the wider whole of what came to be known as 'the Great Church'. The
main point is that the norm of interpretation is the tradition as received
by the whole Church. After his long section on the Roman Church,
Irenaeus briefly cites the agreement with it in faith of the Church of
Smyrna, as represented by Polycarp, and the Church of Ephesus, and
finally the 'barbarian' churches which guard the same tradition orally,
without paper and ink.[52] The starting point of his theology is this 'rule
of truth',[53] of which he gives similar and overlapping versions.[54] On
these the whole idea of orthodoxy rests. Within this framework all
interpretation of Scripture must be done. Irenaeus is the first to insist
that Scripture must be interpreted within the tradition of the Church,[55]
and the necessity of this insistence is made clear by the extent to which
he departs from the schools of thought he is criticizing.

For the subsequent history of the Church this principle will remain
important, and especially a matter of controversy at the sixteenth-
century Reformation, when Luther insisted on the contrary principle
of *sola scriptura* (only scripture), with disastrous consequences for any
unity of doctrine.[56] Irenaeus's stance was, of course, one of the cor-
nerstones of *Dei Verbum*, the decree of the Second Vatican Council on
Revelation, which quotes four times from *Adversus Haereses*).[57]

2. One Single God

After the exposition of the teaching of his opponents and his negative
comments on them, Irenaeus advances his own Christology in Book 3.
It is principally this part that has earned him the title of 'the veritable
creator of modern exegesis'.[58] He does not always show the same skills as
the modern biblical scholar, but he is beginning to use the same tools.[59]
It also shows him to be the first Christian theologian to draw from the
New Testament a full and satisfying vision of redeemed humanity. The
picture is built up gradually: one God, the divinity of Jesus, Christ's
redemptive work.

Against the multiple divine emanations of the Gnostics, Irenaeus
demonstrates that the Scriptures postulate only one God, who is both
Father and Son. Here he shows himself the first Christian writer to
elaborate a proof by working systematically through the Scriptures,
Genesis, Exodus, the Prophets, Paul, with a liberal admixture of Psalm
texts. Indeed, he starts from the classic text of Ps. 109.1,[60] the most
quoted of all texts, to prove the exaltation of Christ. Working exclusively
from the Greek Bible, and oblivious to the nuances of the Hebrew, he
begins his proof from 'The Lord said to my lord'. Both Father and Son
constitute one God. Here the inaccessibility of the Hebrew Bible was

a considerable help. Both 'LORD' and 'lord' are translated into Greek as *kyrios*. In fact in 'The LORD said to my lord' the first and second instances of 'lord' translate different Hebrew words, whereas Irenaeus takes the identity of the words to show that both Father and Son are one God. Later theology, equipped with the terms 'person' and 'nature', would struggle to make some distinction within the identity.

The quality of the argument is further shown by the neat little discussion of Pauline style. In order to avoid the appearance of another deity in the expression 'the god of this world' (2 Cor. 4.4), Irenaeus argues with examples that Paul often uses an unusual word order, and that an unwritten comma should be understood. The text, he holds, should read not 'the god-of-this-world has blinded the minds of unbelievers' but 'God has blinded the minds of the unbelievers-of-this-world'. In the introduction to the work Irenaeus claimed to be innocent of rhetorical technique, but this is precisely the sort of argument for which rhetorical training was designed. The literary skills of rhetorical training are beginning to be applied to the interpretation of Scripture.

3. The Divinity of Christ

It is when Irenaeus comes to proving the divinity of Christ that his method really develops and provides a solid and satisfying basis for all future Christology. Against the Valentinian idea that Christ was merely a semi-divine emanation, it was essential for him to prove the identity of Christ with the Father within the Godhead. His first important move was to establish the four Gospels on a firm footing. Marcion had wanted to exclude all the gospels except Luke, whereas the Gnostics embraced a variety of gospels: the Gospel of Philip, of Peter, of Thomas and so on. Christian writers hitherto had been chary of arguing from the Gospel of John because of the use made of it by Gnostics.[61] Irenaeus takes the important step of insisting that four and four only is the canonical number, using the arguments both of the four animals supporting God's throne in Ezekiel 1 (which will become so important in all Christian iconography) and of the need for four-square solidity. Irenaeus does use such symbolic arguments, but does not embrace the extended allegories that later authors would draw from the texts. He uses occasional symbolism, like the symbolic significance of the gifts of the Magi to the infant Jesus,[62] and typology (the water falling on Gideon's fleece in Judg. 6.37–38 is a type of the fruitful moisture of the Spirit on the people of God[63]), but this is a far cry from the allegorical expansions that will become so popular in the Alexandrian school. Besides the symbolic arguments for four gospels, Irenaeus insists on the individual contributions of each as clearly as any modern *redaktionsgeschichtler* could wish, listing, for instance, a whole series of incidents that come in Luke alone.[64]

Irenaeus then works through each of the Gospels in turn, proving from each of them that Jesus is God. There is, of course, as yet no distinction of persons. Again he is helped by the identification of two uses of *kyrios*, the LORD and the lord, which enables him to regard 'the angel of the Lord' in Mt. 1.20 and 2.13 as the angel of the divine Jesus, and Luke's 'prepare a way for the Lord' as a claim to the divinity of Jesus (Lk 1.17). He is on firmer ground in returning again and again to the prologue of John (1.1-18): God created the world through his Word; it was not, as the Valentinians claimed, the work of a corrupt demiurge. Just as modern exegesis will do, Irenaeus sees the figure of God's creative Word in the prologue against the background of God's wisdom, 'holding all things in being' (Wis. 1.7).[65]

It was equally important, against Gnostic theories, to insist on the full humanity of Jesus. In order to avoid the contamination of God by evil matter, Gnostics had held that Jesus passed through Mary 'as through a tube', not taking her flesh.[66] Irenaeus will have none of this, backing up such texts as Mt. 1.1 *Biblos geneseos Jesou Christou* ('Book of the genesis, or birth or becoming, of Jesus Christ'), with a whole series of strong Pauline assertions (Rom. 1.1-4; 9.5; Gal. 4.4-5). The same desire to keep God free of all entanglement with the human predicament had led the Gnostics to deny that Christ had suffered. As a result, they distinguished Jesus and Christ, maintaining that Christ came down on Jesus at his baptism and departed from him before the Passion,[67] an unfounded distinction which Irenaeus strenuously denies. On the contrary, to emphasize the full humanity of Jesus he also draws attention to the Johannine texts that feature Jesus's tiredness by the well in Samaria and his sorrow at the death of Lazarus.[68]

4. Recapitulation in Christ

The stage is now set for the summit of Irenaeus's theology, to which he returns again and again: recapitulation in Christ. The term 'to recapitulate' is used only twice in the New Testament, once to mean simply 'to sum up' a series (Rom. 13.9). Irenaeus follows and develops the other usage, in Ephesians 1.10, 'to sum up all things in Christ', *anakephalaiosasthai to panta en Christo*. In Ephesians this is a glorious phrase, which by its sheer weight dominates the lofty and inspiring language of the great blessing (1.3-14) with which the letter opens. Literally it means 'to head up' or 'to re-head'. In the former sense it signifies providing a head for a body. The head has connotations of authority, of supplying intelligence and nourishment, bringing the body to life and putting it in command of its surroundings, perfectly mastering its task; so it suggests Christ bringing Creation to completion. The latter sense, 'to re-head', adds another overtone, for the initial particle *ana* can signify returning something to a state in which it was before; it therefore implies that Christ brought creation and the human race *back* to the rightful situation in which the human race had once been.

Irenaeus takes this concept and makes it a keyword of his whole theology. He holds that there were four covenants with the human race: with Adam, with Noah, with Moses and 'finally the fourth through the gospel, which renews man and recapitulates all things in the Lord, raises man up and gives him wings towards the Kingdom of Heaven':[69] 'When he was incarnated and became man, he recapitulated the long series of men in himself, in short giving us salvation, so that what we lost in Adam [that is, to be according to the image and likeness of God] we should receive in Christ Jesus.[70]

The point of the Incarnation is that there is an exact parallel to the Fall. The Docetist theory that Christ only seemed to be human will not do, for the resemblance of this Christ to Adam would not be exact. The human race can be saved only by a human. God formed the first Adam from the dust of the earth. The dust was virgin because it had received no rain or moisture. In the same way God formed the second Adam from the Virgin Mary, so that what was recapitulated should be of the same substance and formation. 'Everyone will accept that we are a body received from the earth, receiving a spirit from God. This is what the Word of God became, recapitulating the same formation in himself. This is why he declares himself Son of Man.'[71]

At first sight it might seem that Irenaeus changes the sense of Ephesians. In Ephesians the *anakephalaiosis* takes place through the blood of Christ (1.7), whereas Irenaeus puts all the emphasis on the Incarnation, the Word made flesh. He is, of course, arguing against those who disputed the Incarnation, so it is important for him to underline that the Incarnation is the essential preliminary to the saving act of obedience, which undid the disobedience of Adam. 'The Word of God won the prize of victory by coming down from the Father and becoming flesh and descending even to death'[72] – a clear and detailed reference to the obedience even to death, death on a cross, hymned in Phil. 2.6-11. The same is clear in the shorter and later *Demonstratio*, 31: 'because we were bound to death through disobedience, the bonds of death had necessarily to be loosed through the obedience of him who was made man for us'.[73] In this Irenaeus is closely following the argument of Rom. 5.12-21. Irenaeus stresses the exact parallel of the recapitulation by the symbolic argument that Jesus died on a Friday to recapitulate, by his obedience, the disobedience of Adam, who ate the forbidden fruit on a Friday: 'It is clear that the Lord suffered death in obedience to his Father on that day on which Adam died because he disobeyed God.'[74]

On the matter of obedience, Irenaeus also lays the foundations of Marian doctrine by the application of the same teaching to Mary. As Eve, still a virgin, by her disobedience became for the whole human race a cause of death, so Mary, a virgin, by her obedience became for the whole human race a cause of salvation.[75] Irenaeus rather charmingly deduces the fact that Eve was still a virgin from the fact that the first couple were unembarrassed by their nakedness: they were still children, 'being only recently created, they had no understanding of sex; they still needed to grow up'.

The exposition concludes with a delightfully sensitive interpretation of the story of the Fall. God did not curse Adam and Eve, but only the earth (Gen. 3.17). The full curse fell on the serpent.[76] On the other hand, Cain was cursed because, bad as it was to kill his brother, it was much worse to respond to God with a cheeky and irreverent question, 'Am I my brother's keeper?' Adam, however, showed signs of repentance by making his garment out of scratchy fig-leaves: 'although there were many other leaves which would have vexed his body less, he made a garment suited to disobedience . . . as though to say "Since by my disobedience I have lost the robe I received from the Spirit of holiness, I recognise that I deserve such a garment which pricks and hurts my body"'.[77]

Conclusion

Irenaeus is often represented as a finger-wagging, unimaginative Gnostic-slayer. In fact he represents an important stage in the development of doctrine. He is perhaps the first Christian theologian to present anything like a full and coherent system of doctrine. He also writes with wit, charm and refreshing imagery. Perhaps his most important principle is that all doctrine must use the tradition of the Church as a control. In addition, the broad, Scripture-based canvas of incarnation and redemption is a more coherent and explicit development than was offered by any of his predecessors. Finally, his use of Scripture shows an impressively attractive similarity to modern methods of investigation and interpretation.

Further Reading

Grant, R. M., *Irenaeus of Lyons* (London: Routledge, 1997).
Minns, D., *Irenaeus* (London: T&T Clark, 2010).
Simonetti, M., *Biblical Interpretation in the Early Church* (London: T&T Clark, 1994).

CHAPTER 3

Origen

Introduction

With the next figure to be studied we enter a new era, which would become of enormous significance for the understanding and use – the 'performance' – of Scripture in the Church, 'a figure crucial to the whole development of Christian thought', says Pope Benedict XVI, who occasioned an 'irreversible change of direction'[1] in all Christian thought.[2] Born c. AD 185, Origen has been hailed as the first professional scriptural exegete in the Christian Church. There are grounds for saying that Irenaeus was the first scholarly exegete, but certainly Origen devoted himself heart and soul to the technical subject of Scripture in a way that Irenaeus did not. He evolved techniques (for instance, textual criticism and comparison of the four Gospels) which have continued to serve the understanding of Scripture till the present day. He was methodical in a way that had never been known before, even studying the topography of the Gospels. He uses this to establish the text: 'Since we have been in the places, so far as the historical account is concerned, of the footprints of Jesus and his disciples and the prophets, we have been convinced that we ought to read not "Bethania" [in John 1.28] but "Bethabara".'

Bethania is only 3 kilometres from Jerusalem, whereas there is a Bethabara on the banks of the Jordan. It is, however, significant that Origen considers a more serious reason in favour of Bethabara to be that the name means 'house of preparation', a name suitable for baptism. 'Bethania' suits the story of Martha and Mary since it can be interpreted to mean 'house of obedience'. Scientifically also, a few lines later he settles the textual dispute about the swine rushing off the cliff into the Lake of Galilee by opting neither for Gerasa (Mk 5.1) nor for Gadara (Mt. 8.28), but for Gergesa, beside the lake, which has a convenient cliff.[3]

Perhaps his single best-known achievement was the Hexapla, an

Old Testament in six vertical columns, by which six different basic versions could be minutely compared.[4] This was the beginning of textual criticism, an essential tool for establishing the text of the Bible at a time when – quite apart from the differences between the Hebrew and Greek versions of the Bible – there was a vast range of variations between manuscripts of the Greek text itself. In his homilies Origen sometimes comments on both variants of a text.[5]

Origen seems to have been the first Christian writer to turn from the Greek Bible back to the Hebrew text and to recognize its importance. This initiative is in itself sufficiently impressive. As we have seen, Irenaeus's attempts to dabble in Hebrew were chaotic; Origen has at least a working knowledge of Hebrew. He could at least transcribe it into Greek, and could handle (sometimes inaccurately) the etymology of Hebrew names.[6] He was the first Christian to write commentaries on the books of the Old Testament; one might even say he was the first Christian scholar to take the Old Testament seriously for its own sake. He frequently mentions learning from Jews about matters of Hebrew, not only when he is in Palestine, but already when he was still resident at Alexandria.[7] It was in fact principally in order to have a biblical text acceptable to the Jews with whom he was in conversation that Origen set about assimilating the text of the Septuagint (hereafter abbreviated to LXX) to the Hebrew of his day. In an exhaustive survey of Origen's use of Hebrew, G. Bardy,[8] though praising his 'zeal for truth and desire to cull information from the best sources',[9] concludes that he had 'only a superficial knowledge of Hebrew'.[10] This element of his scholarship would nevertheless have a crucial influence on Jerome's recourse to and preference for the Hebrew text, which in its turn would have such a decisive effect on Christian use of the Bible. Jerome similarly was much affected by his contact with Jewish biblical scholarship.

Origen was also a world figure in the field of Christian scholarship, invited by the syncretistic empress-mother Mammaea to instruct her in Christianity, and was also in demand to give authoritative rulings in cases of disputed doctrines. As an established teacher, he was invited to a synod at Bosra to consider the teachings of Beryllus, and to another in the presence of both Pope and emperor. Perhaps the most important factor of all about his importance in the life of the Church is Origen's insistence that Scripture must be read with prayer: scriptural reading is a means to knowledge of God. This is the basis of *lectio divina*, the reflective reading of Scripture. Origen writes to Gregory: 'Pay special attention to the reading of Scripture. Much concentration is needed for this reading, and while you study these divine works with a believing and God-pleasing intention, knock at that which is closed in them and it shall be opened to you by the porter, of whom Jesus says, "To him the gatekeeper opens". While you attend to this *lectio divina*, seek aright and with unwavering faith in God the hidden sense which is present in most passages of the divine Scriptures. And do not be content with knocking and seeking, for what is absolutely necessary for understanding divine things is prayer.'[11]

Origen the Teacher

The life story of a person is always important for understanding their writings, but there is space for no more than a brief introduction to Origen. From an early age he was always a teacher. His life is told by Eusebius, Bishop of Caesarea, in AD 315 (a mere half-century after Origen died there), in his *History of the Church*, Book VI. It is always difficult to know to what extent such a history of a saint is factual and to what extent merely conventional.[12] Eusebius relates how wholehearted Origen was in his studies, often studying late into the night, exceeding even his father's ambitions for him, and rigoristic in his ascetic practices; these items may well be conventional. Besides sleeping on the floor with minimal covering, he is also said to have sought to conquer sexual temptations by self-castration.[13] Martyrdom can never have been far from his mind: his father was martyred and all his property confiscated when Origen was 17, leaving the family in poverty. In these persecutions at Alexandria the young Origen not only visited the Christians in prison but greeted them on their way to execution, infuriating the hostile crowds to such an extent that he had to keep changing his place of residence, moving from house to house. All his life he longed for martyrdom as the truest form of baptism, a longing that was partly satisfied, for at an advanced age he himself was viciously tortured during the Decian persecution in 250 AD; he died soon afterwards, possibly as a result of this torture.

Christian teaching was the background of his whole academic career. Having become a *grammaticus*, a teacher of grammar and literature, at the age of 18, he was soon head-hunted by Demetrius, the Bishop of Alexandria, to become his catechist. Alexandria had long been the home of the 'spiritual', that is, non-literal, understanding of Scripture, a tradition initiated by the first-century Jewish scholar Philo, and seen also in the work of Clement of Alexandria around 200.[14] Most significant, therefore, was Origen's division of his catechumens: he entrusted the beginners to Heraclas, while he himself taught the more advanced catechumens, no doubt extending to them the learning he had imbibed at the University of Alexandria. Before long he was peremptorily invited to expound the Scriptures at Caesarea in Palestine. There he took up residence, especially after becoming *persona non grata* at Alexandria, by accepting priestly ordination without the permission of Demetrius, his own bishop at Alexandria. He seems to have expounded the Scriptures publicly each day. Earlier Christian writers had, of course, quoted and discussed the Scripture, but Origen was the first to produce thorough and consecutive commentaries on continuous texts. For this he used all the tools of contemporary scholarship in a way that set a standard and an example for all future commentators. The volume of his homilies and his written commentaries is immense,[15] but it was only towards the end that he allowed shorthand writers to take down his homilies. Such was his facility that he could turn to the bishop and ask which of several passages he should comment on.[16]

To complete this introduction it is worth quoting two passages, one from Origen himself to show how seriously he took his responsibility and loyalty as a teacher in the Church, and another from one of his students to show – in extremely flowery language – the impression made on students. Commenting on Mt. 5.30 ('If your right hand causes you to stumble, cut it off and thrust it from you'), Origen says, 'I, who seem to be a right hand to you and am named as a presbyter and seem to preach the word of God, if I should do anything against the teaching of the Church and the rule of the gospel, so that I create a stumbling-block for you the Church, may the whole Church with one accord, acting in concert, cut me off and fling me, their hand, away.'[17]

As a teacher he was clearly demanding and inspirational. He did not confine himself narrowly to Scripture but made use of his wider skills, 'for example the knowledge of literature or the theory of grammar, as geometry or mathematics or even the discipline of dialectic'.[18] As to its effects, his pupil, later the Bishop of Neo-Caesarea, writes long afterwards (c. AD 340) about his instruction: 'Like a spark landed in the middle of our soul, the love for the most attractive Word of all, and for this man who was his friend and confidant, was kindled and fanned into flame. After he had come to think that there was something in us, he hoed, dug, watered, did everything he could and succeeded in taming us. On occasion he would trip us up in speech, challenging us in thoroughly Socratic fashion, every time he saw us fighting the reins like unbroken horses. At first it was hard for us and not without grief, as he was introducing us novices, who had never practised following an argument, to his own reasoning, and purifying us at the same time'.[19]

Origen and the Hidden Sense of Scripture

In the first Christian century the Jewish philosopher Philo of Alexandria set about explaining Judaism in Hellenistic terms, aware that many Jewish beliefs and practices would seem absurd to the pagan Roman world. Amply aware that time could not exist before Creation ('It would be a sign of great simplicity to think that the world was created in six days, or indeed at all in time, because all time is only the space of days and nights'), he concentrates on interpreting the number six as the perfect number. He also interprets the creation of heaven and earth symbolically, based on the Platonic theory of ideas: 'Speaking symbolically he [Moses, as author of Genesis] calls the mind "heaven", since the natures which can be comprehended only by the intellect are in heaven, and sensation he calls "earth" because it is sensation which has obtained a corporeal and somewhat earthy constitution.'[20] He interprets the Paradise of Eden both literally and symbolically: 'Symbolically taken it means wisdom, intelligence both divine and human, and the proper comprehension of the causes of things, since it was proper to establish a contemplative system of life.'[21] In the same way, he interprets biblical laws symbolically; for example, 'By the command that the feet of the victim should be washed it is figuratively shown that we must no longer walk upon the earth, but soar aloft and traverse the air, for the soul of the man who is devoted to God springs upward and mounts from earth to heaven.'[22]

Against this background it is important first to establish Origen's priorities in understanding the biblical text. The modern historico-critical scholar at the beginning of the twenty-first century would set about establishing the literal meaning of the text and then might attempt to understand the text by some exercise of demythologization. The seven days of Creation are not a historical account but an analysis of the relationship of the visible world to a creator, a statement of the unique position of human beings, expressed in the framework of a claim that the regulations for the Jewish Sabbath are part of the very constitution of the universe. The temptation of Jesus on the top of a very high mountain from where he could see all the territories of the world is an expression of Jesus rejecting a wrong conception of the office of messiah, while at the same time contrasting Jesus with Moses, who was also taken to the top of a very high mountain from where he could see all the territory of the land he was not allowed to enter.

The modern exegete would feel justified in thus departing from a literal historical understanding of the text without casting any doubt on the absolute inspiration of the text. So also would Origen, for he doughtily insists on the verbal inspiration of Scripture 'up to every last letter',[23] for the divinity of Scripture extends to the whole of it.[24] He holds also that there can be no error in Scripture, so he goes into meticulous and often valuable detail about such tricky problems as arrangements in Noah's Ark for waste disposal and for feeding carnivorous animals.[25] This is not the same as saying that every detail of Scripture is historically correct. Origen joins Philo in rejecting the literal historicity of the account of the Creation. Some of the laws cannot be taken literally, such as the prohibition of eating a vulture, for no one, he thinks, even in the direst need, would want to eat a vulture![26] He goes further than a modern literary critic would allow by refusing to accept poetic expression and metaphor as literally true. Along with his very careful study of the letter, and insistence that every word of Scripture, even the definite article,[27] has its meaning, goes a hypercritical blindness to figures of speech and poetic modes of expression. So he mocks those who expect the prophecies of messianic peace in Isaiah 11 that 'the lion will eat hay like the ox', or of divine retribution expressed as 'divine anger burning like a fire' (Jer. 15.14), to be literally fulfilled.[28] Indeed, in his early writings all anthropomorphic references to God are unpalatable to him. Some decades later, in a rather charming passage, he grants that God's seeming anger is not really anger at all but a pretence in order to frighten sinners into conversion, as though speaking to children, adding, 'And you will find many such human expressions in the Bible'.[29] In his early writings he is less flexible: 'If God is represented as walking in the evening in the Garden and Adam hiding under the tree, no one can doubt that this is not meant in a material sense, but that in a transferred sense some mystery is indicated. And as for Cain fleeing from the face of God . . .'[30]

Even a cursory reading of Origen's homilies brings it home to the reader that, despite his care in establishing the text and its literal, material meaning, for Origen the literal truth is simply unimportant. Occasionally impatience with historicity becomes explicit. Commenting on 'Abraham stood by them under the tree' during the divine visit to Abraham (Genesis 18), he explodes, 'What does it help me who have come to hear what the Holy Spirit teaches the human race if I hear that Abraham was standing under a tree? Let us rather see what this tree is, under which Abraham stood.[31]

Abraham stood under the tree of Mambre, and 'mambre' (by a rather tortuous etymology) means 'sharpness of sight' or 'insight'. Since Abraham was pure of heart, this enabled him to see God. This is typical of Origen's moralistic interpretation of many of the factors in both Old and New Testament. The real meaning of the stages of the journey of the Israelites through the desert at the Exodus is the stages of the soul's ascent towards God.[32] His impatience also overflows into impatience with literalists. Origen accuses Melito of teaching that God was corporeal,[33] and sarcastically responds that if God has seven eyes (as in Zech. 4.10), and if 'you will find shelter under his wings' (Ps. 90.4), we are not made in the image of God, as we have only two eyes and no wings. If the earth is his footstool, should we look for God's feet here or in the Antipodes?[34]

In the New Testament, also, after a skilled and detailed discussion of the difference between the first three Gospels and John about precisely when Jesus went down to Capernaum, he cuts short, declaring, 'Anyone who examines the gospels carefully to check disagreement over historicity will grow dizzy, and will either altogether abandon the truth of the gospels or, not daring altogether to set aside confidence about our Lord, prefer one of them at random or admit that their truth does not lie in their material characteristics.'[35] Soon afterwards he simply drops in mid-flow an excellent discussion of the positioning of the cleansing of the temple in the synoptics and John; presumably he felt this was a question that he could afford to leave unresolved. Where his interest lies becomes clear when he announces the principle of the evangelists: 'Their intention was to speak the truth spiritually and materially at the same time where that was possible but, where it was not possible in both ways, to prefer the spiritual to the material. Spiritual truth is often preserved in material falsehood, so to speak.'[36]

This final 'so to speak' is a sort of apology. Elsewhere Origen goes further, asserting that the Word of God deliberately contains passages scandalous[37] and impossible in both law and history in order to alert the reader to 'spiritual' truths. The true meaning of Scripture should not be accessible to those who are unwilling to take the trouble to discover the meaning.[38] Sometimes only a few phrases are materially untrue; sometimes more.[39] Origen holds that some passages of Scripture have no literal meaning at all, but in any case the spiritual meaning is to be preferred. What is the justification for this easy escape route?

Serious exegete that he was, Origen seeks scriptural justification for his understanding of Scripture. His explicit point of departure is Pauline and double. First, he repeatedly quotes or refers to 2 Cor. 3.6: 'The written letter kills, but the Spirit gives life.' Paul is in fact contrasting the two covenants. Origen, however, against his Neoplatonic background, inherited from Philo and the Alexandrians, regards the 'letter' as being akin to the 'body', since both contrast with 'spirit'. It is by these channels that we see entering the Church the tendency, which will become more and more important, to reject the body in favour of the spirit (or the Spirit). In Platonism, 'ideas' (pure concepts), are all-important, and the material or bodily expressions of them are grossly inferior. A presupposition of Platonism is that there are two levels of being, above and below. The real level of being is above, comprising ideas or forms, the true form to which a word refers, and of which the corresponding material reality below is no more than an inferior and partial copy. Ideas can, of course, be seized only by the spirit. Since the same word, *pneuma*, is used for the human spirit and the Spirit of God, it is easy to equate the affairs of the spirit with the affairs of the Spirit and regard the affairs of the body as grossly inferior. This is a fundamental change from Hebrew anthropology, in which all creation, including material things, is good.[40] Origen regularly uses *somatikos*, 'bodily' or 'material', in unfavourable contrast to *pneumatikos*, 'spiritual'. It is the *pneumatikos*, 'spiritual' sense of Scripture that matters; even if there is a *somatikos* ('bodily' or 'material') sense, this is less important. The Neoplatonic preference for mind over matter has, therefore, by a subtle change, gone to the root of Origen's attitude to Scripture, because the literal or material sense is regarded as less important than the spiritual or transferred sense.

His second point of departure is the word 'mystery' in Scripture.[41] The Pauline sense of 'mystery', used in the singular, was the great apocalyptic revelation, to be made clear at the end of time (Rom. 11.25; 16.25; 1 Cor. 2.1; 15.51; Eph. 1.9; 3.3-4; 6.19; Col. 1.26; 4.3). The same sense occurs in Mk 4.11: 'To you is revealed the mystery of the Kingdom of God, but to those outside everything comes in parables.' With a slight, but highly significant, adjustment, this was understood by Matthew and Luke to refer to separate mysteries of the Kingdom; namely, each of the parables. In their passages parallel to Mk 4.11, Mark's singular 'mystery' is exchanged for the plural, and the parables are classed as the myster*ies* of the Kingdom of Heaven: 'To you is granted to understand the mysteries of the Kingdom of Heaven, but to them it is not granted' (Mt. 13.11). This understanding of the word 'mysteries' is combined with the fact that some of the parables in the Gospels are in fact allegories, in which each element in the story has a corresponding significance in the meaning of the parable. The parables are, then, mysteries that cannot be understood without some explanation. This is particularly frequent in Matthew. Obvious examples are the parables of the sower (Mt. 13.4-9), to which a 'key' is given in 13.18-23, and of the wheat and darnel (Mt. 13.24-30, keyed 13.36-43). Matthew tends to adjust parables, such as the wicked tenants, which in Mk 12.1-8 is hardly an allegory, inserting a number of allegorical traits (Mt. 21.33-39). However, some story-parables, such as the crafty steward of Lk. 16.1-8, decidedly have no allegorical features. Scripture scholars still dispute whether the parables used by Jesus have only a single point of comparison rather than the multiple points of comparison found in allegory, or whether (as Adolf Jülicher famously held) Jesus never used allegory, and allegory was introduced only by the evangelists. Nevertheless, this single meaning can validly be classed as a 'hidden' meaning.

This double point of departure founds the conception that the salvific and 'real' meaning of Scripture is not the surface and obvious meaning but a hidden meaning, something mysterious and difficult to decipher, accessible only to those with special insight or special instruction, like the clues of a crossword puzzle. The basis for this understanding of Scripture, then, is not (as in the Pauline use of 'mystery') that the meaning and purpose of Scripture will be made clear at the end of time, but that each element in Scripture has a hidden meaning. Origen sees this also in the idea of 1 Cor. 13.12: 'Now we see only reflections in a mirror, but then we shall be seeing face to face,' though Paul is in fact contrasting our earthly knowledge of the things of God with the full knowledge of heaven (as also in Col. 2.16, 'shadows of things to come').

Origen's full theory is most clearly set out in *De Principiis*, 4.2.4. As his starting point he quotes Prov. 22.20 in the Greek LXX form, which includes the word 'triply' or 'threefold'. This he takes as a justification of his understanding of precisely three senses of Scripture.[42] This is backed up by an allusive argument from *The Shepherd* of Hermas, though Origen himself coyly admits that the work is 'despised by some people'. There a perfectly straightforward injunction to make two further copies of the message that has been given, handing one copy to the presbyters, is allegorized to indicate three senses of Scripture, intended for three different sorts of people. This is used to justify three types of interpretation of Scripture. On this basis, Origen then cites four Pauline examples to show the correct way that Scripture should be understood.

- 1 Cor. 9.9: Paul argues from the law that oxen are not to be muzzled during threshing to the right of a missioner to sustenance with the riposte 'God is not worried about oxen!'. Origen therefore regards the true meaning of the text of Deuteronomy to be the missioners' rights, rather than the obvious 'literal' or 'somatic' meaning.[43]
- 1 Cor. 10.11: the rock from which water was struck in the desert is seen as a type or foreshadowing of Christ, the source of the water of life.
- Heb. 8.5: 'See that you work to the model shown to you on the mountain.' Here the author of Hebrews is arguing that earthly realities are only a copy or reflection of heavenly realities. Again the word 'type' is used, signifying the mould or stamp that gives metal its shape, and is the pattern on which the finished metal product is moulded.
- The allegory of Hagar and Sarah in Gal. 4.21-31.

In each of these cases Origen regards the transferred, typological or allegorical meaning as the true meaning of the text, bypassing any literal meaning. These, however, form a slender base on which to found a whole doctrine of interpreting the Scripture, so slender that it immediately suggests that it is not the real basis of Origen's thought, but only a justification for ideas already lodged in his mind. This is indeed the case, for the real basis is the Alexandrian tradition of interpretation, stemming from Philo, whose influence Origen generously admits.

Whatever the source of Origen's thinking, the result of the search for hidden meaning is overwhelming. Passing over the *somatic* or material meaning of the text, Origen concentrates on allegory, moral and typological meanings. 'The doctrine of the Law and the Prophets at the school of Christ is like this; the letter is bitter, like the skin; secondly, you will come to the shell, which is the moral doctrine; thirdly, you will discover the meaning of the mysteries, with which the souls of the saints are nourished in the present life and the future.'[44] So in the book of Joshua, the crossing of the Jordan is a type of the sacrament of baptism and the moral lesson is drawn, 'then, when the Jordan is parted, you will enter the land of promise by the services of the priests'.[45] Commenting on the passage in the book of Joshua about the sun standing still, the lengthening of the day and the huge hailstones that ensured Joshua's victory (Josh. 10.11-12), Origen does not linger on the historical problems or the miraculous phenomena, or point out that this is a snatch of poetry, but immediately passes to the symbolism: 'until all Israel may be saved the day is lengthened and the setting is deferred and the sun never sinks down as long as the sun of righteousness pours the light of truth into the hearts of believers'.[46] Just afterwards, Joshua's (that is, Jesus's, for in Greek it is the same word) opponents, the five kings immured in the cave at Makkedah, are the five senses by which people fall into sin – again a moral meaning.

In the New Testament the parable of the workers in the vineyard (Mt. 20.1-15) may serve as an example. The attraction of allegory is such that Origen interprets it allegorically, giving a detailed 'key': the early workers are those who respond to Christ's call in childhood, continuing to the 11th-hour workers who respond only in old age. Irenaeus had already used allegory to interpret the parable, but attached the interpretation to the different eras of world history.[47] Origen takes the message of the parable to be that it is zeal rather than length of service that matters.[48] In fact, a standard modern interpretation sees the series of repeated invitations to work in the field as a merely literary feature, not intended to be allegorized. The real meaning of the parable is not in this: 'For Matthew our parable represented the reversal of rank which would take place on the Last Day.' In Jesus's mouth the lesson was simpler still, but relates to the generosity of the landowner: 'the behaviour of a large-hearted man who is compassionate and full of sympathy for the poor. This, says Jesus, is how God deals with men.'[49]

In the same way, commenting on Jesus's saying in Jn 2.19, 'Destroy this Temple and in three days I will raise it up', Origen does not discuss such matters as Jesus's original meaning, the relationship of the saying here to the accusation in the synoptic trial scene, or how this constituted a 'sign'. Nor, having raised the question,[50] of considerable interest both historical and theological, whether the cleansing of the temple occurs at the beginning of Jesus's ministry (as in John) or at the end (as in the other Gospels), does he reach a conclusion or theological evaluation.[51] Instead, he continues, 'Both the temple and Jesus' body appear to me to be a type of the Church, in that the Church, being called a "temple" is built of living stones, becoming a spiritual house for a holy priesthood, built upon the foundation of the apostles and prophets, Christ Jesus being the chief corner-stone. And through the saying "Now you are the body of Christ and members of it", even if the harmony of the stones of the temple appears to be destroyed, all the bones of Christ appear to be scattered in persecutions and afflictions, as it says in Psalm 21.'

Here again the interest is all on the 'hidden meaning' of the temple and Christ as a type of the Church and the moral lesson of the unity of the Church. Perhaps Origen's single most important application of this method concerned the New Jerusalem of the book of Revelation, 20–21. An interpretation until then widespread in the Christian Church[52] was that Christ would literally reign on earth for a thousand years before the final resurrection. This 'millenarian' interpretation was based on a literal understanding of Rev. 20.1-10. Origen would have none of it, criticizing this as understanding Scripture 'in a Jewish way'.[53] He interpreted the 'precious stones' of the heavenly Jerusalem (Rev. 21.19) as faithful Christians. Such was his authority as a teacher that millenarianism seems to have waned from that moment, never again to be taken seriously in the Church, though periodically revived by fringe groups in the Middle Ages and beyond.

Conclusion

Despite his condemnation as a heretic in AD 553, the influence of Origen has been immense. He was, as his appeal to Paul's argument and the extensive use of allegory in both Melito and Irenaeus show, not the first Christian interpreter to appeal to allegorical or typological meanings in Scripture. What was new was the balance: Origen changed the balance of power by exalting the 'hidden' or 'mysterious' meaning above the literal or 'somatic' sense of the Scriptures. This was to have a powerful – some would say catastrophic – effect for centuries to come.

Origen has always been a deeply controversial figure. To the great fourth-century historian Eusebius he was a hero, but at the end of the century Epiphanius (c. AD 315–403), the arch-heresy-hunting Bishop of Salamis in Cyprus, stirred up furious opposition to him (as we shall see, p. 52). It cannot be denied that many of his speculations were judged to be unacceptable to Christianity, largely because of the Neoplatonic philosophical background against which he understood the Bible. In the sixth century he was condemned as a heretic by the Emperor Justinian, and in his wake by the Second Council of Constantinople. It is, however, surely unjustified to brand him as a heretic for his theological speculations in areas where no firm traditional interpretation yet existed. To confine parallels to figures mentioned in this study, Melito was not so branded (p. 20 above) for his Christology, nor Bernard of Clairvaux for his opposition to the Immaculate Conception of Mary, as it was defined seven centuries later.[54]

Opinion is still divided about the value of his biblical interpretation. The most thorough study of Origen as a biblical scholar is Hanson's *Allegory and Event.*[55] Hanson praises many qualities in Origen's work, perhaps especially his openness and objectivity. However, he also criticizes Origen heavily for his lack of historical sense. By undervaluing the literal, historical sense of the text and leaping immediately to the 'spiritual' sense, whether typological, allegorical or merely moral, Origen shows himself 'virtually blind'[56] to the importance of history in the process of revelation. For Origen, says Hanson, 'history can be no more than an acted parable, a charade for showing forth eternal truths about God'.[57] 'Allegory rendered him deplorably independent of the Bible', since 'he used it as a magic ring whenever he did not agree with the Bible',[58] loading his own ideas onto the text with irresponsible freedom. However, in his introduction to the re-issue of Hanson's book, Joseph Trigg points out that Hanson was himself reacting to the excessive praise of Origen by Daniélou and de Lubac. Trigg himself stresses the value of Origen's grasp of the whole thrust of Scripture. Although Origen often sees the great sweep of Christian teaching in biblical books where it cannot have been the intention of the original authors, scholars more modern than Hanson are less concerned with the impossible task of establishing the mind of the original authors than with viewing the Bible as one single, developing witness to divine revelation.

Bibliography

Most of the works of Origen used here are available in English translation in the series *Fathers of the Church* (Catholic University of America Press). For others, the French *Sources Chrétiennes* series has been used.

Further Reading

Daniélou, J., *Origen* (London and New York: Sheed & Ward, 1955).
Trigg, J. W., *Origen* (London: Routledge, 1998).
Von Balthasar, H. U., *Origen, Spirit and Fire* (Washington, DC: Catholic University of America, 1984).

CHAPTER 4

Jerome

Introduction

The way of reading the Bible in the Western Church was radically altered by Jerome, in several ways. First, he gave the Western Church its Latin text – an imperfect text perhaps, but vastly superior to any preceding Latin version. Second, he was the first scholar in the West to read the Scriptures against their Jewish background, making widespread use both of Jewish knowledge and interpretations and of the original Semitic languages. Third, by introducing a much firmer knowledge of the material meaning of the text he made notable progress in diminishing the prevalence of concentrating on allegorical and symbolic meanings of Scripture, which had become so dominant under the influence of the Neoplatonism of the Alexandrian school of exegesis.

Early Formation

Jerome was not an attractive character. Hypersensitive to criticism from others, he seems to have lacked any ability to criticize himself. Prone to exaggeration and the highest flights of brilliant rhetoric, he could swing from extravagant praise of his predecessors and sources to virulent abuse. He had a talent for making enemies. In his letters, which were widely diffused at the time, he invented nicknames for those he regarded as his enemies: Origen was Adamantinus (the unrivalled – that was all right); Vigilantius (the vigilant) became Dormitantius (the sleepy); his long-term friend and later enemy Rufinus became Grunnius (the grunter). He made no secret of his dislike of his venerable older contemporary, Ambrose of Milan. He patronized his younger contemporary, Augustine of Hippo, with sarcastic courtesy. At the same time, it must be accepted that his output was astonishing. Despite constant eye trouble, which made him rely on expensive stenographers and copyists (financed by his aristocratic sponsors), he produced enough material for his surviving works – and we know of others that have not survived – to fill eight volumes of Migne's *Patrologia Latina* (*PL*). He worked amazingly fast,[1] translating the book of Judith in 'one little night's work'.[2]

Tempting as it is to give a full biography of this fascinating, albeit not particularly attractive, character, we must keep to the subject of the interpretation of Scripture, introducing only those aspects of Jerome's biography that are relevant. The first is his sophisticated rhetorical education. Jerome was born into a rich family, which could afford to provide him not only a full education in the Latin classics but also the money to continue buying books – an expensive commodity in those days of laborious copying by hand. His absorption in classical learning occasioned his famous dream as a young man, in which he was castigated for being a Ciceronian rather than a Christian. This seems to have occasioned his conversion to serious Christianity:

> In the middle of Lent I caught a fever, which seized hold of my exhausted frame and left it no peace. Incredible to say, I was no more than skin and bone. They were getting ready for my funeral, since my body was so cold that the only place where the breath and heat of life could be felt was my still warm, wasted chest. Suddenly I was caught up in spirit and dragged to the tribunal of the Judge. There was so much light and such dazzling splendour from those standing around that, falling to the ground, I did not dare to look. Asked my religion, I replied that I was a Christian. The Presider said, 'You lie. You are a Ciceronian, not a Christian, for where your treasure is, there too is your heart.' At that I fell silent, and amid strokes of the whip (for he had ordered me to be flogged) I was even more tormented by the fires of conscience, thinking over that verse, 'In hell who will give you praise?' However, I began to cry out and howl, 'Have mercy on me, Lord, have mercy on me.' This cry resounded among the blows of the whip. In the end those present knelt before the Presider and begged him to pardon my young age and grant me space to repent my error. Punishment could be exacted later if I ever again read books of pagan literature. In such a tight spot I would have been willing to promise even more, and began to swear by his name, saying, 'Lord, if I ever have or read secular books, I will have denied you.' At the words of this oath I was dismissed and returned to the upper world.[3]

Whether he kept his promise never again to read books of pagan literature or not, he certainly continued to fill his own writings with classical quotations and allusions. This he does even at the opening of the preface to his *Hebrew Questions on the Book of Genesis*: 'Although I ought to set out at the beginning of books the subject of the work which is to follow, I am compelled to take a tip from Terence by first replying to abuse, for in his plays he gave over the prologues to self-defence. For Lucius Lanvinus, like our Lucius, used to press him and accuse him of being a poet who stole from the public treasury. The Poet of Mantua also underwent the same treatment from his rivals in being accused of stealing from the ancients when he translated literally a few verses of Homer. He answered them that it needed exemplary strength to wrest the club of Hercules from his hands. Tully, too, who stood at the apex of Roman eloquence, king of orators . . .'.

This full grammatical and literary training stood him in good stead when it came to the linguistic work that first set him on his course of translating. His first serious attempt in this direction (in AD 380) was a translation and supplement of Eusebius's *Chronicle*, a sort of world history. In the preface to this work he writes of the difficulty of translation, and the importance of following the sense rather than the precise words, citing classical precedents for this. Most significantly, he already points out that the LXX Greek translation of the Bible, which had been the Bible of the Church for so long, signally fails in this, so that it is considered by many 'harsh and jarring to the ear'.[4] He goes on to point out that in the Latin translation some of the most beautiful poems of the Bible are 'utterly incoherent'. There was obviously work to be done!

Jerome in Rome

The occasion came when he left the East for Rome. His first recorded contact with Pope Damasus had been a letter he wrote from Antioch in AD 377. In fact he wrote twice (Letters 15 and 16) in quick succession, protesting his loyalty to Rome and asking Damasus for a ruling on a theological problem.[5] The letters are a tissue of neat biblical allusion and flattery. When he arrives in Rome as an interpreter or go-between for an Eastern delegation, he is soon found working for Damasus as drafting secretary,[6] and also answering Damasus's own biblical questions. He sends Damasus a very careful and competent reply on the meaning of 'Hosanna',[7] which displays a detailed knowledge of the Hebrew factors involved. He also sends Damasus a full exegesis of the parable of the two sons.[8] It is significant that Jerome avoids two contemporary tendencies, anti-Semitism and allegorization. Damasus had asked who and what each element in the story was; that is, he had asked for an allegorizing interpretation. Jerome avoids allegorizing the two sons (as Damasus had suggested) as the Jews and the gentiles, interpreting them[9] more generally as *sanctus et peccator*, and seeing the story as a third consecutive example in Luke of welcome to a sinner.

It was not long before a much more significant step was taken. In 383/84 Damasus entrusted Jerome with the task of 'restoring the New

Testament to its Greek original'.[10] Since Latin had become the language of the Church in Africa and Italy, a variety of translations had sprung up, known as the Old Latin, highly diverse and of varied merit. The first translations of the Greek Bible into the Latin of the West had been made in the second century. Two centuries later there were 'almost as many forms of the text as there are copies', says Jerome. With typical exaggeration Jerome claims to have completed the task, though in fact he revised only the four Gospels.[11] He later makes the same exaggerated claim to universality for the Old Testament, claiming that he translated 'the Old Testament' from the Greek, though in fact he translated only some of the wisdom books from the Greek (Psalms, Job, Proverbs, Ecclesiastes and Song of Songs). He would be glad that only the first of these has survived.

In his revision of the Gospels, he worked hurriedly, taking little care to highlight the similarities and differences between the different Gospels, or to translate the same Greek word by the same Latin word – both qualities of a translation considered so crucial in any modern translation. Perhaps the most remarkable achievement of the translation is the simplicity of style, a quality he will later show in his translation of the Hebrew Old Testament, and an impressive contrast to the polished high-flown rhetoric of his own writings, embellished in every paragraph with oratorical figures and classical allusions. Before his conversion Jerome had found the 'uncultured' style of Scripture so repellent that he had taken refuge in Plautus.[12] Now he was well aware of the need for this simplicity. In the early stages of his translation of the Old Testament he writes, 'If you read my translation you will appreciate the difficulty of understanding holy scripture, and especially the prophets. Do not seek in simple works the eloquence which in Cicero you despise for Christ's sake. A translation for Church use, even if it has linguistic charm, ought to disguise and avoid it, so that it may speak not to the idle schools of philosophers and their few disciples, but to the whole human race.'[13]

The next step, however, did not occur until other, less happy, circumstances had intervened. As Jerome expected and predicted in his dedicatory *Preface* to Pope Damasus,[14] when his revision of the Gospels appeared howls of protest and accusations of 'sacrilege!' greeted his changes from the familiar old texts. A change to familiar and well-loved texts is never welcome. However, Jerome's mildest reply to the protests was that there is no point in playing the lyre to a donkey;[15] he did not take criticism lying down. 'If they don't like the stream from the purest fountain, let them drink the muddy puddles.'[16]

From Rome to Bethlehem

Worse was to come. In AD 384, not long after the completion of the translation of the four Gospels, Pope Damasus died and Jerome's situation changed dramatically. He had been (or so it seemed to him) on the crest of a wave: 'I was called saintly, I was called humble and learned. In practically everyone's judgment I was considered worthy of the Papacy.'[17] In fact, when Damasus died, far from being elected Pope, Jerome was swiftly expelled from Rome. The circumstances are not clear, since we have only Jerome's account, but there must have been an official decision. Jerome mentions darkly the 'senatus Pharisaeorum'[18] as being responsible, no doubt a senate of the Roman clergy. His reputation was tarnished by his relationships with a number of aristocratic ladies, who supported him and kept him in funds, and to whom he acted as spiritual advisor. Jerome continually insisted that his relationships with these women were beyond reproach and that he encouraged their single-minded devotion to virginity and the ascetic life. It may, however, be questioned whether it was wise to write to a young girl, encouraging her in virginity in such erotic imagery as he used (drawing on the Song of Songs): 'Let the hidden places of your bedroom ever guard you. Let your Spouse always play with you within them. If you pray, you are speaking to your Spouse. If you read, he is speaking to you. When sleep overcomes you, he will come from behind the wall, put his hand through the hole and touch your belly. Roused, you will arise and say, "I am wounded by love".'[19]

Despite his indignant protestations of innocence it seems that Jerome had no choice but to leave Rome. After some wanderings he set up a monastic settlement, male and female, in Bethlehem. The joys and vicissitudes of this settlement, where Jerome spent the rest of his life, are not our subject. The importance of the move, however, was that it brought him into closer contact not only with Origen's great textual work, the *Hexapla*, at Caesarea a few kilometres away, but also with the Jewish tradition.

The Controversy over Origen

Jerome had long been a devotee of Origen and throughout his scholarly life continued to make widespread use of his writings. In his commentaries on books of the Bible Jerome repeatedly, with or (more often) without acknowledgement, borrows from Origen. One of Jerome's most important early achievements was to translate Origen's works into Latin, so making them accessible to the non-Graecists of the West, a work he continued spasmodically throughout his life. In his early period in Rome Jerome is unreserved in his praise of Origen. Having listed his

13 books on Genesis alone, Jerome continues: 'Do you not see that he equally surpassed all the Greeks and Latins by his labours? Who could ever read as much as he has written? But what reward has he had for all his sweat? He stands condemned by his bishop Demetrius, only the bishops of Palestine, Arabia, Phoenicia and Achaia dissenting. The city of Rome agreed with his condemnation, assembling a synod against him, not because of the novelty of his opinions or any heresy (as the ravening hounds against him cry nowadays) but because they could not bear the glory of his eloquence and of his knowledge. When he spoke everyone else seemed dumb.'[20]

In his book *On Famous Men* (AD 392) he still praises Origen's 'immortal genius'.[21] Later, Jerome becomes less fulsome. Controversy against Origen was reignited by Epiphanius, Bishop of Salamis, in AD 393, who accused Origen of being the spiritual father of Arius, the arch-heretic. This was largely based on Origen's interpretation of the two seraphim in the vision of Isaiah 6 as the Son and the Spirit, in attendance on God and therefore (argued Epiphanius) inferior to God. Origen was also accused of heresy for saying that the Son could not see the Father.[22] Controversy, not to say mayhem, broke out in the Holy Land, the defenders of Origen being led by Bishop John of Jerusalem and Rufinus (a boyhood friend of Jerome's and now leader of a monastic community in Jerusalem), and the opponents of Origen being led by Epiphanius, allied to Jerome.[23] At one stage Bishop John accused Jerome of being the cause of all the trouble, being an admirer of Origen. A former guest of Jerome's, Vigilantius, accused Jerome in Rome of being a full-blooded Origenist, to which Jerome replied expressing dignified loyalty to Origen, mixed with characteristic personal abuse of Vigilantius:[24] 'Origen is a heretic, true. What does that detract from me, since I do not deny that in many ways he is a heretic? . . . If I did not allow that he has erred, or if I did not daily anathematize his errors, I would be a partner in his errors. For are we not obliged to accept what is good in his writings without being bound to reject what is bad? He interpreted well many things in the scriptures, explained obscurities in the prophets and brought out the greatest mysteries both in the Old and the New Testaments. I have taken over what is good, and what is bad I have cut out or corrected or passed over in silence.'[25]

After a stand-off of three years, Jerome was induced in 397 to write a full treatise aimed at Bishop John in which he listed eight unacceptable points in Origen's *De Principiis*.[26] Origen's erroneous speculations listed are:

1. the Son and the Spirit cannot see the Father
2. souls are imprisoned in the body (a standard doctrine of Neoplatonism)
3. the devil and his company will eventually reign with the saints

4. the garments of skin with which God clothed Adam and Eve after the Fall were their bodies, before which they had no flesh, nerves or bones
5. the risen body is not in all respects the same as the earthly body, and is sexless
6. the biblical description of Paradise, the Garden of Eden, is to be understood figuratively rather than literally (Jerome says 'historically', by which term he normally means 'literally')
7. the waters above the heavens are heavenly virtues, and those below are the opposite
8. at the Fall human beings lost the image and likeness of God for which humanity was created.

It is tempting to defend Origen on several of these points. For instance, the first seems to be a crass blindness to Origen's real point in *De Principiis* about the immateriality of God, for he grants immediately afterwards that both Son and Spirit know the Father. Some of the other points would nowadays seem harmless, or at least to contain some truth. For instance, number 5 is an attempt to evaluate Jesus's teaching about the absence of marriage in heaven (Lk. 20.36) and Paul's teaching on the risen body (1 Cor. 15.42-44). Number 6 is on the way to stating an understanding of the Creation story in accordance with modern historico-critical thinking. Number 8 is an exaggerated way of describing the consequences of sin. Numbers 6 and 7 arise from Origen's studied lack of interest in the literal meaning of a text, and his preference for various symbolic and moral meanings. Understood literally, these two assertions are absurd; as poetry some might find them helpful. Number 3 may be seen as groping towards the truth that in the fullness of the Kingdom there will be no room for evil. It is arguable that the most dangerous point is number 2, which implies – in a way standard to all Neoplatonic understanding of the world – denial of the goodness of the material creation.

To me there seem to be three chief lessons to be drawn from the controversy over Origen. First, theology and the understanding of revelation advances step by step. It is the task of a theologian to speculate and to seek new ways of expressing Christian truth. Early expressions of a problem in theology often need to be reformulated. This is better done by sympathetic discussion aimed at discerning the truth of the inadequate formulation rather than by hostile name-calling. Origen was striving towards the expression of important truths, which he did not wholly succeed in reaching. It was therefore unfair and unhelpful of Epiphanius to brand him a heretic, for a heretic is one who chooses and adopts a point of view other than that of the tradition of the Church, not one who espouses a point of view which the Church will later judge to be unsatisfactory. Second, the Neoplatonic opposition of 'spirit good – body bad' is inherently dangerous, suggesting an anthropology and a world view that are difficult to reconcile with Christianity. Third, it is important to distinguish between the literal meaning of a text and its moral or symbolic application.

Before long Jerome and John were reconciled, but Jerome's relationships with Rufinus never recovered, becoming increasingly bitter and vitriolic on both sides. Jerome continued to side with Origen, if somewhat more explicitly discerningly: 'Does anyone want to praise Origen? Let him do so, as I do myself. . . . I have praised him as an exegete not as a teacher of dogma, his mind not his faith, as a philosopher not as an apostle. . . . I grant that I collected his works, and that is why I do not follow his errors, because I know everything he ever wrote. . . . I did read, yes, I did read Origen. If there is any crime in that, I confess! Indeed, these Alexandrian writings have emptied my purse [because their copying was so expensive]. If you believe me, I was never an Origenist. If you don't believe me, I have ceased to be now.'[27]

At any rate, among the debris of spoiled friendships Jerome retained his loyalty to his academic leader and guide. In discerning true and false in Origen, Jerome likened himself to a good money-changer who scrutinizes the coins offered to him, accepting the genuine and rejecting the counterfeit.[28]

Bethlehem: *Hebraica Veritas*

The development most important for the understanding of the Bible resulting from Jerome's move to Bethlehem was Jerome's transfer from translating from the Greek LXX to translating from the Hebrew Bible. From the time of the composition of the New Testament onwards, the Greek of the LXX had been the master text of the Church. Already in the New Testament most of the quotations of the Old Testament use this version, and some of them do not make sense in any other version. For instance, the famous text in Mt. 2.23, 'The virgin shall conceive and bear a son', quotes Isa. 7.14 in the LXX version, whereas the Hebrew text has simply 'The young woman shall conceive and bear a son'. The passage of Job 19.25 so freely used by the early Fathers to prove the bodily resurrection, 'I know that my Redeemer liveth', etc., is much less explicit in the Hebrew than in the Greek of the LXX. For this reason, the LXX was widely held to be an inspired translation; that is, the guidance of the Holy Spirit had watched over not only the original composition of the texts but their preservation as far as the translation itself. This belief was expressed in the legend of the *Letter of Aristeas*: the 70 translators commissioned at Alexandria by Pharaoh Ptolemy (probably Ptolemy Philadelphus, 285–247 BC) to translate the Pentateuch had each produced an identical translation. Just as in medieval times the Vulgate Latin version was simply 'the Bible' and it seems not to have entered anyone's head that it was not the original, or that there could be anything behind it,[29] so in the early Church the LXX was simply 'the Bible'. We have seen the total ignorance of Hebrew in the West at the time of Irenaeus (p. 26). We have also seen the revolutionary work of Origen at Caesarea in turning to the Hebrew text, and the linguistic limitations in Hebrew of even such a great scholar as himself (p. 36). Even so, in the West the work of Origen was hardly known until Jerome began to translate his commentaries and homilies. It was, accordingly, to the Greek LXX, not to the Hebrew, that Jerome was originally commissioned to restore the corrupt Latin texts. However, once he was resident in Bethlehem, and increasingly in contact with Jewish scholars, he became increasingly dissatisfied with the LXX.

In his early years Jerome had been compelled to learn Syriac (which he lampoons as *barbarus semisermo*, 'barbarous gibberish') for want of any other means of communication during his stay in Syria.[30] He also devised a novel expedient for overcoming sexual temptations; namely, learning Hebrew and its 'rasping and gasping' sounds from a Jewish convert to Christianity.[31] 'What labour I undertook, what difficulties I underwent, how often I despaired, how often I gave up and – in my determination to learn – began again!' he there admits. In Jerusalem he was tutored by another Jew, Bar Aninas; '*Quo labore, quo pretio!*' (What labour, what a price!) he complains.[32] Even in Rome he maintained his contact with Jewish friends, breaking off a letter to Pope Damasus in his excitement at the arrival of a parcel of books from the synagogue.[33] Now in Bethlehem he became increasingly aware of the differences between the LXX and the Hebrew. Continuing to associate with and learn from Jewish scholars, he was upset by their criticism of the 'inaccuracies' of the LXX (*PL* 28, 464 on Joshua; 1321 on Chronicles). So in his *Preface to the Psalms* he accepts that the LXX is perfectly acceptable for prayer, but not for controversy with the Jews, for which accuracy is required.[34]

Some of the differences between the Hebrew and the Greek are indeed the product of inaccuracy or of inferior textual readings used by the LXX, and the purpose of Origen's great *Hexapla* was to establish the most ancient text through comparison of a range of translations. However, the extensive septuagintal studies of the last half-century have established – rather too late for Jerome – that in many cases the reverse is true, and that the Hebrew relies on a text inferior to that which the LXX translated.[35] In many cases also the LXX offers a different or more developed text, representing a different historical or theological tradition. Modern scholarship no longer searches for an 'original' biblical text as *the* correct version of which all others are distortions. It is recognized that the biblical text continued to grow and develop, and that the LXX is an important element in and witness to that growth and variety. At the end of the fourth century, however, such researches were far in the future, and Jerome's Jewish colleagues and mentors bullied him into believing that the Hebrew text they held in their hands was the authentic text of the Bible and the LXX a degenerate offshoot. At first sight they were obviously correct, for the Greek text is only the translation of a Hebrew original. The Hebrew original from which it was translated was, however, at least four or five hundred years older than the Hebrew texts held by Jerome and his contemporaries. A more stalwart defence of the LXX could claim that (1) in half a millennium errors and changes could have crept into the Hebrew text, no less than into the Greek; and (2) the Hebrew text on which the LXX was based in some cases represented a different tradition to that of the fifth-century Hebrew texts. It was not, therefore, self-evident that the Hebrew was more 'correct' than the LXX. In some cases the Hebrew might be corrupt, in others the Greek, while in yet others the two texts might simply reflect different traditions, and both be 'correct' though different.

The Purpose of Biblical Study

Even though he became convinced that the Hebrew text was superior, Jerome had to be careful of censuring the highly respected LXX version, universally used in the Christian Church and widely held to be inspired. In the book in which he first used the term *Hebraica veritas* (Hebrew truth), he excuses any faults in it by accepting – or at least quoting – the Jewish opinion that the 70 translators deliberately concealed messianic passages, on the grounds that they did not want to give even the appearance of compromising monotheism: 'Neither do we charge the Seventy translators with error, as our rivals snarl, nor do we regard our labours as being a correction of them, since they did not wish to present to Ptolemy the king of Alexandria all the mysteries of the sacred scriptures, and especially those which promised the coming of Christ, lest even the Jews should seem to worship a second God, since he – being a follower of Plato – valued them precisely because they were monotheists.'[36]

Occasionally Jerome gives a passage where this argument holds. For example, in Letter 57[37] he quotes Hos. 11.2, where the LXX could be understood as suppressing a reference to Christ:

> *Hebrew:* When Israel was a child I loved him and called *my son* out of Egypt.

LXX: When Israel was a child I loved him and called *their sons* out of Egypt.[38]

Recent scholarship confirms that Jerome's instincts (or his informants) were not wholly inaccurate. The original translation of the Pentateuch into Greek probably dates from the mid-third century BC (the 'Ptolemy' of the Aristaeus legend is probably Ptolemy II Philadelphus, 285–247 BC). Since then the LXX had had a very chequered history, two elements of which had been the insertion and then (in the second century AD) the removal of Christian elements, a removal which Jerome attributes to the original translators. The purpose of Origen's great work through the *Hexapla* had been precisely to establish a stable, even an authentic, text of the LXX.[39]

Jerome's Christological argument does not hold universally. It is, however, an important indication of his two chief interests in Scripture. The first is his pursuit of accuracy. Origen had considered the literal sense (if there was one, which was not always the case, see p. 41) to be less important that the spiritual senses. Jerome, as his very careful investigations in such works as *Hebrew Questions on Genesis* shows, was prepared to take endless trouble to establish the literal (or, as he called it, the 'historical') sense of the Scripture. He insists that the literal sense must be the foundation of any 'spiritual' sense.[40] Jerome's other interest in Scripture is, however, chiefly Christological: he sees one of the most important aspects of the Old Testament to be typological, the foretelling of Christ[41] and (less frequently) of the Church. We may deduce this double focus of interest perhaps most fully from his letter to Paulinus of Nola, urging him to Scripture study and giving reasons for doing so. When allowance has been made for the rhetoric and classical allusion that pervade all his letters, it is possible to discern what he sees to be important in each of the books of Scripture.

An introductory section of the letter insists repeatedly that it is impossible to begin the study of Scripture without a guide,[42] and it soon becomes clear that the function of the guide is to teach the meaning of the 'mysteries' contained in Scripture. Just as Irenaeus insists on the rule of faith, so Jerome insists that you must first learn before you can teach. He inveighs with his customary vehemence against 'the garrulous old woman, the weak-minded old man, the wordy sophist' who lacerate the Scriptures before they learn, and against that 'most vicious form of teaching, twisting the reluctant scriptures to their own meanings'.[43] This indicates caution and discernment in interpretation, limiting the arabesques of allegory, though Jerome himself is not enough of a theoretician to give positive guidance on what is and is not acceptable. Jerome differs from Origen by the influence he received from the Antiochene school: for Origen the literal meaning of the Scripture (if

there is one) is subordinate to the applied or 'mystical' meaning; for
Jerome the literal meaning is always supremely important. Nevertheless,
the section of this letter characterizing each of the books repeatedly
stresses that the books are full of 'mysteries' (Exodus, Numbers, Job),
'typical meanings far different from their literal meanings' (Hosea, the
Twelve Prophets); 'the Apocalypse of John has as many mysteries as
words'. In Job he specifies the prophecy of bodily resurrection; in other
books the imagery of the Christian Church, the abolition of the old
law, the struggle of the Church against heresy, salvation to the gentiles,
Christ on the Cross. In the Psalms, David sings of Christ, Solomon (the
putative author of the wisdom literature) unites Christ and the Church.
Esther is a type of the Church. Jerome's interest in the Old Testament
is therefore not so much in the history, guidance and development of
the people of Israel, or in the gradual revelation charted in the Old
Testament itself, as in a 'prequel' to the New Testament and to the
time of Christ and the Church.[44] This is in fact the angle from which
his commentaries on the prophets function, so that Hab. 3.19 'I will
rejoice in *God* my saviour' (in both Hebrew and LXX) is translated
'*exaltabo in Deo* Jesu *meo*', and in his commentary[45] Jerome comments,
'The prophet is speaking of the apostles and of the people who believe
in Christ'. In the commentary on Jonah, not only is Jonah's three days
in the sea-beast a type of the Lord's resurrection, but the prophet's
flight to Tarshish is explained Christologically: 'We can say about our
Lord and Saviour that he left his house and homeland and, by taking
flesh, in some way fled from heaven and came to Tarshish, that is, into
the sea of this world.'[46]

This, however, does not mean that Jerome was blind to the literal
meaning. Thus in commenting on Ezekiel's vision of the dead bones he
steers a very careful course. The prophecy, he maintains, is not about
the general resurrection, though he does not deny that the general
resurrection is a scriptural teaching; it is a prophecy of the restoration
of captive Israel.[47]

The truth is that Jerome was in a cleft stick, straining for accuracy
according to the Hebrew text, but acknowledging the place of the
LXX in the Christian Church. On ecclesiological grounds Origen had
refused to reject the LXX as it was used in the Churches, writing, 'Are
we to suppose that Providence, which has provided for the edification
of all the Churches of Christ through the medium of the holy scriptures, has not taken proper care of the needs of those for whom Christ
died?' Jerome reiterates, 'Yet the LXX has rightly held its place in the
churches, either because it is the first of all the versions, made before
the coming of Christ, or else because it was used by the apostles, though
only where it agrees with the Hebrew.[48]

The claim that the New Testament ('the Apostles') follows the LXX only where it agrees with the Hebrew is astonishing, for Jerome knows full well that there are dozens of places where a New Testament quotation of the Old differs from the Hebrew text. He is perhaps arguing that a translator is obliged to give the sense and not the exact words of a passage, for he goes on to give a bewildering list of scriptural passages where Hebrew, LXX and the commonly accepted Latin version differ from one another. His fullest defence of returning to the Hebrew comes in the *Apology*:

> Our Origen (I call him 'our' not because of the accuracy of his teaching but because of the genius of his learning) in all his books, after the LXX translation explains and teaches the interpretation of the Jews. Eusebius and another contemporary, Didymus, do the same. The apostolic writers use the Hebrew scriptures. It is obvious that the apostles and evangelists do the same. Whenever our Lord and Saviour mentions the Old Testament he gives examples from the Hebrew books. We say this not to revile the LXX, but because the authority of the apostles and Christ is greater, and wherever the LXX do not depart from the Hebrew the apostles use their translation, but wherever they diverge they put in Greek what they have learnt from the Hebrews.[49]

Here again the claim is astonishing: the apostles and evangelists use the LXX only where it does not diverge from the Hebrew text. Respect the LXX though he did, this respect did not prevent him turning directly to the Hebrew for his major work of translation. He considered the *Hebraica veritas* to be the only fully authentic text.

What, then, of the biblical books that had never been written in Hebrew? Previous Church authorities had distinguished three classes of books revered in the Church. The early Church, being Greek-speaking, had adopted the 'Alexandrian' canon of the Alexandrian Jews, consisting of 22 sacred books, which included the Deutero-canonical books, those that existed only in Greek: Wisdom, Ecclesiasticus,[50] Judith, etc. The parts of this Bible existing only in Greek were excluded by official Judaism at about the turn of the first/second centuries AD. Jerome translated – or at least revised – the so-called books of Solomon (Proverbs, Ecclesiastes and the Song of Songs), devoting three days to the work after a long illness.[51] He treated the short stories in the same – or even more – cavalier way. In a characteristically aggressive preface he claims that he translated Esther from the Hebrew 'word for word',[52] but he turned to Tobit and Judith only in response to pressing requests from friends, and rather against his better judgement. He had texts only in Aramaic, a language he did not know, so he persuaded a Jewish friend to translate them orally into Hebrew, which he then translated into Latin. The process took him one day for Tobit and 'one little night's work' for the 16 chapters of Judith. This was not careful work, even by Jerome's standards.[53]

The experience of the howls of disapproval he had received as a result of his corrections of the Gospels remained in his memory, but Jerome was not one to wilt at criticism and adverse comment. In the preface to his translation of Isaiah he parries feistily: 'Nor am I unaware what labour it requires to understand the prophets. No one can easily make a judgment on interpretation without first understanding what he reads. We have laid ourselves open to the teeth of many who, spurred on by envy, despise anything they cannot themselves achieve. So I thrust my hand into the flames knowingly and after forethought. Nevertheless I ask this of critical readers. . . . Let them first read and then despise. Otherwise their condemnation of what they do not know will clearly be based not on judgment but on the presupposition of hatred.'[54]

Jerome was entirely correct about the opposition that his return to the Hebrew would occasion. The great St Augustine, Bishop of Hippo, was rash enough to suggest to Jerome that on ecumenical grounds he would have preferred a translation based on the LXX, since the return to the Hebrew would drive one further wedge between Eastern and Western Churches. In fact Augustine considered that both the Hebrew and the LXX versions of the Bible were inspired, so that from this point of view both could be used as sacred Scripture.[55] Before concluding his letter to Jerome with fulsome compliments and praise, he goes on to describe the tumult provoked in North Africa by a reading from Jerome's translation of the book of Jonah:

> A certain bishop, one of our brethren, having introduced in the church over which he presides the reading of your version, came upon a word in the book of the prophet Jonah, of which you have given a very different rendering from that which had been long familiar to the senses and memory of all the worshippers, and had been chanted for so many generations in the church.[56] Thereupon arose such a tumult in the congregation, especially among the Greeks, correcting what had been read, and denouncing the translation as false, that the bishop was compelled to ask the testimony of the Jewish residents (it was in the town of Oea [now Tripoli]). They, whether from ignorance or from spite, answered that the words in the Hebrew manuscript were correctly rendered in the Greek version and in the Latin one taken from it. What further need I say? The man was compelled to correct your version of that passage as if it had been falsely translated.[57]

Needless to say, this provoked a furious reply from Jerome, who complained that a previous (unanswered) letter from Augustine seems to have become known all over Rome before he had received it himself, and twice asked Augustine to 'desist from annoying an old man who seeks retirement in his monastic cell'.[58] Nor does he hesitate to explain painstakingly and patronizingly to Augustine that Augustine is too stupid to understand the conventions of Origen's *Hexapla*. To Augustine's polite concluding suggestion that he is ready to accept from Jerome any correction of scriptural interpretations, Jerome replies that he has never read Augustine's works with attention and has few of them, 'which if I were disposed to criticise, I could prove to be at variance, I shall not say with my own opinion (for I am nobody) but with the interpretations of the older Greek commentators'.[59]

Conclusion

Despite such explosions the translation Jerome produced became the standard version of the Bible all over the Christian West for a thousand years. Jerome was not responsible for the whole of the 'vulgata' or 'common' version of the Bible, yet his work lay at the base of it. We do not know the source of the other New Testament books apart from Jerome's translation of the four Gospels. Yet it was Jerome's version of the Scriptures that dominated Western Christianity all through the Middle Ages and beyond. There is a fascinating contrast between his own sophisticated, high-flown, rhetorical style and that of his translation of the Scriptures, which speaks volumes for his respect for the Scriptures. He was aware that the translator should not impose his own personality, and that, especially in scriptural translation, the simplicity and directness of the Scripture should be reflected in the style of translation.[60] Previous translations of the Old Testament had been not only based on faulty readings of the LXX, but had reflected the reverence for Hebrew grammatical forms and Hebrew expressions, which dominate the LXX. Translations of the Gospels were so varied and imprecise that there simply was no authoritative text. Jerome made the Scriptures available and intelligible to the Western reader of Latin like never before. His text was so authoritative that it was virtually forgotten that any other version of the Bible existed in any language: the Vulgate simply was the Bible, even up to the Council of Trent in the sixteenth century.

However, another consequence of Jerome's work was less happy. His preference for the *Hebraica veritas* was exhumed by Luther in the sixteenth century, largely on doctrinal grounds, since the Greek books of the Old Testament contained doctrines against which he was protesting (e.g., praying for the dead in 2 Macc. 12.42-45). This led to a general Protestant rejection of the Greek books and passages of the Bible. In many circles these are still relegated to a secondary category, 'the Apocrypha', whereas the Roman Catholic appellation is 'the Deutero-canonical' portions. This divergence on the canonical Scriptures remains an important point of division between the Churches.

Bibliography

Many of Jerome's works are available in English in the series *Nicene and Post-Nicene Fathers*. For uniformity, however, I have given the reference to Migne's *Patrologia Latina*, which has them all.

Further Reading

Kelly, J. N. D., *Jerome* (London: Duckworth, 1975).
Rebenich, S., *Jerome* (London: Routledge, 2002).
Steinmann, J., *Saint Jerome* (London: Geoffrey Chapman, 1959).

CHAPTER 5

St Bede

Introduction

St Boniface, the apostle of Germany (c. AD 675–754), was described by Christopher Dawson as having had 'a deeper influence on the history of Europe than any Englishman who has ever lived'.[1] For Boniface, as he travelled round Germany on his mission, the reading of the Bible was a vital sustenance. In his old age, when his eyes were no longer capable of reading by the dim light of a candle, he asked his old master, Daniel, the now blind Bishop of Winchester, for a particular book he remembered from long ago, a copy of *The Book of the Prophets*, six prophets bound together in clear letters, since 'with my failing sight it is impossible for me to read small, abbreviated script', and such books cannot be obtained in Germany.[2] Towards the end of his life, in about 746, he also asked insistently first Archbishop Egbert of York and then Abbot Huetbert of Wearmouth to send him the treatises of Bede, 'who lately shone in your midst, a light of the Church'.[3] Huetbert replied touchingly that the winter had been so cold that their frozen fingers had been unable to do the work of copying,[4] so Boniface wrote again to Archbishop Egbert: 'We beg you from the bottom of our heart to comfort us in our sorrow, as you have done before, by sending us a spark from that light of the Church which the Holy Spirit has kindled in your land; in other words, be so kind as to send us some of the works which Bede, the inspired priest and student of sacred scripture, has composed – in particular, if it can be done, his book of homilies for the year (because it would be a very handy and useful manual for us in our preaching), and the Proverbs of Solomon.'[5] He reinforces the request by accompanying the letter with 'two small casks of wine, asking you in token of our mutual affection to use it for a merry day with the brethren'.

An Outline of Bede's Life

As a representative of the use of the Bible in the so-called Dark Ages, the Venerable Bede stands out. He was a monk of the double monastery of Wearmouth and Jarrow, and tells us all he thinks we need to know about him at the end of his monumental *Historia Ecclesiastica Gentis Anglorum*.[6] (Such biographical notes, as also the titles of books, were commonly put at the end rather than the beginning of books. It was, incidentally, this book which earned Bede the title of 'Father of English History'. It is an invaluable source for understanding the steps by which the Saxon peoples were converted to Christianity, and the significance of that development).

> I was born in the territory of this monastery. When I was seven years of age I was, by the care of my kinsmen,[7] put into the charge of the reverend Abbot Benedict and then of Ceolfrith, to be educated. From then on I spent all my life in this monastery applying myself entirely to the study of the scriptures; and amid the observance of the discipline of the Rule and the daily task of singing in the church, it has always been my delight to learn or to teach or to write. At the age of nineteen I was ordained deacon and at the age of thirty priest, both times through the ministration of the reverend Bishop John on the direction of Abbot Ceolfrith. From the time I became priest until the fifty-ninth year of my life I have made it my business, for my own benefit and that of my brothers, to make brief extracts from the works of the venerable fathers on the holy scriptures, or to add notes of my own to clarify their sense and interpretation.

To this outline a few more biographical details may be added. Bede was born in 672 or 673. He must be the boy mentioned in the anonymous *Life* of Abbot Ceolfrith. In 686 a plague struck the monastery of Jarrow: 'All who could read or preach or recite the antiphons were swept away, except the abbot himself and one little lad nourished and taught by him, who is now a priest of the same monastery. The abbot, deeply saddened by this visitation, ordained that, contrary to their regular practice, they should, except at vespers and matins, recite the psalms without antiphons. When this had been done with many tears and lamentations on his part for a whole week, he could bear it no longer, but decreed that the psalms should be restored to their proper order with the antiphons. This was done with no little labour on the part of himself and the aforesaid boy.'[8]

The monastery must have been quickly replenished with monks, for, by the foresight of its abbot, it soon became a centre of learning. Contact between the Church in England and Rome was particularly strong, no doubt stimulated by the Synod of Whitby, which decreed the adoption into the English Church of several Roman customs, including the date for the celebration of Easter. Journeyings to Rome were so frequent that a Saxon hostel was founded by King Ina in 727; it has given the name to that part of the bank of the Tiber nearest the Vatican, the Lungotevere in Sassia, though the hostel itself has given way to the Hospedale S. Spirito. In the same period Abbot Benet Biscop made several visits to Rome, bringing back with him painters and stained-glass artists. The Pope himself (*ipse papa apostolicus*) sent with Biscop the papal cantor, who stayed for a whole year to instruct the monks in the singing of the liturgical cycle.[9]

More relevant to our theme, he may well have brought back the copy of Cassiodorus's *Pandect,* which Bede attests that he actually saw.[10] The books of the Bible were at this date normally copied separately or in small groups. Cassiodorus (485–580), a century before Bede, seems to have been the first to put all the books of the Bible together into a single volume (*pandect,* meaning 'hold all'). It is a sign of the seriousness of the approach to the Bible in Bede's monasteries that no less than three pandects were produced there, one for Wearmouth, one for Jarrow and one that Abbot Ceolfrid set out to present to the Pope; he died in 716 in France on the way to Rome. The book disappeared and was rediscovered in the fifteenth century in the monastery of Monte Amiata in Italy. This *Codex Amiatinus* is now in the Laurentian Library in Florence and is now accepted as being Ceolfrid's third pandect. It is so huge that it requires two or even four men to carry it. Of the other two pandects only a few leaves remain, housed in the British Library.[11] It has been calculated that 500 calf-skins would have been needed for each volume, a not inconsiderable expense. Furthermore, two little elements, a verse in honour of St Jerome and the caption for an illustration of Ezra copying, contain reminiscences of Bede's own writing, suggesting that Bede himself may have been directly connected with the project.[12]

A final biographical detail must be the account of Bede's death, which he approached with typical devotion. This deserves to be quoted at length because it shows not only the love and respect his community had for Bede, but also both the monastic and prayerful context of his studies and his own devotion to the Scriptures. He died on the eve of the Ascension.

> He was very cheerful and thanked God that he should have deserved such weakness. He often said, 'God punishes every son whom he accepts,' and quoted the saying of Ambrose, 'I have not lived in such a way that I should be ashamed of living among you, nor am I afraid to die, because we have a good God.' In those days, apart from the lessons which we daily received from him and the recitation of the psalms, he was keen to finish

two notable little works: he had translated into our language for the use of the Church the Gospel of John from the beginning up to the words, 'what is that among so many?', and certain extracts from the books of Bishop Isidore, saying, 'I do not want my sons to read a lie and thereby work fruitlessly after my death.' But when the third day before the Ascension came round he began to have especial difficulty in breathing, and slight swelling appeared on his feet. Nevertheless, he taught all that day and merrily dictated, and several times said (among other things), 'Learn quickly, for I do not know how long I shall live, or whether my Maker will take me quite soon.' However, we thought that he well knew the time of his death, and that was why he kept vigil in thanksgiving right through the night. When the morning began to dawn, that is on the Wednesday, he told us to write earnestly what we had begun, and this we did until mid-morning. From then on we went in procession with the relics of the saints as the custom of that day demanded. One of us stayed with him and said to him, 'There is still one chapter missing from the book which you were dictating, but I think it is difficult to ask you for any more.' But he replied, 'It is not difficult. Take your pen and ink and write quickly.' And this is what he did. In mid-afternoon he said to me, 'I have some treasures in my box, some pepper and prayer-cards and incense. Run quickly and gather the priests of our monastery, so that I may distribute to them the little gifts which God has given me.' This I did with some fear and when they arrived he spoke to each of them individually, encouraging them and asking them to offer Mass zealously and pray for him. They answered willingly, but they were sad, and all wept, especially at what he had said, since they reckoned that they would not see his face much longer in this world. But they rejoiced at his saying, 'It is time, and so it seems good to my Maker that, released from the flesh, I should soon come to him who, when I did not exist, made me from nothing. I have lived long, and the kind Judge has given me a good life. My time is over, and my soul longs to see Christ my king in his glory.' This and other things useful for our edification he said until the evening. And the boy I have mentioned, called Wilberch, said, 'Dear master, there is one sentence you have not yet dictated.' 'Very well,' he said, 'write!' And after a little the boy said, 'Now it is written.' He said, 'Good, it is complete, you are right. Take my head into your hands, for it gives me great pleasure to sit opposite my holy place in which I used to pray, so that I may sit and call upon my Father.' And so, on the floor of his cell, singing 'Glory be to the Father and to the Son and to the Holy Spirit' and so on, he breathed his last.[13]

Bede's Learning

Bede spent his whole life in the monastery. We know of only three visits elsewhere: one to Hexham, one to the neighbouring monastery of Lindisfarne, and the third to York, where his pupil Egbert had, in about 732, become bishop. But his great *Historia Ecclesiastica* is peppered with references to other people, both within his own monastery and beyond, from whom he had acquired knowledge of some incident or segment of church history; he must have had an extraordinarily wide circle of correspondents.[14] He continued to learn late in life, and it is interesting to see how much his knowledge of Greek has advanced between his early commentary on the Acts of the Apostles and his later commentary; named the *Retractatio in Actus Apostolorum* in imitation of St Augustine's work of that name.[15] In the former work there was no first-hand discussion of the Greek text. In the latter, on Acts 1.6, he explains how the case of the definite article is the clue to the correct interpretation of the indeclinable noun 'Israel'.[16] At Pentecost he points out that the Greek has literally 'they spoke in *other* tongues' (not the Latin Vulgate's *various*), thus fulfilling Isaiah's prophecy. In the *Retractatio* he corrects himself for having formerly interpreted the name 'Stephen' as 'crowned', now knowing that the Greek name in fact means 'crown'.[17] In what is surely a humorous passage, he corrects the spelling *Pentecostem* to *Pentecosten,* and proceeds to run through the declension of the Greek word like any schoolboy.[18]

Another passage that shows his sense of humour is the delightful saying of Bede handed down by Alcuin:[19] 'I know that the angels attend the canonical hours and the assemblies of the brethren. What if they should not find me there among them? Would they not say, "Where is Bede? Why does he not come to the prayers prescribed for the brethren?"' Another light-hearted passage occurs at the beginning of his treatise *De Ratione Temporum.*[20] Bede explains the method of communicating letters by raising the corresponding number of fingers, which he says can be used for a game. So, to a companion whom you wish to warn to be careful [compare the old schoolboy warning of '*Cave!*' 'Look out! Be careful!], you signal '3, 1, 20, 19, 5, 1, 7, 5', or '*Caute age*'.

Bede can also be charmingly down-to-earth, using imagery from building and cooking. There would have been a great deal of building in the monastery at that time, from which Bede draws the image, 'As courses of masonry are supported by one another, just so in the Church each of the faithful is supported by the just who go before them, and in their turn support the just after them.'[21] Reminiscent of meals in the monastic refectory is the image of the various ways of examining the Scriptures: 'We are being fed upon food roasted on a gridiron when we understand literally, openly and without any covering, the things that have been said or done to protect the health of the soul; upon food cooked in a frying pan when by frequent turning over of the superficial meaning and by looking at it afresh we comprehend what there is in it that corresponds allegorically with the mysteries of Christ. Afterwards we search the oven for the bread of the Word when by exertion of mind we lay hold of the mystical meanings in the scriptures.'[22]

We do not have any library list from the monastery, but perusal of a couple of pages of his commentaries is enough to convince a reader that the monastery library was well stocked, for the range of Bede's learning is staggering, as he quotes one Church Father after another. He interprets the name of the disciple Justus as 'sparing', following Jerome's *Book of Hebrew Names* (Bede himself knew very little Hebrew), and immediately adds that Clement of Alexandria (c. AD 150–215), 'a man most learned on every subject', says that he was one of the 70 disciples sent out by Jesus. This book of Jerome's was one of his stand-bys, providing all kinds of snippets of information, such as that the Tigris is so named because the speed of its flow is reminiscent of the tiger.[23] One can hardly dip into Bede's work without finding his indebtedness to that distinguished (but often incorrect) natural scientist Isidore of Seville.[24] As the biographical snippet at the end of the *Historia Ecclesiastica* makes clear, Bede is vividly aware that he is a man of the Church, and that it is his duty to transmit the tradition of the Church. There is no need to strive for originality. Indeed, in the preface to his commentary on Luke he explains his duty to give the interpretation of the Church Fathers.[25] He openly acknowledges his debt to them by putting in the margin an abbreviation for the name of the four great Western Church Fathers[26] whom he is following, and asks any scribe to transcribe these as well. He defends himself for questioning the meaning of a passage by saying that he was not giving his own ideas but merely using the words of 'that holy and completely unerring master Gregory Nazianzen'.[27] On the one hand, he can transcribe practically word for word his older contemporary Adamnan's work *On the Holy Places* (which Adamnan derived from that inveterate traveller to the Holy Land, Arculf).[28] On the other hand, he is no slavish follower of authorities, and can give a lively dispute of Origen's interpretation of Isa. 24.21-23 that even the wicked will eventually be saved.[29] A few lines later he argues against the view proposed 'in the name of Melito' of Sardis (he clearly does not like to argue against Melito of Sardis himself!) that at the death of Mary one year after the Ascension the Apostles were carried through the clouds to Jerusalem from the countries to which they had been dispersed. They could not possibly, he argues, have finished their mission in Judaea and Samaria in such a short time.[30] So, while he sees it as his task to transmit the tradition of the Church, he does not do so uncritically.

Bede and Numbers

Bede is a vital link in the traditional exegesis of the Church, not only in his reliance on it but also in his furtherance of it. One of the chief ways in which the tradition of the Church was transmitted during the Middle Ages was by the *glossa ordinaria*. This was the standard medieval commentary on the Bible. On each page of a Bible the biblical text would be given in the central portion of the page, surrounded by a large amount of marginal and interlinear commentary drawn from the Fathers. Bede was the latest of these Fathers who could be quoted as an authority, for the patristic tradition was considered to end with him.[31] On several books of the Old Testament Bede is the principal source of the *glossa ordinaria* (Ezra-Nehemiah, Tobit, Proverbs, the Song of Songs), as well as for the Gospels of Mark and Luke.[32] For the book of Acts the commentary is based almost exclusively on his work and that of one other writer (Rabanus Maurus, c. AD 780–856).

Besides the use of Bede's commentaries for these books, Bede's fascination with numbers was such that he always sees in them some symbolism, which is regularly transcribed into the *glossa ordinaria*. Thus in his commentary on John, the six water-jars at the marriage feast of Cana are the six ages of the world. The water-jars hold two or three measures: two because the prophets speak only of Father and Son, three in order to mention the Trinity. The transformation of the water into wine signifies the completion of the law in Christ.[33] A little further on the Samaritan's five husbands have triple significance: the five books of Moses, the five bodily senses, and the woman's five inadequate answers to Jesus.[34] Then the five porticoes of the Pool of Bethzatha are again the five books of Moses, and the pool itself is the Jewish people, supported on all sides by the guardianship of the law.[35] As for the 153 fish from the Lake of Galilee in Jn 21.11, nothing could be more obvious! Add together each of the numbers from 1 to 16 and you get 136. Add to this the 10 commandments of the Law and the 7 days of creation (the 7th day, which God sanctified by resting, yields the 7 sanctifying gifts of the Holy Spirit) and you reach 153.[36]

The Four Senses of Scripture

To say that such symbolism is taught by or even contained in Scripture raises such difficulties for the modern mind that it is important to attempt to penetrate into what is really meant by this form of exegesis. We have met it before, especially in the Alexandrian school of exegesis stemming from Origen. Origen spoke of a 'spiritual', 'hidden' or 'figurative' sense of Scripture in addition to the 'somatic' or 'material' sense. Explicitly, and relying on Prov. 22.20 (LXX), he distinguished

three senses of Scripture (p. 43). Next Augustine mentioned the 'quad-
riform pattern of all sacred scripture': (1) eternal things intimated/
hinted (*intimentur*); (2) facts narrated; (3) future events foretold; and
(4) actions prescribed or advised.[37]

It fell, however, to Bede[38] to elaborate the full theory of the fourfold sense of Scripture, which was to become classic and dominate all
medieval exegesis. He also changed the order from that of Augustine:
Augustine's second is Bede's first, Augustine's fourth is Bede's third;
Augustine's first and third spring from a different method of categoriza-
tion, only partially coinciding with Bede's second and fourth.

1. **History**: is when something is reported straightforwardly as having
    been done or said (e.g., how the people of Israel built a *tabernaculum*
    in the desert for the Lord). This is straightforward enough.
2. **Allegory**: is when the presence of Christ or the sacraments of the
    Church are mystically indicated, either in words or in deeds:
    a. in words, as Isaiah says (Isa. 11.1), 'A rod will come forth from
        the root of Jesse and a flower will grow from its root', which in
        clear language is saying the Virgin Mary will be born of the stock
        of David and Christ will arise from her stock
    b. in things, as when the people saved from slavery in Egypt by the
        blood of a lamb signifies the Church, set free by the Passion of
        Christ from domination by the devil.
3. **Moral (or tropological**: the Greek word *tropos* signifies a way of life or
    a way of behaving) – the establishment or correction of behaviour,
    expressed either:
    a. openly (e.g., 'Children, our love must be not just words or mere
        talk, but something active and genuine', 1 Jn 3.18), or
    b. figuratively (e.g., 'At all times, dress in white and keep your head
        well scented', Eccl. 9.8, which in clear language means, At all
        times let your actions be clean and your heart full of love).
4. **Anagogical (i.e., leading to higher things)**: which refers to sayings
    about future rewards and life in heaven, either:
    a. openly (e.g., 'Blessed are the pure of heart, for they shall see
        God', Mt 5.8), or
    b. figuratively (e.g., 'Blessed are those who will have washed their
        robes clean, so that they have the right to feed on the tree of life',
        Rev. 22.14; that is, Blessed are those who purify their thoughts
        and actions, so that they may be able to see Christ the Lord).

The difficulty is that, to the modern mind, the figurative senses (2, 3b,
4b) are far from obvious, leaving much more latitude for interpretation than a clear statement should. Indeed, even Bede's own example
in 2a is difficult. He is no doubt influenced by the verbal similarity
of the Latin *virgo* (virgin) and *virga* (rod). Is it really an allegorical

prophetic statement? It was, after all, Joseph rather than Mary who was said by the Gospel (Mt. 1.6-16) to be of the stock of Jesse. Similarly, in the context of the book of Ecclesiastes, the quotation in 3b could be more accurately understood to mean, 'Enjoy life and be sure to look your best'. Furthermore, with regard to 4b, in the context of the book of Revelation, it may well be considered that Rev. 22.14 refers to martyrdom rather than the more general purity of thought and action. In the case of all these 'figurative' statements, the meaning is read back into the statement from independent Christian belief rather than expressed in the statement itself; the meaning is read back into the statement by the commentator rather than expressed by the biblical author. Certainly, in some instances there may be a further sense, not intended by the author (known in modern exegesis as the *sensus plenior*), but visible in the light of the revelation given by the whole of the Bible.[39]

However, the allegorical meaning (2) has its special difficulty. Further, in Bede's definition the two words 'sacraments' and 'mystically' require interpretation. 'Sacraments' is obviously not to be confined to the liturgical sacraments of the Church, but must include a much wider range of sacred entities, as is clear from the example Bede himself gives. Both Christ and the Church are commonly referred to as sacraments in the sense of revelations of, or means of communication with, God. Bede understands the word still more widely to include all the teachings of the Church. Perhaps it should be translated simply as 'sacred things'. 'Mystical' is used by Paul and other first-century authors in the clear sense of 'a secret or mystery finally revealed by God at the end of time' (Rom. 16.25). Here it is used in a much more general sense, meaning little more than 'religious'.

In fact Bede himself makes little use of the fourfold division, and concentrates chiefly on two senses, the 'material' and the 'spiritual' or 'allegorical'. He takes meticulous care over explaining such matters as the construction of the Tabernacle because he regards an investigation of the material details to be an important preliminary to an advance towards the allegorical meaning. Having described in outline the dimensions of the Tabernacle, he goes on: 'Having by way of explanation made a preliminary tasting of these matters, let us examine the words of the story themselves, so that by these we may be able to penetrate more deeply and more openly to the meaning of the allegory.'[40] The literal meaning is important, but more important, and the real object of the search, is the 'hidden' meaning. Similarly at the beginning of the explanation on the books of Samuel he remarks – alluding to Mt. 13.52 – that a scribe learned in the Kingdom of Heaven must be able to bring out both new and old. He continues, not without humour:

If we make it our business to bring out from the treasury of scripture only the old, that is, to follow the shapes of the letters in the Jewish manner, what edification among the daily sins, what consolation among the increasing cares of the age, what spiritual instruction among the manifold errors of this life will we gain by reading or listening? For example, as soon as we open the Book of Samuel, we find that Elcanor had two wives. According to the custom of the ecclesiastical way of life, we have long refrained from the embrace of a wife, and firmly intend to remain celibate. If we do not know how to carve out from this and similar statements some allegorical sense, how will this restore us inwardly by correction, instruction and consolation?[41]

For Bede, then, the purpose of studying Scripture is to derive edification against sin, consolation amid care, and instruction against error. Perhaps the prime example of Bede's application of this method is to be found in his allegorical interpretation of the book of Tobit.[42]

The Allegorical Interpretation of the Book of Tobit

Bede introduces his exposition with the promise that the book abounds in examples and counsels for the moral life. 'Anyone who knows how to interpret it allegorically will find that its interior sense goes beyond the simplicity of the letter no less than apples go beyond leaves, for if it is understood spiritually it is found to contain the greatest sacraments of Christ and the Church.' It would be as well, already at this stage, to bear in mind that such an approach is not exactly that favoured by modern exegetes. The contrast is stark. Modern exegesis regards the book as a Jewish novel – Luther called it a comedy – full of irony, farce and other humour. It principally makes fun of Tobit's absurdly fussy and meticulous observance of the law, contrasting this with his wife's sensible, practical and reverent religious observance. Another figure of fun is Tobit's son, the naïve and ineffective Tobias, guided at every step of his journey to retrieve his father's money by an angel, whom he fails to recognize as such. The crowning burlesque is the scene where Tobias and the dolorous Sarah (whose previous seven husbands had all died on their wedding night) piously interrupt their wedding night – while Sarah's father is digging a grave for Tobias, just in case – to get out of bed and offer a long prayer together.

In Bede's exegesis Tobit himself, the hero of the book, stands for the people of Israel, serving God with right faith and good works amid the gentiles given over to idolatry. There is, however, plenty of detailed 'spiritual' meaning. For example, at one point

Tobit (in 2.10) is so exhausted by his good works that he takes a siesta under the eaves, where he is blinded by the droppings of swallows. For

Bede, Tobit here represents one who fails to stay awake in faith (like the five sleepy wedding attendants in Mt. 25.1-13). The swallows, because of their airy flight, represent levity of heart, which blinds those whom it dominates.

Tobias sets out on his journey to recover his father's money, followed by his faithful dog. The dog represents Christian teachers, who follow Christ and defend their Master's household and sheep from unclean spirits and heretics. In the course of his journey he goes down into the Tigris to wash his feet. A huge fish springs out to devour him. This is, of course, Jesus' descent into death, and the devil's attempt to overcome him. Tobias shrieks for help to the angel, who tells him to grab the fish. Tobias kills and guts the fish. This is Christ's victory over the devil, after which the devil's wiles are exposed. On the return journey the dog runs ahead, wagging its tail.

Christian preachers go ahead, followed by the Lord, who cleanses hearts. The extremity of the dog's body suggests the final accomplishment of the good work and the consequent rejoicing.

Conclusion

By modern canons of literary criticism it would be impossible to say that these are the meanings of the various elements in the story of Tobit. Neither this exegesis nor the foregoing interpretation of numbers in the biblical text could, by modern criteria, be held to be the meaning of the texts. Bede's purpose, however, is different. He does not claim that the lessons he puts forward are freshly learnt from the text. His attitude is more that this is a story which can call to mind the various events and virtues of the Christian life. The Christian story and the story of Tobit run along parallel lines, so that the story of Tobit serves the Christian reader as a reminder of the lessons taught by the Church. In this Bede's is the perfect example of the Christian exegesis of his day. Furthermore, through the dominant role that Bede's commentaries play in the formation of the *glossa ordinaria*, he is also the influence that continues to shape the understanding of the Bible in the high Middle Ages. However, the last word should perhaps remain with Canon Jenkins: 'a reader who has no taste for allegory had better leave Bede's commentaries alone'.[43]

Further Reading

Bede, the Venerable, *Ecclesiastical History of the English People*, tr. Leo Sherley-Price (Hardmondsworth: Penguin Classics, 1990).
Ward, B., *The Venerable Bede* (London: Continuum, 2005).

CHAPTER 6

The High Middle Ages – Bernard of Clairvaux and Thomas Aquinas

Bernard of Clairvaux

Bernard the Monk

Approaching St Bernard we move several centuries forward, leaping regretfully almost entirely over the so-called Dark Ages. Again it is important to situate the person before considering his interpretation and use of Scripture. Bernard was born of aristocratic parents near Dijon in 1090, one of seven children dedicated to God by their mother, who died when Bernard was 14 (which may have some connection to his great personal devotion to the Mother of God). The twelfth-century renaissance was already beginning to bud when he received his education. He quotes Juvenal and Horace with ease and aptly. His style shows not only a natural genius and fluency but also a mastery of the techniques of rhetoric, which can only be the result of an education that included classical oratory, for it abounds not only in balance,[1] alliteration and anaphora, but also in the more formal rhetorical techniques of *praeteritio, prosopopoiea*, etc.[2] In his mature writings Bernard is heir to a style of Christian writing inherited from Augustine.[3] The perfection and easy fluency of this style is not achieved overnight, and his correspondence shows that he could spend long years revising and polishing: the *Apologia* to Abbot William went through several stages and revisions, and the *Sermons on the Song of Songs* were 18 years in preparation.

The decisive move came when Bernard, obviously a natural leader, accompanied by some 30 friends and close relations, entered the small and strict monastery of Cîteaux, founded in 1098 by Robert of Molesmes and currently under the rule of Abbot Stephen Harding. In the daringly short time of three years he was sent to make a foundation at Clairvaux. This was only the beginning of his public life, in which he became one of the most influential figures of his age: advisor to popes and monarchs, arbiter in disputes, preacher of the disastrous Second

Crusade, sending warm letters of friendship and approval or of frank and fiery denunciation of abuses, dispatching monks to make dozens of foundations all over Europe. He journeyed extensively on various missions, tolerating the discomforts and hardships of medieval travel, despite having been so broken in health by his early austerities that he was dogged by sickness and was hardly able to digest any solid foods.

Fundamentally, however, Bernard was a monk, living according to the Benedictine Rule. This way of life forms the background to his whole mode of thinking, writing, understanding and use of the Bible. However much he travelled, negotiated, engaged in external affairs, his centre of gravity remained the monastery, and he returned there for long stretches of time.[4] According to the Rule, the monk's day (and much of the night) is to be punctuated by the singing of the *Opus Dei* (now known as the Prayer of the Church), which would generate intimate familiarity with the prayer of the Psalms. In addition, the Rule provides for notable stretches of *lectio divina*, the meditative reading of Scripture and the Fathers of the Church (see Chapter 13). In a world without the distractions and excitements of modern life it would be expected that the monk's imagination, thoughts and language would be marked – indeed shaped – by these readings.

Controversy with Cluny

The principal source for Bernard's use of Scripture are his homilies on biblical texts. We will, however, begin with a rather more light-hearted and even humorous and satirical use of the Scripture.

The controversy was deadly enough, and half Europe seems to have watched on the touch-lines.[5] It began with a letter[6] from Bernard to his young first cousin, who had been promised by his parents to the monastery of Cluny, but nevertheless entered Cîteaux, made his profession and went with Bernard to Clairvaux. After some time he decided to defect to the easier way of life at Cluny, making his excuse (as Bernard sees the matter) the dedication made by his parents. This first letter is full of scriptural quotation and allusion. Bernard's purpose, by means of these constant allusions, is to show himself a loving apostolic father in the Lord, who will welcome back the erring young man. References to the story of the return of the prodigal son abound. The early part is subtly based, in a way that no monk could miss, on Paul's reproaches to the Corinthians: Bernard presents himself as the Apostle, affectionately chiding his erring converts. When the monk reads 'Sorrow is not careful to count the cost; it is not ashamed; it does not depend on calculation, does not fear loss of dignity, does not keep strictly to the law', he must immediately think of the famous 'hymn' to love in First Corinthians 13. When he reads the exquisite sentence, 'Changed, you will find me changed; him whom you used to fear as a master, you will embrace in security as a comrade,'[7] he will find echoes of Paul's Letter to Philemon about the returned slave, Onesimus (v. 16). 'You fled my severity, return to my gentleness'[8] must remind him of Paul's blandishments to the repentant Corinthians in Second Corinthians 2. When he hears, 'You foolish boy! Who has bewitched you not to fulfil the vows which adorned your lips?' Paul's reproach to the Galatians must spring to mind: 'You fools! Who has put a spell on you?' (Gal. 3.1). The letter is studded with further echoes: 'if you have many masters in Christ, yet you have few fathers. . . . I begot you in religion. Then I nourished you with the milk which was all you could take' (1 Cor. 4.15; 3.2).

> Would that if I were to die you, at least, might live [cf. Rom. 9.3]! But how could this be? Does salvation consist rather in soft raiment and rich food than in frugal fare and moderate clothing? If warm and comfortable furs, if fine and expensive cloth, if long sleeves and ample hoods, if fur coverlets and soft shirts make a saint, why do I delay and not follow you at once? But these things are comforts for the weak, not the arms of fighting men. Behold, those who wear soft raiment are in kings' houses [Mt. 11.8].

The affair was not over, for further in the letter Bernard unashamedly accuses the Prior of Cluny of luring the boy away, and the community at Cluny of flattering the boy with special treatment, before going on to detail (and lampoon) the luxurious way of life he considers the monks of Cluny lead.

Not surprisingly, the superiors at Cluny took offence at this treatment from a fellow abbot, and Bernard was prevailed upon by Abbot William of St Thierry to write an apologia to correct the scandal he had caused. It was as well that Peter the Venerable, Abbot of Cluny AD 1122–1156, was a personal friend of Bernard's,[9] for the resultant 'apologia' is full of outrageous satire and piquant sarcasm – and all dripping and glittering with scriptural quotation. The importance of harmony between the monastic establishments is vigorously stressed[10] by a scintillating passage on the seamless robe of the Saviour, whose symbolism is enriched by a chain of other scriptural references and allusions, a passage in itself noble and inspiring. There follows another biblical development about splinters and logs, outlawing judgemental criticism. Then somehow within a couple of pages we find ourselves slipping from biblical allusion to rollicking caricature of the monastic meal at Cluny:

> When we come together, to use the apostle's words, it is not to eat the Lord's supper [1 Cor. 11.20]. No one asks for the bread of heaven, no one gives it. No hint of the Bible, no hint of the salvation of souls. Idle fripperies and laughter and words thrown to the wind. At table, the ears

are fed with gossip as much as the mouth with food. Focussed on this, you forget all moderation in eating. Course follows course. Only meat is lacking, and to compensate for this, two huge servings of fish are given. When you are gorged with the first and taste the second, you lose all memory of the first. The cooks prepare everything with such skill and cunning that, when you have already eaten four or five courses, the earlier ones do not impede the later, and being full does not impede your appetite.

And this is illustrated by a delightful passage, full of Bernard's greatest art of mockery, with alliteration, asyndeton, anaphora, on the variety of ways in which eggs are cooked there. Later Bernard turns his attention to the church of Cluny itself, then the largest church in Christendom: 'I say nothing about the immense heights and immoderate lengths and superfluous widths of the oratories, nothing about their expensive decorations and exquisite images, which catch the eye of the worshippers, impede their devotion, and somehow remind me of the ancient rites of the Jews.'[11]

Controversy with Abelard

This is no place to enter into the machinations and hostilities generated over the controversy between Bernard and Peter Abelard (AD 1079–1143), whom Bernard thought a dangerous heretic and pursued with his utmost vigour, writing a series of letters to cardinals and bishops, which effectively destroyed all Abelard's chances of defending himself. It is, however, relevant that Bernard presented matters enveloped in scriptural imagery in such a way as effectively to implant in these high-ranking ecclesiastics a particular understanding of the situation. One example must suffice, the letter written by Bernard to Pope Innocent in 1140 (I have inserted the scriptural references; to the original readers they would have been obvious).

All night long she is weeping, the bride of Christ [2 Cor. 11.2], tears running down her cheeks. Not one of her lovers remains to comfort her [Lam. 1.2]. While the Bridegroom delays [Mt. 25.5] the woman of Shunam [Song 7.1] is entrusted to you, my Lord, in the land of her exile. To no one does she acknowledge her hurts more intimately, to no one does she reveal her anxiety and her groans more secretly [Ps. 37.9] than to the friend of the Bridegroom [Jn 3.29]. For because you love the Bridegroom you do not despise [Ps. 50.9] the bride when she cries to you in her need [*Salve Regina*], in her trouble. Amid all this variety of enemies by whom the Church of God is besieged like a lily among thorns [Song 2.2], nothing is more dangerous, nothing more troublesome than when she is torn within by those whom she holds in her lap, whom she feeds at

her breast. In such circumstances and about such people is that saying of
the sorrowing and groaning Church, 'My friends and neighbours have
closed in on me and stand against me' [Ps. 37.12]. Indeed no plague is
more effective to harm than an intimate friend [Ps. 40.9]. For proof is
the intimacy of Absalom [2 Samuel 15], the kiss of Judas.[12]

By means of the scriptural allusions, the Pope is seen as John the Baptist,
the friend and herald of Christ, the sole defence of the Church as the
beloved bride, in ultimate peril from the most malicious and dangerous type of treachery from within. Bernard then neatly goes on to
characterize Abelard as both the lion and the snake ('On the lion and
the viper you will tread' [Ps. 90.13]): the roaring of Peter the Lion has
been silenced already, and the hissing of Peter the Snake must now be
dealt with similarly.

Bernard was, of course, far from unique in using the Scripture in
this way to create an interpretation. Only his skill and delicacy are
unrivalled. In the collection of Bernard's letters is included one from
the Archbishop of Rheims and other bishops to Pope Innocent about
Abelard, 'who was tested by fire [1 Pet. 1.7] by the legate of the Roman
Church because iniquity was found in him [Mal. 2.6]. Cursed be one
who rebuilds the walls of Jericho [Josh. 6.26]. That book of his has
risen from the dead, and with it many heresies which had fallen asleep
have risen and appeared to many [Mt. 27.53]'.[13] At least the first and
last of these references, used in a sense opposite to that of the original,
may be considered at best indelicate, at worst blasphemous. Not only
knowledge of the Bible but considerable skill are required for apt use
of this genre.

Bernard's Scriptural Writings

Bernard's way of using the Scripture is quite different to those we have
considered in earlier chapters. It is not primarily doctrinal, seeking to
understand and formulate the mystery of Christ or Christianity. It is
certainly not historical, seeking to understand the history or experiences of the people of God in Old or New Testaments, or even to learn
lessons from these. It is not exegetical, seeking to explain literary,
linguistic, historical or geographical puzzles in the text. It is not moral-
izing; that is, seeking to draw lessons for Christian living from the text,
possibly by allegory. Much more, it is monastic. Bernard presupposes
an easy familiarity with the whole Bible, which has been developed
by prolonged and habitual meditative reading and reflection on the
text. It is rhetorical and allusive. Bernard's mind is so permeated by
the Bible that, to a listener familiar with the Bible, almost every phrase
receives a little tweak which evokes a passage of Scripture. His mind

is permeated not only with the Scripture itself, but also with the great interpreters of previous ages, in such a way that it is often impossible to know whether his primary source is the actual scriptural text or the homilies of Origen (in Latin version), Jerome or Gregory the Great. Another frequent influence is, of course, the monastic liturgy. This is, no doubt, the reason for the preponderance of the psalms and their mode of expression in all his writing. Furthermore, he often quotes the Bible in the slightly variant versions used in antiphons or responses of the monastic liturgy of the hours, versions that stem either from pre-Vulgate translations or from adaptations to musical requirements. Bernard receives the biblical text very much from within the tradition of the Church.

A characteristic passage, which is full of scriptural quotation and allusions, and in which Bernard lays out his attitude to Scripture, comes in the first of the *Homilies in Praise of the Virgin Mary*, one of Bernard's most popular works:[14]

> What does the evangelist mean by so deliberately giving so many proper names in this passage? Why this? Do you think any of them is given to no purpose? Far from it! If no leaf falls from a tree without a cause and no sparrow falls to the earth without the heavenly Father, should I think that any word flows superfluously from the evangelist's lips, especially in the story of the Word? I do not. Indeed, all are full of heavenly mysteries, each overflowing with celestial sweetness if they have a careful reader who knows how to draw honey[15] from the rock and oil from the hardest stone. Certainly in that day the mountains dripped sweetness and the hills flowed with milk and honey, when the heavens poured down dew and, while the clouds rained the just one, the earth opened, joyfully begetting the Saviour.

There are at least a dozen quotations or allusions in this passage. More important, however, are the attestation that every word (even the names) is to be treasured as full of heavenly mysteries, and the image of the careful reader drawing honey from the rock and oil from the hardest stone. It is, however, only the loving and attentive reader who can benefit from the Scripture and be led on to this experience. Bernard never tires of quoting the saying '*Anima justi sedes sapientiae*' (the soul of the just is the seat of wisdom).[16] It is only the just, well intentioned and loving who can penetrate to the true wisdom of the Scriptures. So Bernard speaks with obvious annoyance of those whose attention is only on the intellectual meaning of the Scriptures: 'I must warn those present whose agile minds outstrip my thoughts, and in every sermon anticipate the end almost before they have grasped the beginning, that I am obliged to adapt myself primarily to minds that are less keen. But my purpose is not so much to explain words as to move hearts.'[17]

The cascade of biblical images enriches the mind and the imagination. The primary object is to lead not to bare knowledge or intellectual or academic understanding, but to fruitful spiritual nourishment – an experience. The reader 'recognizes in himself what is being said',[18] or 'what he hears aloud he feels within'.[19] For the effect of Scripture Bernard constantly uses the images of eating, drinking, nourishing: 'I ruminate on these things sweetly,' he says, 'and they fill my inner parts. They nourish my inmost being and all my bones bring forth praise.'[20] Elsewhere he expresses the same idea: 'At the table of Catholic doctrine plentiful food is put before everyone according to their measure of understanding.'[21] This is Bernard's comment on Gregory the Great's delightful image, 'In the sea of holy scripture the lamb can walk and the elephant can swim.'[22] Bernard sees as his task 'to draw on the manifest streams of the scriptures and from them serve the needs of each individual'.[23] Or again, 'I must draw water and offer it as a drink, a task I shall achieve not by a spate of rapid comments, but by careful examination and frequent exhortation.'[24] Scripture must be chewed meditatively: 'As food is sweet to the palate, so does a psalm delight the heart. But the soul that is sincere and wise will not fail to chew the psalm with the teeth as it were of the mind, because if he swallows it in a lump, without proper mastication, the palate will be cheated of the delicious flavour, sweeter even than honey that drips from the comb. Let us with the apostles offer a honey-comb at the table of the Lord in the heavenly banquet. As honey flows from the comb so should devotion flow from the words; otherwise if one attempts to assimilate them without the condiment of the Spirit, the written letters bring death.'[25]

The result of this 'chewing' and assimilation of Scripture, leading to personal enrichment, frequently becomes clear in Bernard's writing. He uses the Scripture to assess and explain both to himself and to others his own situation, as is shown by another passage of the *Sermons on the Song of Songs*:

> To make a short digression, there have been times when I have sat at the feet of Jesus sorrowing [Ezra 9.3] and offering the sacrifice of a troubled spirit [Ps. 50.19] as I remembered my sins, and certainly in the rare moments when I have stood at the head of Jesus rejoicing in remembrance of his generosity [Mt. 26.8], I have heard people saying, 'Why this waste?' They were complaining that I lived only for myself, though they thought I could do good to many. They said, 'This could have been sold at a high price and given to the poor [Mt. 26.9].' But it would not have been a good bargain for me, even if I were to gain the whole world, to lose myself and suffer harm [Mt. 16.26]. Therefore, realizing that these words were the ones of which scripture speaks [Eccl. 10.1], 'dying flies which spoil the

perfume of ointment', I remembered those divine words, 'My people, those who praise you lead you into error' [Isa. 3.12]. Those who accuse me of idleness should listen to the Lord, who excuses me and answers for me, 'Why do you pester this woman?' [Mt. 26.10]. That is, you look at the surface, and that is why you judge superficially [Mk 12.14]. It is not a man, who can put forth his hand to great deeds, but a woman [Prov. 31.19]. Why do you try to load a burden on him whom I see to be too weak [Acts 15.10]? He is doing a good work for me [Mk 14.6]. Let him remain in the good work until he develops strength for better. If ever he advances to manhood, the perfect manhood [Eph. 4.13], he will be able to embark on the work of perfection.[26]

The presence of 13 quotations or allusions in so few lines leaves no doubt that Bernard's whole thinking – and indeed his decision-making – was shaped by meditation on the Scriptures. In a way it is a perfect example of Bernard's personal and private use of Scripture. He is meditating on his own predicament of being pressed to use his spiritual talents and influence in a more proactive way, rather than pursuing his own goal of personal holiness in the monastic state.[27] His answer to the challenge is based on meditation on the Gospel story of the woman who was reprimanded by the Disciples for wasting precious ointment on anointing Jesus (to which five allusions are made), together with scriptural reflection on the need to advance further in his own spiritual development before running the risk of stretching too far his limited spiritual resources.

Indeed, this series of *Sermons on the Song of Songs* provides the perfect example of Bernard's style. The dramatic context of these sermons is monastic, for they purport to be delivered in the abbot's daily homilies after prime, the short liturgical office at the beginning of the working day. They often begin with an 'As I was saying yesterday' and often end with some practical remark about the monks needing to go off to work, or Bernard needing to go to welcome guests who have been announced – or indeed a complaint that Bernard has noticed that some of the monks fall asleep at the night office (*Sermon 7*). Dom Jean Leclercq, in his authoritative 'Introduction' to Volume 2 of the Sermons,[28] concludes that the style is often too elaborate to be entirely oral, and the enquiries from friends about their progress too frequent to suggest that they were spontaneous. Nevertheless, the dramatic context of the sermons remains that of the daily monastic conference by the abbot at the end of the liturgical celebration of prime, before the monks dispersed to their manual labour.

There is almost a mesmeric quality about the sermons as the scriptural words, scriptural phrases and scriptural images flow over the listeners like a series of waves beating on the shore, or even battering against rocks. The monks were to depart for their day's work with their imaginations filled with these images, their ears ringing with striking phrases. The Song of Songs is in any case passionate, emotional and indeed often erotic poetry about young lovers, seeking, losing, finding, teasing each other, playing together, finally – with great delicacy and allusion – consummating their love. The second sermon uses the opening words of the girl as a sort of oft-repeated mantra, 'Let him kiss me with the kiss of his mouth'. The monk, lover of Christ, is placed in the position of the lover in the song, clearly intended to depart to his silent and meditative work in field or craft shop with this passionately emotional image ringing in his ears for his reflection during the day. The third sermon, coloured by that consciousness of sin that is never far from Bernard's thoughts, takes up again and develops the same image of kissing. It begins with the penitent kissing of the feet of Jesus by the repentant sinner (as in Lk. 7.38, but without any explicit quotation of that passage, presumably superfluous to the listeners). It advances by degrees, mounting to the humble kissing of Christ's hand before rising to receive the kiss of his lips.

Here enters another feature of Bernard's use of the Bible, the background of medieval court imagery. Kissing the hand is not a biblical gesture, but in the Middle Ages was a gesture of feudal fealty, the expression of loyalty from a subject to an overlord, an acknowledgment of subjection and indebtedness. Even Bernard is stumped for a biblical image, resorting to a completely alien psalm-verse, 'You must kiss his hand, that is, you must give glory to his name not to yourself [Ps. 113.9]. First of all, you must glorify him because he has forgiven your sins, secondly because he has adorned you with virtues'. This medieval feudal background frequently protrudes. In the same way, in *Sermon 2 on the Ascension* he dramatically imagines himself as a spectator in a medieval court procession and enthronement scene as Jesus proceeds to enthronement at the right hand of the Father.

As always, one image leads on to another. Though Bernard continues to use the same imagery of the feet and the kiss, his application of it in the *Sermons on the Song of Songs* becomes almost whimsical as he talks of the two feet of God, one of which is mercy and the other judgement, as God – further mixing the uses of the image – walks among his followers and makes his enemies his footstool. The kiss is sometimes the incarnation, sometimes the kiss, of the Holy Spirit through the risen Christ breathing upon his Disciples in the Upper Room (Jn 20.22), and the bride becomes the soul passionately desiring the kiss of Jesus. This is clearly not literal or pedestrian interpretation of Scripture; rather, it is weaving arabesques coloured by biblical imagery. By the time we reach Sermon 9, Bernard has even set up an animated little dialogue between the bride and her friends. The two breasts of the bride*groom*

have become his patience and his welcoming mercy towards the penitent sinner, and the psalm is said to describe both his breasts by 'slow
to anger and rich in mercy' (Ps. 102.8). Next, Bernard reverses the
imagery of the sexes to express the fruitfulness of Christ's kiss: 'so great
is the potency of that holy kiss that no sooner has the bride received it
than she conceives and her breasts grow rounded with the fruitfulness
of conception'.[29] Even further, the breasts of the bride become the
guidance of the spiritual director: one full of the milk of consolation
in sadness and the other of encouragement in eagerness.[30]

One of Bernard's most forceful techniques is a sort of dramatic
prosopopoiea, addressing and imagining the subject of his thoughts. He
slips into this particularly easily with Mary. So on the martyrdom of
Mary, in a sermon on the Assumption:

> And indeed after your Jesus (the Jesus of all people, but especially yours)
> gave up his spirit, the fierce lance which opened his side (not sparing
> him in death, though he could suffer no hurt) touched not his soul but
> yours. His soul was no longer present, but yours could not by any means
> be torn away. The pang of sorrow therefore pierced your soul, so that we
> rightly call you more than a martyr, in whom the effect of compassion
> transcended the bodily suffering. Did not that saying, 'Mother, behold
> your son' more than the sword, truly pierce your soul and touch even
> the division between soul and spirit? What an exchange! In place of Jesus
> John is given to you, a servant in place of the Lord, a disciple in place of
> the master, a son of Zebedee in place of the Son of God, a mere man in
> place of the true God. How could it be that hearing this did not pierce
> your most affectionate heart, when the mere memory of it breaks even
> our hearts, stony or even iron though they be?[31]

By this dramatic apostrophe the listener is brought to share intimately
in the experience of Mary, to appreciate and participate in her emotion
with profound empathy. If the purpose of meditating on the Scriptures
is not so much intellectual understanding as experience, then this is
a powerful means of achieving that purpose. In the four *Homilies in
Praise of the Virgin Mary* the moment of the Annunciation, while the
world waits for Mary's reply, offers an incomparable opportunity for
such dramatization:

> The angel is awaiting an answer. It is time for him to return to the One
> who sent him (Tob. 12.20). We too wait for the moment of pity, O Lady,
> we who are wretchedly oppressed by the sentence of damnation. And see,
> the price of our salvation is offered to you. If you consent, straightway will
> we be freed. In the eternal Word of God were we all made, and see, we
> die. In your brief answer we can be refreshed and brought back to life.

This contrite Adam asks from you, gentle Virgin, cast out from paradise
with his wretched descendants. This Abraham, this David, this all other
holy Fathers beg from you, your own fathers, who themselves are living
in the land of the shadow of death (Isa. 9.2). This the whole world awaits,
prostrate at your knees, and rightly too, since on your lips hang consolation of the wretched, redemption of captives, freedom for the damned,
lastly salvation for all the children of Adam. Hurry, O Virgin, to give your
answer. O Lady, answer with the word which the earth, which the underworld, which the world above also awaits. (Homily 4, 8)

By this masterpiece of breathless suspense, itself a prayer, as time stands
still, are expressed the firmness of Christian hope, human longing for
salvation from the depths of sin, devotion to the Virgin, and countless
other experiences of the Christian life.

Thomas Aquinas

The Birth of Universities

In the Middle Ages the pace of change was far less rapid than today.
Thomas Aquinas was born hardly more than a century after Bernard.
Between the late nineteenth century and the beginning of the twenty-
first staggering changes in the world have taken place: space travel,
electronics, globalization serve as headings to introduce a whole raft
of changes of attitude and material circumstances. In the century and
a third between 1090 and 1225 no such striking material changes had
occurred. Yet the change in universities and in intellectual life had
proceeded apace. Bernard represented a monastic world, founded on
prayer and contemplation. He had fought against the nascent intellectual movements of logical and scientific enquiry represented in his
day by Abelard, for he found them irrelevant to the search for God. He
had won a small personal victory against Abelard himself, but the movement had continued. Universities – groups of scholars teaching pupils
and pushing back the barriers of knowledge, scientific, religious and,
perhaps above all, legal – sprang up in the course of the half-century
1150–1200: Oxford in the 1170s, Cambridge, Bologna, Paris, and a
papal school in Rome soon followed. Since Latin was the language of
learning throughout Europe, and most of the scholars belonged to religious orders who had representatives at all these universities, there was
an easy transition of personnel and a rapid transmission of knowledge
between them all. In this spread of learning the newly founded orders
of friars (Franciscans founded 1208, Dominicans 1215), and especially
the Dominicans, played an important part.

Thomas himself, born perhaps 1225, was entrusted for his education

to the monks of Monte Cassino near Naples at the age of five, and proceeded from there to the University of Naples at the age of 15. In 1245
he broke through parental opposition to join the Order of Preachers,
and was soon sent to Paris to continue his studies, probably still 'the
liberal studies' (that is, general education), though his future tutor,
St Albert the Great (c. AD 1195–1280), was teaching at Saint-Jacques
at Paris during this period, and Thomas may have attended lectures
there. At any rate, he accompanied Albert when he moved to Cologne
in 1248, remaining there with him till 1252. His later writings show how
important an influence on him Albert was. It was no doubt through
Albert that he first encountered the growing influence of the Greek
philosophy of Aristotle. Returned to Paris, he received the degree of
Master and taught there for three years. There his primary duties would
have been teaching Scripture, as well as lecturing on the *Sentences* of
Peter Lombard, a compendium of theology compiled by Lombard
(later Archbishop of Paris) about a century earlier. Thomas's output
was always prodigious, and it is from this early period that date not only
his commentary on the book of Isaiah, but also philosophical works
such as *De Ente et Essentia* (On Being and Essence).

His grasp of different disciplines was remarkable. He has become
known as the theologian *par excellence* of the Roman Catholic Church.
Yet philosophers also claim him for their own, and he is accounted
chiefly responsible not only for the revival at this time of Aristotelian
studies and their integration into Christian theology, but also for the
interest in and appropriation of the Arab philosopher-theologians
Avicenna (AD 980–1037) and Averroes (AD 1126–1198). At the same
time, biblical scholars point out that the primary object of his teaching,
as of all theology, was the Bible. In his early years of teaching at Paris he
would have lectured on the Bible every morning for a couple of hours.
The first subject to be studied in his theology course was how to use the
Bible. Thomas's inaugural lecture, which won him his title to teach,
was a commentary on the Psalm-verse *Rigans montes de superioribus suis*
(watering the mountains from above) (Ps. 103.13). This he applies to
the teaching of Scripture, stressing the need for personal qualities of
both teacher and pupil in a way that would have earned him Bernard's
approval. The teacher of Scripture must, like the mountain-tops, be
raised up from the earth, yearning for heavenly things, and first illuminated by the rays of the sun. The personal qualities of teachers are also
important; they must be blameless, intelligent, fervent and obedient to
God's will. The listeners, in their turn, must be humble, willing to learn,
and fruitful; that is, able to carry the teaching further, with a certain
inventiveness, 'through which the good listener, hearing a little, will
proclaim much: "Give the wise man a chance and he will learn more
wisdom" (Prov. 9.9)'.[32]

Apart from this period of formation, Thomas's life story has little to tell us about his approach to Scripture. After three years in Paris he was summoned back to Italy, where he continued – apart from a brief return to Paris – to teach and write at various centres of learning, as well as setting up a number of studia and travelling, always (as the rules of the order prescribed) laboriously on foot, until his death on the way to the Council of Lyons in 1274. The notes for his full course of theology were written up (by him, completed after his death by disciples) as *Summa Theologiae*, a work so comprehensive and compelling that it has remained to this day probably the most important basis of any theology course in the Roman Catholic Church.

Scriptural Commentaries

Thomas's commentaries on the Bible reveal a distinctive method. It would, of course, be a mistake to suppose that his theology course consisted merely of biblical knowledge laced with philosophy. At every turn he also quotes from the Fathers of the Church. His knowledge of the Fathers of the Church was such that he was commissioned by Pope Urban IV to assemble a truly marvellous commentary on the four Gospels drawn from the sayings of the Fathers, justly known as the *Catena Aurea*, or Golden Chain. He works, therefore, from deep within the tradition of the Church, but independent-mindedly, his writings drawing their authority from their respect for the tradition of the Church as well as their brilliant clarity and satisfying argumentation.

Literal and mystical senses

Fundamental to all Thomas's commentaries is a clear distinction between the literal and the 'mystical' sense of Scripture. In the preface to his *Commentary on Job*, Thomas attests that he proposes to comment on the text literally, since Gregory the Great has commented so subtly and judiciously (*tam subtiliter et discrete*),[33] on the 'mystical' elements. He begins, therefore, by commenting on Job's sex, residence, name, earthly reality and rectitude – all of which set the scene for what he considers to be the book's thesis: a demonstration of how human affairs are ruled by divine providence. The whole tone is utterly different from Bernard's affective commentaries, intended to convey an experience of the text and to bring out the richness of the text in all the ways it has been understood and applied in Christian tradition. Although Thomas does not rule the 'mystical' sense out of court, he is here giving full preference to the literal (or what has sometimes been described as the 'historical') meaning. Thomas's mindset and emphasis will become clear when he leaves no doubt about the utter priority of the literal sense and the insufficiency of the unaided spiritual sense. In much of contemporary scriptural exegesis and commentary the spiritual sense had run wild. In Thomas the value and importance of the spiritual senses is strictly subordinated to the literal sense. Again and again he insists that nothing can be established from Scripture unless it is present in the literal sense: 'As Augustine says,[34] there is nothing taught in a hidden way in scripture in one place which is not taught openly in another. Therefore a spiritual explanation (*expositio*) must always be supported by some literal explanation of the scripture, so that there is no possibility of error.'[35]

Elsewhere the same thing is expressed differently: 'Nothing necessary for faith is contained in the spiritual sense which the scripture does not elsewhere express openly.'[36] As Spicq says,[37] 'The genius of St Thomas was to moderate the uncontrolled exuberance of allegorical interpretations by defining the rules for their discernment.' While not denying the usefulness of allegorical senses for intensifying the appreciation of the Christian message, Thomas insists that such senses must always remain secondary to the primary, literal sense.

Thomas is quite happy to point out the 'mystical' sense, but is always careful to distinguish it from the literal. Three examples from the *Commentary on John* may be quoted:

- On Jn 1.27 he first gives a literal explanation about the Baptist and Jesus's sandal, and then says, 'There is also a mystical explanation'.
- On Jn 5.13 he gives the literal explanation that Jesus hides himself after healing the sick man because it is not good to parade one's good works, and then gives the 'mystical' explanation that this disappearance symbolizes and promises his turning to the gentiles.
- On Jn 6.51, in a wonderful passage, he again makes a clear distinction between the spiritual and the literal senses:

This saying ('Unless you eat the flesh of the son of man and drink his blood you will not have life in you') can be referred to spiritual and to sacramental eating. Referred to spiritual eating the saying has a clear sense. One who eats the flesh of Christ and drinks his blood partakes of the unity of the Church which comes about by love [Romans 12.5]. You are all one body in Christ. Anyone who does not eat in this way is outside the Church and consequently outside love, so does not have life. [1 John 3.4] 'Anyone who does not love remains in death.' Referred to sacramental eating the saying contains a doubt, for [in John 3.5] it is said, 'Someone who is not born again of water and the Spirit cannot enter into the Kingdom of Heaven'. But in the same way this saying is put forward, 'Unless you eat the flesh, etc.'. Therefore while baptism is the necessary sacrament, it seems that the Eucharist is also necessary. And this indeed the Greeks accept, and so they give the Eucharist to children who are baptized, and for this they have the authority of Denys, who says that the reception of every sacrament reaches its summit in Eucharistic communion, which is the summit of all the sacraments.

An understanding of Christ and the Church

Whatever the senses of Scripture, Thomas is constantly aware of the often-quoted saying of the *glossa ordinaria* (the generally accepted medieval commentary on all Scripture): *Nihil est in divina scriptura quod non pertineat ad Christum vel ad Ecclesiam* (There is nothing in holy scripture which does not relate to Christ or the Church). He was always searching to penetrate more deeply into the Christological or ecclesiological meaning of the texts. For Thomas and the scholastic circles of the high Middle Ages, such penetration consisted of analysis in intellectual and philosophical terms, leading finally to *cognitio intelligibilium*, as he says in his discussion of the nature of theology.[38] Theology makes use of the sort of images that make poetry delightful (*ibid.*, 1 ad um), but these are a veil through which the 'ray of divine revelation' is seen. The mind cannot be satisfied with this and must progress to *cognitio intelligibilium* (properly intellectual knowledge).

His early *Commentary on Isaiah* is delightfully crisp, argumentative and factual. On Isaiah 7 he explains the historical situation of the prophecy in detail, even to detailing (with medium accuracy) the three water-pools of Jerusalem, before entering into specific controversy with the Jews over the interpretation of the sign of the virgin. After this he comes to the relationship to Christ. He sees Isa. 7.14 as a 'sign of the incarnation', although he is perfectly aware that the Jews have multiple objections to this view, objections he refutes one by one. First, though he has been chided for his lack of knowledge of Hebrew[39], he explains that the Hebrew has עלמה for 'young woman' (Thomas gives it in transliterated form, *alma*) in Isa. 7.14, whereas 'virgin', which occurs in the Greek and Latin texts, would require בתולה, *bethula*. Second, by a complicated calculation of ages, he shows that the 'sign' could not refer to Ahaz's son Hezekiah – again the sort of meticulous literal explanation that would have been entirely foreign to Bernard's methods. It must therefore be understood in the Christian sense as pointing to the Incarnation.

The Contribution of Philosophy

Typical of Thomas's use of philosophy, and particularly the anthropology of Aristotle, is the commentary on the crucial passage about
original sin in Rom. 5.12. Far from wishing merely to convey an experience of the redemptive love of God expressed in the text, as Bernard
would have done, Thomas is seeking an intellectual or philosophical
understanding of the doctrine. The whole exegesis makes vital use of
Aristotle, for Thomas's anthropology is formed by Aristotle. (Not surprisingly, as it stands it would hardly pass muster in a modern medical
textbook.) Typical also of his method as a philosopher is the method,
so fully used in the *Summa Theologiae*, of starting from a difficulty, the
resolution of which will throw light on the positive explanation.

> It seems impossible that sin should be transferred from one to another
> through fleshly origin, for sin is in the rational soul, which is not passed on
> by fleshly origin. Also because the intellect is not the actualization of any
> body. So it cannot be caused by means of bodily seed, as the Philosopher
> [Aristotle] says in the *Book on the Origin of Animals*. Also because the
> rational soul is something existent in itself; it operates by itself and is not
> destroyed by the destruction of the body. Consequently it is not generated
> by bodily generation, like other forms which cannot exist independently,
> but rather is caused by God. Consequently it seems that sin, which is a
> quality of the soul, cannot be transferred by fleshly origin either.
>   A reasoned response to this is that, although the soul is not in the seed,
> the seed nevertheless contains a disposition of the body to receive a soul.
> When the body receives the soul, the soul is in its own way conformed
> to the body, because everything is received in the mode of the recipient
> [another Aristotelian maxim]. So we see that children resemble their par-
> ents, not only in physical defects (as a leper begets a leper and someone
> with a defective foot begets a child with a defective foot) but also in defects
> of the soul (as an irascible person begets an irascible person, and a men-
> tally unbalanced person a mentally unbalanced child). Even though the
> foot, which is the subject of the defect, is not in the seed, nor is the soul,
> which is the subject of anger or madness. Nevertheless the seed contains
> a force which forms the bodily members and disposes the soul.
>   But a difficulty still remains, for defects passed on from a distorted
> origin are not culpable, since they deserve not punishment but sympathy,
> as the Philosopher says about someone born blind or deficient in some
> other way. This is because it belongs to the notion of blame that it should
> be voluntary and under the control of the person to whom blame is
> imputed. So if any defect comes to us from an origin in our first parent,
> it is in us a matter not of blame but of punishment.

By applying such categories of Aristotelian philosophical analysis to the sacred text, Thomas has taken the crucial step towards a separation of the interpretation of the Bible and an independent science of systematic theology, integrating the analysis of revelation into the intellectual categories of that great age of discovery of Aristotle, Avicenna and Averroes. It is this which will in due course excite the ire of the brilliant young Augustinian scholar Martin Luther.

Conclusion

This has been a frustrating chapter! Both Bernard and Thomas have so much more to them than their use of Scripture that it has been difficult to confine the discussion strictly. Bernard is a towering figure in the history and movements of his age, and Thomas is a towering figure in the wider development of theology. However, the two of them offer scintillating examples of the use made of Scripture in the high Middle Ages, each typifying their own time. Bernard is the culmination of the monastic sheer love of God in the Scripture, of *lectio divina*, earning the title of Doctor Mellifluus. Aquinas, the friar, has moved on to an age of philosophy and reasoning, applying to Scripture the burgeoning development of the sciences, earning the title of Doctor Communis for the widespread use of his writings by theological students everywhere. Yet Scripture remains at the heart of his study. The reward of this chapter is to show that, philosopher though he was, his philosophy was fed by the Bible.

Further Reading

Bernard of Clairvaux, *Selected Works* (New York: Paulist Press, 1987).
Davies, B., *The Thought of Thomas Aquinas* (Oxford: Clarendon Press, 1992).
Evans, G. R., *Bernard of Clairvaux* (Oxford: Oxford University Press, 2000).
Geisler, N. L., *Thomas Aquinas* (Grand Rapids, MI: Baker Book House, 1991).
Kenny, A., *Aquinas* (Oxford: Oxford University Press, 1980).
Leclercq, J., *Bernard of Clairvaux and the Cistercian Spirit* (Kalamazoo, MI: Cistercian Publications, 1976).
McCabe, H., *On Aquinas* (London: Continuum, 2008).
Pieper, J., *Introduction to Thomas Aquinas* (London: Faber & Faber, 1963).

CHAPTER 7

Two Norfolk Ladies

Introduction

The latter part of the fourteenth century was not a tranquil time. Europe had been ravaged by the Black Death, first in 1348 but recurrently since then, reducing the population of Europe and of England by some 50 per cent. It has left its mark in a nursery rhyme sung even today:

> Ring a ring of roses
> A pocket full of posies
> 'A-tishoo, a-tishoo'
> We all fall down.

The first line refers to the circular red marks on the skin which preceded lesions, the second to attempts to evade the smell of death and burning corpses, the third to the sneezing which soon developed, and the fourth to the inevitable outcome. A more immediate consequence was a disastrous shortage of labour, which led to widespread agricultural unrest, and in England to the Peasants' Revolt of 1381, brutally suppressed. One of its more important outbreaks was around Norwich, where Geoffrey Litster forced his way into the city, only to be captured and executed by the bishop (after hearing his confession). Norwich was at this time possibly the greatest city in the kingdom and its most important centre of trade (particularly the wool trade); the south coast had been largely disabled by the Hundred Years War with the French, while trade from Norwich with the Netherlands continued to flourish. In the wider world, after the return of the papacy to Rome, the Church was split by the Great Schism. The 'fighting bishop' of Norwich, Henry Despenser, played an active but ineffectual part in seeking to put an end to it by military force, though in effect reconciliation was achieved only at the Council of Florence in 1417.

In the spiritual sphere the *devotio moderna*, encouraged by the Brethren of the Common Life, founded in the Netherlands by Gerhard Groote (1340–1384), brought a new warmth of devotion to the humanity of Christ in reaction to the intellectual speculation of the schools. Visually and in art, this change was marked by a change from the popularity of the victorious Christ on the Cross, dating from Saxon times (e.g., the pre-Norman Langford Rood), to a preference for the pietà, or representation of Christ brought down from the Cross and cradled in his mother's arms. From a literary point of view it issued in not only such lasting and popular works as *The Imitation of Christ*, but also in a wave of mystical writing, especially in England, from authors such as Richard Rolle (1290–1345), Walter Hilton (author of *The Ladder of Perfection*, died 1396), and the anonymous *Cloud of Unknowing* (late fourteenth century).

We shall concentrate on two women among these authors, namely Julian of Norwich and Margery Kempe, and how they saw the Bible. Both were natives of Norfolk, Margery Kempe of the town now known as King's Lynn, some 80 kilometres from Norwich and similarly an important port. Both meditated devotedly on the Scriptures and especially on the Passion of Christ. Both their affective and lovingly personal relationship to Jesus and to the events of his Passion are touching. They both meditated on and cherished every detail. They met each other, for one of Margery's less extensive journeys was to consult Julian in her anchorhold. In almost every other way they seem to have been utterly different in character.

Julian of Norwich

About Julian's exterior life we know almost nothing; she did not wish to tell us much. Even her personal name is unknown. Principally we know that she was an anchoress, living a rigorously restricted life in a cell attached to the church of St Julian in Norwich. Such a way of life was not uncommon and was carefully regulated. Those who lived it commonly adopted the name of the church to which they were attached. The rules were strict, such an anchoress remaining immured in her cell but able to communicate with others by a window into the church and by another window (covered with a curtain) for communication with people who might come for advice or spiritual counsel. She herself tells us that in 1373 she was 30 years old. The very full civic records of Norwich mention various small bequests to an anchoress Julian, of which the latest is in 1416. Unless another anchoress had adopted the same name, this tells us that she was still alive at this date. She tells us also that she was 'a simple unlettered creature' or, according to some manuscripts, 'a simple creature that cowde no letter', but the meaning of this remains disputed. Literary critics aver that her work is too well organized, too full of references backwards and forwards, to have been simply dictated, and that 'unlettered' must mean 'unliterary', in the sense that she lacked a university education or knew no Latin. It has even been argued that Julian's protestation is purely conventional: 'It is very evident that she was a learned woman. . . . We can only make conjectures about how she acquired her Latin and her learning.'[1] Such suggestions rest upon supposed literary allusions to the Latin Vulgate and other works, which could be accounted for also by an attentive memory and by close attention to the liturgy. There are occasional Latin grammatical errors, such as '*Benedicite Dominus*',[2] presumably a mishearing for '*Benedicite Dominum*'. Julian's humility is simple and unaffected. She does not exaggerate or denigrate herself, and several times simply stresses that she did not earn or deserve the 'showings': 'I am not good because of this showing, but only if I love God better. And in so much as you love God better, it is more to you than to me.'[3]

Julian's Revelations of Divine Love

The record of the revelations she received exists in a short form, written soon after the event, and a long form, written after a score of years of reflection, and considerably developed. At one stage[4] she mentions that she did not receive full understanding of the vision until 20 years after the original 'showing', no doubt as the fruit of years of meditation. However, the visual memory of these 'showings' remains so bright – the world 'the size of a hazel-nut in the palm of my hand, and as round as a ball',[5] and the visually realistic description of Christ dying on the Cross in sections 16 and 17 – that they remain fresh and expressive to any reader, with the vividness of the colouring of medieval art. Perhaps the most vivid pictorial description is the blood of Christ: 'great drops of blood fell down from under the garland like pellets, and as they emerged they were brown-red (for the blood was very thick) and in the spreading out they were bright red; and when the blood came to the brows, there the drops vanished.'[6] Julian's description of the workman is thoroughly reminiscent of the pictures in the margins of medieval manuscripts: 'His clothing was a white tunic, thin, old and all soiled, stained with sweat of his body, tight fitting for him and short, as it were but a hand's width below the knee, undecorated, seeming as it would soon be worn out, about to be turned to rags.'

But the vividness of all the 'showings' of the Passion[7] is matched only by the tenderness and love with which Julian narrates them. There is nothing pretentious about her, so that she can say, 'The number of these words surpasses my wit and all my understanding and all my abilities. And therefore the words are not explained here, but every man according to the grace that God gives him receive them in our Lord's meaning.'[8]

The valuable background[9] to her revelation is that it was preceded by a desire for three gifts from God: the memory of Christ's Passion; bodily sickness at 30 years of age; and three 'wounds', namely true contrition, compassion and yearning for God. The purpose of the first two gifts (which she says passed from her memory) was that she should share more fully in the Passion of Christ. She desired a bodily sight of the Passion and the pains of Christ, and a sickness that should be so severe that it would help her to understand and share in the Passion of Jesus. This sickness would seem mortal; she would herself expect to die, and would receive all the last rites of the Church. The Passion of Christ is the key to all her thought and prayer.

In her 31st year she underwent just such a bodily sickness, and on the third night seemed to be at the point of death:[10] 'Thus I endured till day, and by then my body was dead from the midst downwards as regards my feeling. My curate was sent for to be at my ending, and by the time he came I had cast my eyes upwards and could not speak. He placed the cross before my face and said, "I have brought thee the image of thy Maker and Saviour. Look thereupon and comfort thyself with it." I consented to fix my eyes on the face of the crucifix if I could, and so I did. After this my sight began to fail, and it grew all dark about me in the chamber as if it had been night, except on the image of the cross on which I beheld an ordinary light, and I know not how.'

Her pain eased, 'Then came suddenly to my memory that I should desire the second wound of our Lord's gracious gift, that my body could be filled with the memory and feeling of his blessed Passion, as I had prayed before. Suddenly I saw the red blood trickling down from under the garland, hot and freshly and most plenteously, just as it was at the time of his Passion when the garland of thorns was pressed onto his blessed head.'

Julian and the Bible

It is clear that all Julian's thought is based on the Bible, though her vivid word-pictures of the Passion of Christ go well beyond the sober or even reticent accounts of the Gospels. The evangelists are concerned not so much to feed the visual imagination as to interpret the events of the Passion in the light of the Old Testament. Similarly, the enchanting picture of Jesus's young mother, 'the maiden who is his dearworthy Mother',[11] takes as its starting point the Annunciation. In the Middle Ages, betrothal often took place at an age almost as early as in first-century Galilee, and she pictures Mary as little more than a child: 'I saw her spiritually in bodily likeness, a simple maid and humble, young of age and little grown beyond childhood, in the stature that she was when she conceived with child. Also God showed me in part the wisdom and the truth of her soul. And this wisdom and truth caused her to say full humbly to Gabriel, "Behold me here, God's handmaiden".'[12]

The words of Scripture spring readily to Julian's lips: 'In times of joy I could have said with Saint Paul, "Nothing shall separate me from the love of Christ". And in the pain I could have said with Peter, "Lord, save me, I perish".'[13] There is, however, no doubt that she is much more deeply formed by biblical reading and meditation than this. Apart from her burning personal allegiance to the suffering Christ and her joy in his joy, the most pronounced element in her thinking is the salvation of all people in Christ. 'Truly our Lover desires that our soul cleave to him with all its might, and that we evermore cleave to his goodness, for of all things that heart can think, this pleases God most.'[14] It is a message full of optimism; she insists that there is no anger, only forgiveness, in God,[15] for wrath is incompatible with peace and love. This springs from a deep understanding of Scripture, for in the Old Testament the Divine Name is explained as 'God of mercy and forgiveness' (Exod. 34.6), a reading which echoes down the Scriptures: in 1 Tim. 2.4 God 'wants everyone to be saved'. In this conviction she is profoundly puzzled by the contradiction between the conviction that we are sinners and her inability to see our sin in God, for, 'I saw our Lord God showing to us no more blame than as if we were as pure and as holy as angels are in heaven'.[16]

Perhaps Julian's most original and lively piece is the great parable of the lord who has a servant in section 51; it also illustrates the extent to which her thinking is formed by the New Testament, and in particular by Paul, as well as by the poems on the suffering servant of the lord in Isaiah. The lord 'looks upon his servant most lovingly and sweetly, and humbly he sends him to a certain place to do his will'. The servant 'suddenly leaps up and runs in great haste because of his love to do his lord's will. And immediately he falls into a deep pit and receives very great injury. Then he groans and moans and wails and writhes, but he cannot rise up nor help himself in any way'. The lord does not blame the servant, since his fall was the result of his very eagerness. On the contrary, the servant is to be rewarded 'to such an extent that his falling and all the woe that he had received from it would be transformed into high and surpassing honour and endless bliss'.

Julian's conception of the redemption combines the theology of Romans 5 and Philippians 2 with that of Hebrews 10. In Romans 5, Paul presents Jesus as the second Adam, whose obedience undoes the disobedience of the first Adam. In Philippians 2, Christ is exalted because he has first humbled himself to take on human nature and to die on the Cross. In Hebrews 10, Christ is the high priest who stands before God to say, 'Here I am, I come to do your will'. Julian's conception is a synthesis of these passages. The servant is Adam; 'when Adam fell, God's Son fell',[17] for

> Adam fell from life to death into the pit of this miserable world and after that into hell. God's Son fell with Adam into the pit of the womb of the Maiden (who was the fairest daughter of Adam) and that in order to obtain for Adam exemption from guilt in heaven and on earth. And he mightily fetched Adam out of hell. . . . He stood before his Father as a servant, willingly taking upon himself all our burden, and he leaped up wholly ready at the Father's will, and soon he fell most lowly into the Maiden's womb, having no regard for himself nor for his harsh pains. . . . And I saw the Son standing, saying in his meaning, 'Behold, my dear Father, I stand before thee in Adam's tunic all ready to jump up and to run, I am willing to be on the earth to do thine honour when it is thy will to send me.'

This same passage in section 51 is permeated with other scriptural allusions, which enrich its meaning and show how meditation on Scripture has formed Julian's thinking: Christ as the wisdom of God (1 Cor. 1.24), 'he is the head and we are the members' (1 Cor. 12.12), an end to sorrow and pain (Rev. 21.4).

A little further on, Julian uses the Pauline teaching on the body of Christ to show that Mary is the mother of all Christians. 'Thus our Lady is our mother in whom we are all enclosed and out of her we are born in Christ, for she who is mother of our Saviour is mother of all who shall be saved within our Saviour.' She carries this further, seeing Christ also as mother: 'And our Saviour is our true mother in whom we are endlessly born and never shall come to birth out of him.'[18] This imagery may be dependent on St Anselm's use of it in his Hymn to St Paul. For Julian, the whole of the Trinity is involved: 'In our creation God all Power is our natural Father, God all Wisdom is our natural mother, with the Love and the Goodness of the Holy Spirit, who is all one God, one Lord.' The relationship is carried further, into the spouse-imagery of Ephesians 5: 'He is our most true Spouse, and we are his beloved wife and his fair maiden; with this wife he is never displeased, for he says, "I love thee and thou lovest me."'

So does Julian extend her loving meditation on the 'showings' of the Passion of Christ by means of Pauline imagery to illustrate the relationship between Christ and the Christian? She shows the same dependence on Paul in her advice to Margery Kempe when that lady came to consult her. It is striking that in the short account of Julian's advice to her given by Margery, each of the counsels given by Julian is explicitly based on a biblical text:

- to be certain and steadfast in her way, without any hesitation – based on the Letter of Jas 1.6: 'the person who has doubts is like the waves thrown up in the sea by the buffeting of the wind'
- not to be alarmed by the gift of tears – based on Rom. 8.26-27: the Spirit comes to help us in prayer, and 'makes our petitions for us in groans that cannot be put into words'
- in Margery's own words, 'Any creature that has these tokens may steadfastly believe that the Holy Ghost dwells in his soul' (as in 1 Cor. 12.12-13).

So Julian's reliance on the Bible extends not only to her own prayers and meditations, but also to her spiritual counselling.

Margery Kempe

Introducing Margery

Margery Kempe was a very different kettle of fish. She was a practical, busy woman of the world, wife and mother of a large family, who had no hesitation in calling a spade a spade. She really was illiterate, and all her knowledge of sacred literature came from books that were read to her by priests who performed this service for her. The book of her experiences[19] was first written out at her dictation in a mixture of German and English by a scribe whose handwriting and spelling were so bad that it was barely decipherable by the priest-scribe who rewrote it and, at her further dictation, completed it. We have no means of knowing to what extent this priest was responsible for editing the story. He does occasionally insert his own opinions, for example to express his sympathy with Margery's gift of tears.[20] A further question is whether he was responsible for the arrangement of the book, describing her experiences not chronologically but grouped according to subject matter (e.g., her correction of others – often quite sharp, often leading to conversion – her correct predictions, her investigations for heresy). Is this arrangement too coherent for an illiterate?

Margery has no hesitation in describing her own illegitimate sexual advances, made unsuccessfully to a man who had first approached her, and her own subsequent inability to make love to her husband.[21] Nor does she spare the detail about the negotiations between herself and her husband when he wants to have sex with her – despite her long-standing bargain of sexual abstinence if she would pay his debts – on the road between York and Bridlington.[22] In the same bustling, self-absorbed way she frankly relates her strange religious antics and the adverse reactions they provoked from those who witnessed them. Her account is the first autobiography in the English language and presents a lively picture of life in medieval Norfolk. Added to this is the record of her extensive travels to the Holy Land, Norway, Santiago and Italy, though she is much more interested in describing her own behaviour than in any features of these countries. Almost the only 'tourist' detail is about the raising of the Cross in Norway on Easter Sunday at noon, instead of early in the morning, in spite of which 'she had her meditation and her devotion with weeping and sobbing as well as if she had been at home'.[23]

One example of her extraordinary self-absorption is that, having borne 14 children to her husband, she barely mentions them, dwelling only on her stormy relationship with one son. This makes it evident that she is giving us a spiritual rather than a general autobiography. She is happy to tell us that her constant admonitions and threats to him to improve his way of life totally alienated him, and that when he fell ill he regarded this as a result of her curse upon him. He married and lived in Germany[24] and was later warmly reconciled to her, returning with his wife briefly before dying suddenly. His death, followed by that of his father, Margery's husband, are described in a few words and without any emotion, merely as an introduction to the prolonged account of Margery's negotiations with her confessor about her accompanying her widowed daughter-in-law back to Germany.[25]

Margery was born into a prosperous bourgeois family of King's Lynn (then known as Bishop's Lynn) in about 1373. Her father had held a number of civic offices in that flourishing port: member of parliament, five times mayor, justice of the peace and so on. With this background, Margery was quite prepared to defend her own corner, to stand her ground and argue with the Archbishop of York or rebut the charge of Lollardy.

Extreme Expressions of Margery's Devotion

Her story is extraordinary. She tells, seemingly frankly and openly, of a six-month period of madness after the birth of her first child, when she had to be 'tied up and forcibly restrained day and night' to prevent her doing herself serious injury,[26] and of two failed business ventures, brewing and milling.[27] Interspersed in the body of the book are stories of the scornful treatment she received from various people, mostly because of her propensity for being so affected by devotion that she lay on the ground and wept. Not surprisingly, this caused considerable upset, especially because she shouted so loud that she could be heard outside the church. On one Good Friday she made such a disturbance that she had to be carried out.[28] Furthermore, the priest, her confessor, whose sermons most provoked such outbursts, forbade her to attend his sermons.[29] And yet the gift of tears was highly valued at the time, recommended by Bonaventure, Walter Hilton and others, as her priestly scribe stresses,[30] 'part of a well-recognised pattern of medieval devotion'.[31]

There are intimate conversations with the Lord, in which the Lord thanks her and calls her daughter, mother, sister and even spouse;[32] incidents when she was consulted about the future and was proved right; and consultations with various confessors, some named, some unnamed, some known from other documents, some otherwise unknown. One touching series is when she prayerfully pictures herself as maidservant to St Anne during Mary's childhood, attending devotedly on Mary also during the visitation and the early days of Jesus's life until the flight into Egypt;[33] busy housewife and experienced mother that she is, she is very preoccupied with linen and lodgings. In this Margery is conforming to medieval practices of devotion, for St Aelred[34] already recommends that those meditating should imagine themselves as part of the scene – a practice carried further by Ignatius of Loyola.

On the journey to Jerusalem her devotional habits and her constant tears got on her companions' nerves, so much so that they several times tried to be rid of her, though at the same time they showed their awe of her by following her advice and eventually keeping with her. Her extraordinary devotion reached its extreme expression when she was shown round Jerusalem and they came to Mt Calvary (the only detail of Jerusalem mentioned): 'She fell down because she could not stand or kneel, but writhed and wrestled with her body, spreading her arms out wide, and cried with a loud voice as though her heart would have burst apart, for in the city of her soul she saw truly and freshly how our Lord was crucified. . . . And she had such great compassion and such great pain to see our Lord's pain that she could not keep herself from crying and roaring though she should have died for it. And this was the first crying that she ever cried in any contemplation. And this kind of crying lasted for many years after this time, despite anything that anyone might do, and she suffered much contempt and much reproof for it.'[35]

Such extremes of behaviour may be less extraordinary than they seem to us. Felix Fabri, another traveller to the Holy Land in the fifteenth century, describes similar scenes at the Holy Sepulchre, when women threw themselves to the ground and 'screamed as though in labour'; this he finds entirely appropriate and acceptable. However, when she finally gets back to Norwich this extraordinarily loud crying gets Margery into great trouble, so that people said that 'she had a devil within her', or epilepsy. 'Then people spat at her in horror at the illness, and some scorned her and said that she howled like a dog, and cursed her.'[36]

Margery in Rome

Another extraordinary vignette occurs on the return journey through Rome, including four separate elements.[37]

1. She is ordered by her confessor to look after 'an old woman, a poor creature'. This she does for six weeks, and 'served her as she would have done our Lady', fetching wood and water for her, and begging food and drink for her, she herself having no bed to lie on and full of vermin. 'When the poor woman's wine was sour, this creature herself drank that sour wine, and gave the poor woman good wine that she had bought for her own self.'[38]

2. 'When she saw women in Rome carrying children in their arms, if she could discover that any were boys, she would cry, roar and weep as if she had seen Christ in his childhood. And if she saw a handsome man, she had great pain to look at him lest she might see him who was both God and man. And therefore she cried many times and often, and wept and sobbed bitterly for the manhood of Christ, so that those who saw her were greatly astonished at her.'

3. Then there is a scene of a mystical marriage. A mystical marriage is not without precedent in medieval times; for instance, that between God and St Catherine of Siena. In 1367 Catherine underwent a sort of mystical marriage to Christ in which they 'exchanged hearts'. Catherine describes how Our Lady presented her to her Son, who gave her a ring (which only she can see). She was told, 'Apply your lips to the sacred side of the Son of God; from the divine wound issue the fires of love and the blood which takes all our sins away'.[39] This and similar accounts may well have prompted Margery's experience. However, Margery's is remarkable for two factors. First, she is at last daunted and overcome with awe at the idea of marriage to the Father, rather than to the Son. The Son, to whose humanity she is devoted, stands beside, as a sort of Best Man; she would have preferred a marriage to the Son. Remarkable also, but typical of Margery, is the earthiness, even eroticism, of the language. It is far less restrained than the dignified reticence of Catherine: 'The Father took her by the hand in her soul before the Son and the Holy Ghost and the Mother of Jesus, saying to her soul, "I take you, Margery, for my wedded wife, for fairer, for fouler, for richer, for poorer, provided that you are humble and meek in doing what I command you to do."' This resulted for many years afterwards in sweet smells in her nose, sounds and melodies in her bodily ears, 'many white things flying about her on all sides, as thickly in a way as specks in a sunbeam', and a flame of fire of love, 'marvellously hot and delectable and very comforting, never diminishing but ever increasing; for though the weather were never so cold she felt the

heat burning in her breast and at her heart'. There follow some long and intimate conversations, in the course of which God tells her 'when you are in bed, take me to you as your wedded husband, as your dear darling. . . . I want you to love me, daughter, as a good wife ought to love her husband. Therefore you can boldly take me in the arms of your soul and kiss my mouth, my head, and my feet as sweetly as you want'.[40]

4. Finally, she gave away all her money, even money she had borrowed, to make herself destitute for the love of God. Luckily she met up with 'a worthy lady', an Italian whom she had met previously, and there is an amusing little conversation in broken English: '*Margerya in poverté?*' – '*Yea, grand poverté, madame*'. This lady fed her on Sundays, and she was given weekly meals by various other benefactors.[41]

Margery's Self-defence

At other times Margery could show her mettle more pugnaciously. On a visit (unexplained) to Leicester, at the sight of a realistic crucifix the fire of love was such that 'it caused her to break out in a loud voice and cry astonishingly, and weep and sob very terribly, so that many men and women wondered at her because of it'. Before long she was summoned to the mayor, with whom she had a sharp and bold exchange. Though Margery is too wrapped up in her own experiences, and her vigorous self-defence, to give us the context of these trials, the series of investigations makes good sense against the background of the witch hunt against Lollards in 1417. Her trial is apparently a trial for heresy, but it was in fact a political trial, for Lollardy was always as much a political as a theological offence. The trials were conducted by ecclesiastical courts, but the accusations were pressed by the secular authorities. In the background was the Duke of Bedford, brother to the King, and delegated by the King to defend the north against the Scots. Margery was initially accused of being 'Cobham's daughter'.[42] Sir John Oldcastle, Lord Cobham, was the leader of the Lollard movement, accused of a plot against the King in 1415 and finally executed in 1417. Margery had lately come from Bristol, one of the centres of Lollardy. Her charismatic-type behaviour and her appeal to the Holy Spirit could have made some suspect her of Lollardy. Similarly suspect of Lollardy would have been her reputation for correcting sinners – and even priestly sinners. The accusation that she had not been on pilgrimage accords with the Lollard criticism of pilgrimage, and would also have destroyed her alibi, for she claimed to have been abroad in 1415, at the time of the plot against the King.

The trial unfolded as follows. First[43] she is interrogated in Latin by the steward, to whom she replies smartly, 'Speak English, if you please, for I do not understand what you are saying'. The steward then incautiously takes her off into his chamber and 'makes filthy and lewd gestures' till she shocks him by explaining that her speech comes from the Holy Spirit. Next follows an interrogation by the Abbot and Dean of Leicester and an assemblage of clerics before the high altar. This interrogation starts with a leading anti-Lollard question. Lollards, or 'spirituals', stressed the importance of a holy life and campaigned against unworthy priests, denying the validity of sacraments celebrated by a wicked or dissolute priest. To a seemingly innocent and vague question from her clerical interrogators about what she thinks of the blessed sacrament (Lollards were accused of denying the real presence of Christ in the sacrament), Margery neatly replies with a denial of the Lollard view of sacramental ministry, spiritedly asserting the validity of the Eucharist consecrated by a priest 'be he never so wicked a man in his manner of life'. After further unfounded slurs by the mayor, the clerical assembly lets her go.

Perhaps the most remarkable and characteristic feature of this series of events is the initial exchange between Margery and the Archbishop of York:[44] 'Then the Archbishop said to her, "I am told very bad things about you. I hear it said that you are a very wicked woman." And she replied, "Sir, I also hear it said that you are a wicked man".' The robust archbishop confirms her orthodoxy but asks her to leave his diocese. She has the effrontery to bargain with him – successfully – saying that she first wants to say goodbye to friends in York. Further, she is provoked into telling him a rather risqué tale about a wicked priest. Her examiner is shamed by the tale into conversion, but the archbishop 'liked the tale a lot' and gives her a blessing and a safe-conduct, which keeps her out of trouble in several subsequent arrests.

Conclusion

Judgements on this extraordinary manifestation of medieval piety will vary. David Knowles pronounces that there is 'little in it of deep spirituality and nothing of true mystical experience'.[45] Santha Bhattacharji sees her in the context of her time. This feisty woman is not shy about admitting the distaste, criticism and even outrage which her uncontrollable shoutings, groanings and writhings provoked from those around her. Nor is she shy about admitting any of her faults. She was clearly, as the first instance of her madness after childbirth suggests, an unbalanced character, and several times voices her fear of falling back into this state. Even her extreme generosity in giving herself and her (and other people's) possessions to the service of the poor is impressive, but unbalanced. She is so wrapped up in herself and her relationship to the Lord that she is almost unaware of her surroundings, and even of her own children and family, though her distant relationship to her long-suffering husband remains unbroken and even supportive. Yet she is strong enough and self-possessed enough to stand her ground and make her defence before secular and ecclesiastical authorities, and to receive their acquittal, if not their approval. In a society where faith and religion were taken for granted, the attitude to such phenomena is bound to be different from the reaction of modern society permeated by secular and materialist influences.

Margery is a fascinating representative of her own age, and gives us a brilliant picture of common religious practice at that time. It is fundamental that the ecclesiastical authorities who examined her seem to have accepted her wholly, without a word of criticism, though with political caution. The impatience shown by her fellow burghers at her weepings and groanings seems to be annoyance at the disturbance they create rather than criticism of their authenticity or value. She has all the marks of genuine religion that were valued in that age: poverty, asceticism, generosity to those in need. Stressed also is a series of qualities that were considered special criteria of deep religion: her celibacy, her obedience to her confessors, repentance for sin, exhortation leading to conversion of sinners, and, above all, devotion to the Passion of Christ. Unbalanced as a personality she certainly was, but she is touchingly aware of this. Bhattacharji[46] explains her strange behaviour as the result of a 'deep insecurity' resulting from the bout of madness after the birth of her first child. Whether her attitude was based on legitimate use or on abuse of the Bible, it is an instructive, though extreme, example of the popular spirituality of the late medieval period.

Further Reading

Bhattacharji, S., *God is an Earthquake* (London: Darton, Longman & Todd, 1997).

Colledge, E. (ed.), *The Medieval Mystics of England* (London: John Murray, 1962).

Goodman, A., *Margery Kempe and her World* (Harlow, Essex: Pearson Education Ltd, 2002).

Julian of Norwich, *The Revelations of Julian of Norwich* (ed. and trans. Father John-Julian, Order of Julian of Norwich; London: Darton, Longman & Todd, 1988).

Kempe, M., *The Book of Margery Kempe* (trans. B. A. Windeatt; Harmondsworth: Penguin, 1985).

Knowles, D., *The English Mystical Tradition* (London: Burns & Oates, 1964).

CHAPTER 8

Martin Luther

Introduction

It will be impossible to examine all Luther's voluminous works, which fill some 55 volumes in the American translation we use[1] and range over a vast array of subjects. The solution selected is to examine Luther's approach to a couple of particular topics in order to see the use he makes of Scripture on these topics and the place it holds in his theological thinking. The general background to Luther's work is well painted by Hans Küng in the essay on Luther in his contribution to the *Great Christian Thinkers* series. He numbers among the widespread abuses in the contemporary Church, against which Luther was rebelling:

- the absolutist centralism of the Roman curia, its immorality and resistance to reform, and finally – the immediate cause of Luther's explosion – the trade in indulgences for rebuilding St Peter's
- the way in which Church and theology were overgrown with canon law
- the secularization of rich bishops and monasteries, and the abuses caused by pressure towards celibacy
- a terrifying superstition among the uneducated laity
- the success of opposition to reform movements, such as those of Wycliffe, Hus, Ockham and even the humanists.

All these may be seen as important background to Luther's writing. On the other hand, among factors that enabled this to become a significant moment of development in religious history are:

- the intellectual ferment of the time, seen not only in the humanistic revival of classical learning known as the Renaissance, but more particularly in the foundation of a number of universities
- the invention of printing, which made the diffusion of new ideas so much more rapid and easy.

Martin Luther's Early Years

Early Promise

Born on 10 November 1483, and baptized the next day, the feast of St Martin, he was given the name of the day's saint. He was clearly an outstanding student, graduating with his Master's degree in 1505 at the University of Erfurt, second out of seventeen. This outstanding record continued throughout his student days, and his superiors hurried him forward unremittingly, until he was unwillingly pushed into receiving his doctoral degree and the challenge of teaching and independent academic work in 1512 at the youngest permissible age. He had already distinguished himself by being chosen as a substitute teacher for a short spell, teaching Aristotle's *Nicomachean Ethics* at Wittenburg, and being chosen in 1510 to accompany a senior colleague on a mission to Rome. There could be no doubt that this young friar was destined for a distinguished career.

A Dominant Idea

Martin Luther's father changed from being a farmer into a hard-working and successful figure in the copper-mines of Mansfeld. Young Martin was destined for the law when he had the famous thunderstorm experience in 1505. Terrified by the summer storm and a near-miss from a lightning bolt, he vowed to St Anne to become a monk if he survived. Two weeks later, to his father's fury, he entered the Augustinian Hermits. The experience of this terror and his helplessness never left him. It was reinforced by his enthusiasm for the theology of St Augustine, and particularly Augustine's vigorous struggle against Pelagianism. The Briton Pelagius[2] stood for the view that human beings can in various ways work their own salvation instead of receiving it all from Christ the Saviour.[3] By contrast, the dominant emphasis of all Luther's theology became the utter corruption of humanity and the inability of human beings to do any good works. Justification by faith *alone* (the crucial word added by Luther in his translation of Rom. 3.28 – the Greek reads merely 'a person is justified by faith and not by what the Law tells him to do') is an external covering by which God imputes believers to be justified, though they still remain as corrupt as ever. Needless to say, this interpretation of Augustine – and, behind him, of Paul – was not the only possible reading of the great theologian. The greatest humanist of the Renaissance, Erasmus (AD 1466–1536), held a diametrically opposed view of Augustine, fought out with Luther in their respective pamphlets *De Libero Arbitrio* (Erasmus) and *De Servo Arbitrio* (Luther) in 1524–1525.

The Babylonian Captivity of the Church

Luther's use of the Bible may first be illustrated from *The Babylonian Captivity of the Church*. This work was the second of three comparatively short works written in 1519–1520, so an early work, a mere couple of years after Luther's protest began. The immediate background to it was two controversial meetings at Augsburg in 1518 and at Leipzig in 1519. These meetings were the first major salvoes in a battle that had already begun with small-arms gunfire. The abuse of indulgences, and what appeared to Luther to be their unashamed sale to gather money for the building of the Basilica of St Peter's in Rome, had led in 1517 to the publication of the Ninety-Five Theses of the Augustinian friar of Wittenburg. This is generally considered to be the opening shot of the Reformation. Whether they were actually nailed to the church door at Wittenberg is uncertain; it may be a dramatized myth. Luther certainly sent them to the Archbishop of Magdeburg. In any case they were taken as a direct challenge by the Dominicans.

At first it appeared to be no more than another round of the squabble between the Augustinians, whose theology was (of course) based on Augustine, and the Dominicans, whose theology was encapsulated in the works of Thomas Aquinas. Luther was particularly hostile to Aquinas's use of Aristotle, a pagan philosopher about whom his abuse knew no bounds.[4] The Dominican opposition was headed by Johann Tetzel (c. AD 1464–1519), whose approach was to concentrate not on Luther's own preoccupation with indulgences but on the issue of papal authority. Although indulgences were the spark that lit Luther's theses, Tetzel was perfectly correct in his astute assessment of the crucial issue, for the theses are peppered with provocative remarks against papal power: 'The Pope has neither the wish nor the power to remit . . .' (no. 5); 'The Pope has no power to remit guilt . . .' (no. 6); 'The Pope does not understand . . .' (no. 20); 'To hold that papal pardons are of such power that they could absolve . . . is to rave like a lunatic' (no. 75), etc. Luther was summoned to appear at Augsburg before the papal legate, Cardinal Cajetan (AD 1469–1534), who happened to be in Germany on other business. Cajetan could hardly be considered an impartial judge between Augustinians and Dominicans: he was himself a Dominican and had just completed the first full commentary on the whole *Summa* of Aquinas. By the time this meeting actually occurred more fat had been thrown on the fire by a writing forged by Luther's enemies in his name, further disputing papal authority and denouncing venality at Rome, in consequence of which the Pope ordered Cajetan to arrest Luther. After three sessions, initially friendly but marked by deepening misunderstanding and increasing anger, Luther and his team left Augsburg. One can see the inflammatory nature of Luther's contentions from one example: with reference to Christians of the East and of Africa, he asked, 'Who dare deny that one can be a Christian without submitting to the Pope and his decretals?'[5] It would be some centuries before the Church was prepared to welcome the possibility of Christians who did not submit to the authority of 'the Pope and his decretals'.

The second disastrous meeting then took place at the University of Leipzig, the major rival of Luther's own University of Wittenburg. Here Luther's chief opponent was Johann Eck (AD 1486–1543), with whom he had previously conducted a reasonably eirenic exchange of letters. Eck beforehand published 12 theses for discussion, but when it came to the meeting he centred the disputation on his own 13th thesis, on papal primacy. Although Luther subsequently claimed that he 'did not deny the primacy of honour due to the pope',[6] he was goaded into saying that 'I am sure of this, that many of Hus' beliefs were completely evangelical and Christian',[7] thus flying in the face of Jan Hus's condemnation for heresy in 1414 at the Council of Constance. It was this failure to pay adequate respect to papal authority that led to Luther's own condemnation for heresy in the papal bull *Exsurge* (1520). A 'primacy of honour' was not enough. Two days after the promulgation of the bull Luther published his *Babylonian Captivity of the Church*. The whole affair had been characterized by agonizingly intemperate, angry misunderstanding, topped up by a little mischief-making by Luther's enemies.

The importance of the *Babylonian Captivity* is immense. It signified Luther's own definitive break from the Roman Church, for it was a full-scale attack on the sacramental system that was at the basis of Church life. It also provides an excellent example of the use and interpretation of Scripture introduced by Luther. He shows himself to be not only an ebullient controversialist but also a careful exegete. He makes good use of the biblical texts, argues persuasively for their meaning, and illustrates them by the tradition of the Church in the form of early Church writers, frequently citing not only his beloved Augustine and the *Sentences* of Peter Lombard, but other patristic writers for support, while taking others, such as the second-century heretic Marcion, as counter-examples. He even cites his teacher, Cardinal D'Ailly, as the source of his thinking on the Eucharist, for D'Ailly had argued 'it would be much more plausible and would entail fewer redundant miracles if it were asserted that not only the accidents but also the reality of bread and wine remained in the sacrament of the altar – had not the Church determined otherwise!'[8] He departs from the tradition of the Church in only one respect: he does not admit that ecclesiastical authority – and in particular papal authority – has the right to make a decision about the meaning of Scripture. He relies on the fact that the meaning he sees in Scripture must be clear to all.

After half-a-dozen pages of invective against his opponents, chiefly 'a certain Italian friar of Cremona',[9] attempting to underpin with scriptural arguments the current practice of the Church in forbidding the use of the chalice to the laity, Luther launches into his principal thesis, that there are only three sacraments, or rather 'one single sacrament, but with three sacramental signs'.[10] Christ himself is the single sacrament, according to the Vulgate translation of 1 Tim. 3.16, as Luther will explain elsewhere, and the three sacramental signs are baptism, eucharist and (for the moment) penance.

The Real Presence in the Eucharist

First Luther firmly excludes the 'Eucharistic discourse' in John 6 from the discussion, on the grounds that it is speaking not of the sacrament but of faith. This argument is based on the following premises:

- the sacrament had not yet been instituted (therefore, presumably, any reference to it would have been unintelligible)
- the authority of Augustine, 'Believe and you have eaten' – in other words, Jesus is speaking about belief under the image of eating bread
- 'My words are spirit and they are life' (Jn 6.63) show that Jesus was teaching about spiritual, not bodily, eating
- 'Unless you eat my flesh and drink my blood, you have no life in you' (Jn 6.53) would, if it literally meant the sacrament, exclude from eternal life all children and others who died without receiving the sacrament.

In fact most modern exegetes,[11] including Catholics,[12] would agree that the earlier part of the discourse in John 6 focuses on faith, the revelation and acceptance of Christ as the Word, though the final section, 6.51-58, does move on to the sacramental reception of Christ in the Eucharist.

Next Luther moves on to the synoptic account of the institution of the Eucharist at the Last Supper. Here his emphasis is to prove that the medieval Church usage of denial of the cup to the laity is against the command of the Lord, correctly noting that Matthew's account includes the dual commands, 'Take, eat' and 'Drink from it, all of you'. He points out, against all current usage, that 'it is certainly an impious act to withhold the cup from laymen when they desire it, even though an angel of God were to command it'.[13] No one could fault his exegesis, though the Catholic Church took till the liturgical reforms of Vatican II to restore the cup to the laity. After a few pages of angry argument he confirms his exegesis by appeal to Paul (1 Cor. 11.23),

'For I received from the Lord what I also delivered to you', not merely 'what I permitted to you': it is a command, not a mere permission, and so must be observed. Furthermore, he appeals to tradition, in the form of the third-century Bishop of Carthage; namely, Cyprian's testimony that the cup was administered to all, even children.[14]

Luther's next subject of contention is the mode of presence of the Lord. He inveighs against the Thomistic doctrine of transubstantiation, 'a monstrous word and a monstrous idea',[15] a formula sanctioned by the Church at the Fourth Lateran Council in 1215. Vehemently he contests that the scriptural words must be taken 'in their simplest meaning' as real bread and real wine. He invokes as a parallel the image used by Basil the Great of the Incarnation: 'Why could not Christ include his body in the substance of the bread just as well as in the accidents? In red-hot iron, for instance, the two substances, fire and iron, are so mingled that every part is both iron and fire.'[16] This understanding has been termed 'consubstantiation'. No doubt Luther was led by his more general detestation of the 'pseudo-philosophy' of that 'monster' Aristotle to reject this philosophical attempt to analyse the presence of Christ in the sacrament. The truth is that Luther's mind works far more easily with brilliantly evocative imagery (such as the red-hot iron) than with dry philosophy. Several times he shows his impatience with philosophical analysis: 'Let us not dabble too much in philosophy', he says.[17]

He makes the valid distinction between opinions and articles of faith, but does not admit the authority of the Church to change one to the other: 'I saw that the Thomist opinions, whether they be approved by Pope or by Council, remain opinions, and do not become articles of faith. For that which is asserted without the authority of scripture or of proven revelation may be held as an opinion, but there is no obligation to believe it'.[18]

His real insistence was on the presence of Christ, in whatever mode. Within a few years, arguing against those (*die Schwärmer*, or 'the Enthusiasts') who denied the real presence, he was even willing to admit the papal doctrine, though not the binding authority behind it: 'I do not argue whether the wine remains wine or not. It is enough for me that Christ's blood is present; let it be with the wine as God wills. Before I would drink mere wine with the Enthusiasts, I would rather have pure blood with the Pope.'[19] At the Diet of Worms, two years later, he put the principle even more strongly: 'Unless I am convicted of error by the testimony of scripture or (since I put no trust in the unsupported authority of Pope or of Councils, since it is plain that they have often erred and often contradicted themselves) by manifest reasoning I stand convicted by the scriptures to which I have appealed, I cannot and will not recant anything. On this I take my stand; I can do no other' (the famous words, 'Hie stehe ich. Ich kan nicht anders').[20]

In fact Luther's insistence on the real presence of Christ in the eucharistic elements as 'the plain meaning of scripture' was the major source of disagreement between Lutherans and other reformers. So in *The Sacrament of the Body and Blood of Christ* (1526) against the Zwinglians,[21] he says emphatically, 'Because in the sacrament Christ says in clear words, "Take, eat, this is my body, etc." it is my duty to believe these words, as firmly as I must believe all the words of Christ. If he handed me a mere straw and spoke these words, I should believe it. Therefore one must close mouth, eyes, and all the senses and say, "Lord, you know better than I".'[22] More vehemently still in 1528 in *The Confession concerning Christ's Supper*, declaring Zwingli 'un-Christian' and 'seven times worse than when he was a papist',[23] he takes his stand on the literal meaning of the words, refusing to be diverted by 'alleosis, heterosis, ethopoeia or any other trick that Zwingli produces out of his magician's kit'. In Luther's thinking, the words of institution are now joined and confirmed by 1 Cor. 10.16, 'The cup of blessing which we bless, is it not a participation in the blood of Christ? The bread which we break, is it not a participation in the body of Christ?' This verse he calls 'the life-giving medicine of my heart' and 'my heart's joy and crown'.[24] He proclaims repeatedly that the real presence of Christ in the bread and wine is the only possible meaning of this verse, and sees no need to seek any further explanation: 'If we must depend on simple naked words, we would rather depend on the simple naked text which God has spoken to us than on the simple naked interpretations made up by men.'[25] Indeed, he rather glories in its incomprehensibility: 'God's word and works proceed not according to our view of things, but in a way incomprehensible to all reason.'[26]

The Primacy of Scripture

More important, however, for our investigation of Luther's understanding and use of the Scripture is his refusal to accept ecclesiastical authority for its interpretation. For Luther, Scripture validates the Church, not vice versa, even in the matter of the establishment of the canon of Scripture. 'The gospel is not believed because the Church confirms it, but because one recognizes it is God's word.'[27] Even more, Scripture is not validated by the Pope: 'If the article of our faith is right, "I believe in the holy Christian Church," the Pope cannot alone be right; else we must say, "I believe in the Pope of Rome," and reduce the Christian Church to one man, which is a devilish and damnable heresy.'[28]

Scripture is a 'lamp for lighting a way through the dark' (2 Pet. 1.19), and only the godless can fail to understand it. The meaning of the Scripture is plain to believers and needs no confirmation from the Church. He rejects the Letter of James as Scripture because he cannot see how its teaching on faith and works in 2.20-22 is compatible with his understanding of salvation by faith alone. Seemingly, if one does not recognize Scripture as God's word, it is not gospel and must be rejected.

Luther's attitude to the Scriptures is thoroughly Christocentric. Christ is the centre, the King, 'the Lord of scripture',[29] and he grades the books of Scripture according to his view of the immediacy with which they show forth Christ and his salvation, which is received by faith. Thus 'the true and noblest books of the New Testament'[30] are the Gospel of John, First John, Romans, Galatians and Ephesians, because they 'show how faith in Christ overcomes sin, death and hell and gives life, righteousness and blessedness'. By contrast, Revelation and Jude are placed at the bottom of the scale because he can see 'no trace' that Revelation 'was written by the Holy Spirit',[31] presumably since he does not see how it speaks of the Passion, death and Resurrection of Christ, or how this salvation is received by faith.

Similarly, the value of the Old Testament is that it leads to Christ. With another of his wonderful images he says of the Old Testament, 'Here you will find the swaddling clothes and the manger in which Christ lies and to which the angel points the shepherds.'[32] Although he firmly rejects the allegorical interpretation of the Old Testament, which Origen used so liberally, he embraces wholeheartedly the typological sense of the Old Testament: the high priest and the sacrifices are figures that point beyond themselves and signify Christ,[33] and the Passover is a type, pointing to the Christian Easter. This is a thoroughly medieval view, encapsulated in the well-known jingle *Novum in vetere latet, vetus in novo patet* (The New Testament lies hid in the Old, the Old Testament lies open in the New).

Nevertheless, the authority of the Church is not to be entirely dismissed in the matter of interpreting Scripture. Luther has respect for this interpretation, except when it contradicts God's word: 'No one likes to say that the Church is in error; if the Church teaches anything in addition to or contrary to God's words, we must say that it is in error.'[34] How can one tell that the Church is in error? The answer can only be Luther's complacent self-confidence in his own interpretation: 'My teaching lets God be God and it gives God the glory; therefore it cannot be wrong.'[35] This applies even to a council of the Church – and it is to be remembered that in desperation Luther appealed from the Pope to a council: 'Even though saints are present at the Council, still we do not trust personalities but only God's word, since even saints can make mistakes.'[36] Reluctantly one must return to the same problem: who determines when the council is wrong? Only God's supreme word, replies Luther. But who determines the meaning, the 'plain sense' of God's word when there are different interpretations?

Promise and Sign

The third captivity of the Church denounced by Luther is the notion that the Mass is a sacrifice. Here he relies on his insistence that human beings can do no good work that will contribute to their salvation. Insisting that the four accounts of the institution of the Eucharist contain the whole theology of the Mass, he focuses his understanding on the notions of 'testament' and 'for the forgiveness of sins'. A testament, he points out, is the same as a promise, except that it is always brought into effect by the death of the testator. At this stage of Luther's thinking the two essentials of a sacrament are a sign and a promise. Marriage and confirmation are not sacraments because they have no divine promise attached to them. Penance will eventually be rejected on the grounds that it has no divinely instituted sign. The Mass, therefore, is God's promise of forgiveness of sins, which we can only approach in faith and love. So in the Mass nothing is offered, but in the sign the promise is received and grasped in faith. It was not enough, declared Luther in the teeth of the papal bull of excommunication, to say that the sacrament gives grace provided there is no obstacle in the form of mortal sin: 'there must be an unwavering, unshaken faith in the heart which receives the promise and sign'.[37]

He beautifully sets this promise, 'the most perfect promise of all',[38] in the context of the Old Testament promises of God, as the climax of the promises to Adam, Noah, Abraham, Moses and David. 'Who would not shed tears of gladness, indeed, almost faint for joy in Christ if he believed with unshaken faith that this inestimable promise of Christ belonged to him?'[39] This understanding of the Mass is derived from Luther's general theology of human corruption. His principal purpose, plainly, is to remove the possibility that any human work can be efficacious. A particular case of what seemed to Luther to be conceived as a good work was the widespread and repeated offering of Masses for the dead to which, especially since it involved financial abuses, he was inflexibly opposed. Nevertheless, he has no objection to a priest celebrating Mass alone, provided that he is aware that he is not offering the Mass itself. He is only offering prayers for others, not the Mass, and in the Mass itself is receiving the promise, just as would any lay person.[40] The effective action of the Mass itself is that of God, not of the celebrating priest. In confirmation of this, Luther cites the opinion of Gregory the Great that a Mass celebrated by a wicked priest is not less effective than one celebrated by a good priest: 'neither would a Mass of St Peter have been better than that of Judas the traitor'.[41]

The Justice of God

The Babylonian Captivity of the Church was, however, only one highly significant early outburst of the reformer. The thread that runs through all his thinking, already mentioned several times, was his awareness of complete unworthiness and helplessness in the face of God. An early instance of this came in the thunderstorm experience in 1505. His scrupulosity was a worry during his student days. It was completed by two other experiences: lecturing on Paul's Letter to the Romans (in 1515–16, virtually his first teaching assignment after his doctorate), and then the so-called *Turmerlebnis* (the tower experience). Luther's theological writings are nothing if not autobiographical, but he wrote down this experience only at the very end of his life, and we cannot now recover when and where it took place. It is generally thought to have been when he was in protective custody in his patron's Wartburg Castle, just after his excommunication in 1520. His guilty state of mind at the time was clearly linked to Paul's lament in Rom. 7.14-23: 'I know of nothing good living in me, for though the will to do what is good is in me, the power to do it is not; the good I want to do I never do, the evil which I do not want, that is what I do.' The keyword of the Letter to the Romans is 'the justice of God', which seemed to him a dreadful threat of punishment hanging over him, until the liberating *Turmerlebnis*. This key experience must be quoted at length.[42]

> Up till then it was a single word in chapter 1[Rm 1.17] that had stood in my way. For I hated that word 'righteousness of God' which, according to the use and custom of all the teachers, I had been taught to understand philosophically regarding the formal or active righteousness, as they called it, with which God is righteous and punishes the unrighteous sinner. Though I lived as a monk without reproach, I felt that I was a sinner before God with an extremely disturbed conscience. I could not believe that he was placated by my satisfaction. I did not love, yes, I hated the righteous God who punishes sinners, and secretly, if not blasphemously, certainly murmuring greatly, I was angry with God and said, 'As if, indeed, it is not enough that miserable sinners, eternally lost through original sin, are crushed by every kind of calamity by the law of the Decalogue, without having God add pain to pain by the gospel and also by the gospel threatening us with his righteousness and wrath!' Thus I raged with a fierce and troubled conscience. Nevertheless, I beat importunately upon Paul at that place, most ardently desiring to know what St Paul wanted. At last, by the mercy of God, meditating day and night, I gave heed to the context of the words, namely, 'In it the righteousness of God is revealed, as it is written, "He who through faith is righteous shall live".' There I

began to understand that the righteousness of God is that by which the righteous lives by a gift of God, namely by faith. And this is the meaning: the righteousness of God is revealed by the gospel, namely, the passive righteousness with which merciful God justifies us by faith, as it is written, 'He who through faith is righteous shall live'. Here I felt that I was altogether born again and had entered paradise itself through open gates. There a totally other face of the entire Scripture showed itself to me.

From now on Luther felt able to rely entirely on the saving power of God. This is indeed the true meaning of 'the justice of God' in Romans. It is not like human justice: behaviour in accordance with law and due recompense for that. If I drive at the right speed and pay my taxes, that is just. My justice is faithfulness or fidelity, an external standard of behaviour. God's justice, however, is his faithfulness to his own standards, his consistency with his promises. God's justice is God's fidelity to the promises of salvation made to Abraham, so wholly a saving justice, not a retributive justice. In Hebrew poetry (e.g., the Psalms), God's justice is often put parallel to God's salvation, God's saving power, God's forgiveness.

Luther's thinking is also further determined by a very important factor stressed in Romans 4. This whole chapter is a meditation on the text of Gen. 15.6: 'Abraham put his faith in God and this was reckoned to him as justice.' For Luther the phrase 'was reckoned to him as justice' is crucial, for the justice (or righteousness) imputed or reckoned[43] to human beings is Christ's righteousness, in which we are clothed, and which remains alien or external to us: 'Righteousness is our possession, to be sure, since it was given to us out of mercy. Nevertheless, it is alien to us, since we have not merited it. . . . It is thus an alien holiness and yet it is still our own holiness. . . . It is strange indeed that we are to be called righteous or to possess a righteousness which is in us, but is entirely outside us in Christ, and yet becomes our very own, as though we ourselves had achieved and earned it.'[44]

Nothing a human being can do will contribute to this righteousness. It is purely passive, and must be received merely by faith in the word of God. Faith grasps this promise or word of God, so that the Christian's righteousness and Christ's own righteousness are bound together, just as – and again we have the image of the Great St Basil – 'iron becomes red in the fire in which it is heated'.[45] The sinfulness remaining in a human being is not imputed to the believer: 'The sin which is left in his flesh is not imputed to him. This is because Christ, who is entirely without sin, has now become one with his Christian and intercedes for him with the Father. Christ's righteousness, since it is without defect and serves us like an umbrella against the heat of God's wrath, does not allow our beginning righteousness to be condemned. For Christ's sake, the sin that remains in those who believe in him may not be charged against them.'[46]

Such a situation makes possible the stance of *simul justus et peccator* (at the same time just and a sinner). The question then arises as to the part played by good works. Good works are wholly ineffective towards salvation and can contribute nothing to the righteousness of the believer. They are not the cause of righteousness, but the joyful service of God in the neighbour is the inevitable consequence of righteousness in the believer: 'True faith is not idle. We can therefore ascertain and recognize those who have true faith from the effect or from what follows. Accordingly, if good works do not follow, it is certain that this faith in Christ does not dwell in our heart, but is dead faith.'[47] Just as, in Rom. 4.10-11 circumcision was a sign and guarantee that Abraham's faith was reckoned to him as righteousness, so 'works are a sure sign, like a seal on a letter, which make me certain that my faith is genuine'.[48]

The question remains whether Luther reaches the full richness of Paul's Christian anthropology: is the Christian capable of any truly good works? Is the Christian transformed, dipped into Christ, grown into Christ and one with Christ, as Paul teaches in Romans, or is the justification merely external, an 'umbrella' or a cloak that hides the corruption from God's gaze and judgement? It does seem to be more than this, for Luther speaks with great enthusiasm of the transforming power of faith:

'Faith is a divine work in us which changes us and makes us to be born anew of God. It kills the old Adam and makes us altogether different persons in heart and spirit and mind and powers; it brings with it the Holy Spirit. Oh, it is a living, busy, active, mighty thing, this faith! Faith makes someone fulfill their obligations to everyone. For through faith a person becomes free from sin and comes to take pleasure in God's commandments.'[49]

It should therefore be clear that the whole of Luther's thinking on righteousness – the righteousness of God, faith and works – is derived from his reading of Romans. It is an entirely biblical theology.

Free Will and Predestination

The other major controversy that shows Luther's principles and practice of exegesis most characteristically at work is the argument with Erasmus over grace and free will. This problem was destined to assume even greater importance with the other reformers, John Calvin (AD 1509–1564) and Ulrich Zwingli (AD 1484–1531). The controversy sprang from an age-old dispute between Augustine and Pelagius, which has already been mentioned (p. 105). A view akin to that of Pelagius, called 'nominalism', was championed by several outstanding theologians, including

William of Ockham (AD 1288–1347). According to this view, if a human being did *quantum in se est*, 'as much as she/he can', God was bound to respond with the gift of grace. The analogy was used of lead coinage, which was often used by medieval monarchs in liquidity crises: silver and gold coinage would be withdrawn and replaced by lead coinage, with the promise that the base-metal coins could eventually be exchanged for the same face-value of precious metal, just as paper money, virtually worthless, can be exchanged nowadays for the value printed on it. In the same way, God would respond with full-value grace to the puny and inadequate human efforts. Luther's view, however, stemming immediately from Thomas Bradwardine (Archbishop of Canterbury for 40 days in 1349), was more thoroughly Augustinian: no human being can of him- or herself in any way do anything towards meriting salvation. Any salvific action is spurred on by the divine gift of grace and must be attributed to that divine grace.

The preliminaries to the controversy between Erasmus and Luther have already been outlined: Luther was condemned by the Pope in 1520. To this condemnation he replied in 1521 with his vigorous *Assertio*, reasserting all the opinions that had been condemned. Erasmus, the leading scholar of Christendom, but very chary of theological controversy, was prevailed upon to attack one of Luther's propositions, and chose to write a short and moderate treatise called *De Libero Arbitrio Diatribe*[50] (62 pages in Rupp's edition[51]), opposing Luther's assertion that 'whatever is done by us is done not by free choice but by sheer necessity'. This asserts 'bondage of the will', which is rather more than Augustine's adage 'when God crowns our merits, he crowns his own gifts', which indicated that human beings can do nothing salvific of themselves. Here Luther seems to assert that human beings have no free choice at all.

Luther amply replied to Erasmus with *De Servo Arbitrio* (233 pages in Rupp) in his usual aggressive, not to say explosive, style. Our interest is not in Erasmus's booklet but in Luther's reply. The disagreement focuses first on two factors we have already met. Erasmus begins by saying eirenically that Scripture is unclear on the disputed point about the interrelationship between God's knowledge of what is going to happen and the human decision that makes it happen, and that it is not an important point. 'By all means let us entreat the mercy of the Lord, without which no human will or endeavour is effective . . . for there are certain things of which God has willed us to be completely ignorant.'[52] He cites other matters as being obscure and only to be venerated in mystic silence; for example, 'the distinction between the divine Persons and the juncture[53] of the divine and human nature in Christ'. He next[54] complains that Luther's interpretation of Scripture takes no account of the steady interpretation of the tradition. Tactfully, knowing Luther's views, he does not include in his list of over a dozen Church Fathers any Pope,[55] and finally mentions 'supreme pontiffs' only after 'so many authorities of universities and councils'.

Luther returns this courtesy (it seems to me) by playing Erasmus at his own game. Erasmus was the acknowledged European master of classical studies,[56] and within a couple of pages Luther aptly draws on Horace, Vergil, Sallust, Quintilian and Boethius for his argument that the question he had raised is indeed an important one. He repeatedly uses the classical image of steering between Scylla and Charybdis. There is, of course, a fair amount of what seems to us name-calling and abuse, but these are the stock-in-trade of controversy at the time. Luther is politeness itself by comparison to St Thomas More's personal abuse of Tyndale in the same year.

The two most important aspects of Luther's defence are (1) the emphasis on the Spirit; and (2) his grasp of St Paul. With regard to the first, Luther makes emphatic distinction between internal and external clarity. Internal clarity requires understanding of the heart, which leaves nothing obscure, since this comes from the Holy Spirit. On the other hand, external clarity relates to the questions debated by 'sophists' (the name given by Luther to philosophers of whom he disapproves). Luther puts a great deal of emphasis on the Spirit, which gives understanding; but, apart from that, the difficulty is that the two protagonists are simply loosing off tracer-shells past each other. Erasmus says that there are some things one cannot know, such as how the three persons of the Trinity or the two natures of Christ interrelate, and other things on which Scripture is unclear but which we do not need to know. Luther replies that 'to those who have the Spirit of God the meaning of Scripture is clear on everything we need to know. Leave the rest to disputatious sophists! However, to say that it is merely inquisitive and superfluous to delve into questions about the contingent foreknowledge of God and whether our human will accomplishes anything of itself or merely undergoes the divine action of grace, *das ist zu viel*' (that really is too much![57] – in his exasperation Luther lapses from Latin into German). It is the same situation as with the Eucharist: to him the meaning is clear, and he cannot see that to others it may not be. Rupp has an excellent analogy:[58] to some people one argument is convincing, to others another argument; just as A is attractive to C and B is attractive to D. Luther simply could not see that what was immediately clear to him should not be immediately clear to everyone.

What does the Scripture say? For Luther's second defence he launches into a splendid and careful exegesis of Paul's insistence that all people are under the wrath of God: 'This is how Paul, writing to the Romans, enters into an argument against free choice and for the grace of God, "The wrath of God is revealed against all ungodliness and

wickedness of people who in wickedness hold back the truth of God"
[Rom. 1.18]. Do you hear in this the general verdict of all people, that
they are under the wrath of God? What else does this mean but that
they are deserving of wrath and punishment? He gives as the reason
for the wrath the fact that they do nothing but what deserves wrath and
punishment, because they are all ungodly and wicked.'

Luther follows up this passage[59] with careful and apposite comments
about Paul's use of Hebraisms and the force of Greek participles, all of
which would meet only approval from the modern exegete. The only
trouble is that Paul is not writing about the problem in which Luther
is interested. The emphasis of Romans 1–3, which is the whole burden
of Luther's argumentation, is the ineffectiveness of the law to save, and
the consequent need for the merciful promises of God to be fulfilled
in Christ. The Hebrew mind – and, yes, Paul's is a Hebrew mind – was
not concerned with secondary causality. So the Bible can provide no
direct message on the interrelationship of free will and divine grace.
To the Hebrew mind God is the cause of everything, and the problem
of the interrelation of human and divine will simply does not arise.
This is at least part of the reason why, when the problem does arise
in the confrontation between Pelagius and Augustine, it cannot be
definitively solved, and returns in the later Middle Ages to be disputed
between the schools of Ockham and Bradwardine. The tragedy is that
this dispute fed Luther's sense of his own sinfulness, confirming his
conviction that human beings could do no good on their own. He was
so preoccupied with the dispute that he read the first three chapters of
Romans in these terms. There Paul's argument is, however, essentially
Christological. Paul is arguing that all humanity is sunk in sin in order
to show the need for Christ. Without Christ no human being can be
saved. If it were not for Christ's obedience, which has restored humanity to a position of friendship with the Father, no human action could
achieve salvation. In the light of the Pelagian and semi-Pelagian controversies, which were currently so heatedly discussed in Augustinian
schools, Luther read Paul's argument as anthropological, as a statement
about how the human will functions. Consequently he was outraged by
Erasmus's contention that the Scriptures could not provide an answer
to the problem which he saw to be the basis of the whole Letter to
the Romans. In fact Romans provides no answer, for the Pelagian and
semi-Pelagian issue is framed in terms of a philosophy basically alien
and incomprehensible to the Hebrew mindset, which sees God as the
unique cause of everything and does not deal in secondary causality.
Erasmus is the more subtle, and sees the limits of the Pauline teaching.
Luther has a superb grasp of the basic teaching of Paul, but goes too
far by attempting to apply it to the wrong problem.

Conclusion

Brilliant, witty and down-to-earth as Luther's argumentation on the Scripture often is, sundered from the deep trust in the tradition of the Church, to the Catholic it has a strangely maverick quality which taints the whole and radically reduces its value. These early works of Luther have a racy and hard-hitting quality about them which is highly attractive. He knows the tradition of Christian writing but uses it to reinforce his own convictions rather than letting it guide him. It is hard to escape the conclusion that if the Church itself – and, in particular, theology – had been in a better condition and had treated this exciting, original and combative theologian with more sympathy (and he them), his insights and his devotion might have fed into a reform of the Church from the inside.

Further Reading

Chadwick, O., *The Early Reformation on the Continent* (Oxford: Oxford University Press, 2001).
MacCulloch, D., *Reformation* (London: Allen Lane, 2003).
McGrath, A., *Reformation Thought: An Introduction* (New York: Blackwell, 1988).
Todd, J. M., *Luther* (London: Hamish Hamilton, 1982).

CHAPTER 9

The Bible in the Politics of Early Seventeenth-century England

Introduction

Any sketch of the use and interpretation of the Bible in the Christian Church would be incomplete without mention of the use of the Bible in politics. A single chapter, however, must suffice to sketch this theme. The political use of the Bible is no new phenomenon. Indeed, it could well be maintained that political purposes entered into the writing of some books of the Bible. Thus the Book of Daniel was undoubtedly written to inspire the resistance of the faithful Jews undergoing the persecution of Antiochus Epiphanes, assuring them of ultimate deliverance and triumph. It can be dated to the period 167–164 BC by the sudden change in the middle of Daniel 11 from exact historical references to vaguer predictions. Similarly, the Book of Judith, narrating the triumph of the faithful Jewess (in marked contrast to her timorous and despairing male compatriots) over the foreign invader, comfortably fits the category of propaganda of the same period. In the New Testament the book of Revelation falls into the same category, assuring its faithful Christian readers of ultimate triumph over the Roman persecutions and the fall of the Great Prostitute, 'Babylon the Great' (Revelation 17–18). It is, however, arguable that Revelation would more fairly be considered religious rather than political propaganda on the grounds that the chief element of conflict was the strictly religious demand that Christians, like all others (except the Jews), should embrace the cult of Roma and worship the Emperor.

In Christian history the Bible has been widely used as a political tool. Medieval controversies over the relative powers of church and state were centred around the image of the two swords supposedly held by Peter in Lk. 22.38. Afro-American slaves expressed their longing for freedom, in the songs known as Negro spirituals, in terms of Israel's exodus from Egypt. The Dutch Reformed Church of South Africa justified apartheid on the basis of biblical texts beginning with Noah's curse on Canaan, son of Ham, the reputed father of African races, 'He shall be his brothers' meanest slave' (Gen. 9.25). In the present age, Zionist territorial claims have rested on the divine gift to Abraham, 'To your descendants I give this country from the River of Egypt to the Great River' (Gen. 15.18), and the interpretation of biblical history has been slanted by different schools to fit in with political claims to modern possession of the land. During the Second World War the Aryanization of Jesus was an important factor in the retention of Christian loyalties during the ethnic cleansing of the Hitler regime. Even the interpretation of the figure of Jesus in a political or non-political sense has played a large part in the movement of liberation theology, most strongly in South America.[1] It is impossible to examine all of these issues. Instead, two examples have been chosen: the use of the Bible in the political crises of early seventeenth-century England, and the political use of the Bible by the modern State of Israel (Chapter 12).

The Bible in Sixteenth-century England

Translation of the Bible into English was slow in coming. During the reign of Henry VIII the English Bible began to be known, but it was not until the popular spread of the Geneva Bible in the reign of Elizabeth I that it became the common language of the people and a tool in political discussion.

One of the reasons for the delay was itself political. It must, however, be remembered that England was backward in printing. On the Continent the whole Bible had been printed in Germany by Gutenberg as early as 1466, whereas it was not until 1477 that Caxton produced at Westminster the first book to be printed in England, by which time complete Bibles had already been printed in Italian, French and Dutch. A second reason frequently given was that English was felt not yet to be a literary language, not an appropriate vehicle for a translation of the Bible; its advance had been stunted by the prevalence among reading classes (and handwritten books were expensive) of French after the Norman conquest. This second reason was, however, somewhat dubious, for by the beginning of the sixteenth century there was a flourishing English literature in the form of manuals on a variety of subjects such as hawking, cooking, medicine and behaviour; a number of collections of letters, often playful and lively; and devotional works such as *The Scale of Perfection* of Walter Hilton (AD 1343–1396), or Nicholas Love's (he died about 1424) popular *Mirror of the Life of Christ*. When William Tyndale eventually came to make his translation, his command of the language fully gave the lie to this reasoning. The most significant reason was, therefore, probably the political one.

The first attempt at a large-scale translation of the Bible into English

had been under the patronage of John Wycliffe, and had been associated with and tainted by his 'heresy' and political views. Wycliffe
(AD 1330–1384), a highly distinguished Oxford figure and primarily
a philosopher rather than a theologian, had upset the establishment
at the beginning of the fourteenth century by his revolt against the
stranglehold of clericalism on the Church. Two of his major thrusts
were that obedience should not be paid to unworthy and sinful office-
holders in church or state, and that the Word of God should be available
directly to all, not merely through the often ill-informed preaching
of the clergy. These views were shared by the Bohemian reformer Jan
Hus, which increased the suspicion with which they were viewed. When
Wycliffe attracted papal attention by further attacks on the philosophical formulation of the presence of Christ in the Eucharist, and on the
value of religious life, opposition to him increased. The final blow came
when his populist views were taken up by the leaders of the abortive
Peasants' Revolt of 1382, with which he was ever after associated, though
Wycliffe himself was protected by the powerful patronage of John of
Gaunt, Duke of Lancaster.

Wycliffite and Hussite anti-clerical and anti-establishment views
became known as 'Lollardy' and remained highly suspect, the two figures being widely regarded as the two grandfathers of the Reformation.
With this suspicion was associated all translation of the Bible into the
vernacular. In 1407 the Constitutions of Oxford forbade translation
of the Bible unless authorized by the bishop, and made it an offence
to possess such translations.[2] It was clearly considered safer that the
message of the Bible should remain in the hands of the clergy and be
mediated to the people only by them. Despite this, Lollardy grumbled
on throughout the fifteenth century, and with it secret readings of
the vernacular Bible in little conventicles, which are known to us only
through the records of their prosecution. When the ideas of Luther's
Reformation began to penetrate into England, they were seen as a
further outbreak, and the direct successor, of Lollardy.

In the Reformation in England political and personal factors are
inextricably interwoven with religious factors. There can be little doubt
of Henry VIII's steadfast orthodoxy of belief, his stance with regard to
the Church being determined by both his desire to hassle the Pope
into legitimizing his second marriage by the recognized medieval ploy
of temporary withdrawal of obedience, and his desperate need for
money to finance his spendthrift expenditures. Once truly Protestant
ideas began to take hold in the reign (AD 1547–1553) of Edward VI,
the situation was further complicated by fear of foreign dynastic intru-
sion through the Spanish marriage of Mary Tudor in 1554 and that of
Mary Queen of Scots to the French Dauphin in 1558. The production
of Bibles played a significant part in these controversies.

In 1520 William Tyndale (1494–1536) applied to join the household of that Renaissance figure Bishop Tunstall of London, as a translator, offering a translation of the Greek orator Isocrates as a sample of his work. Against the background we have rehearsed, reinforced by the first sparks of the penetration of Lutheran ideas into England (the Oxford bookseller John Dorne lists the sale in 1520 of several copies of Luther's works, and Tyndale was perhaps already tainted by association with Lutheran discussions at Cambridge), Tunstall rejected him. Tyndale therefore took ship for the Netherlands, where he proceeded with his translation of the Bible. When the earliest parts of it began to arrive in England, Tunstall (AD 1474–1559) proved himself an implacable enemy, ordering the burning of the books as they arrived at London Docks, and engaging that most eminent of all Renaissance scholars, Lord Chancellor Sir Thomas More (AD 1478–1535), to write a withering attack on it. After other unsuccessful attempts to silence Tyndale, he was kidnapped, garrotted and burnt at the stake in 1536.

Nevertheless, an English Bible was badly needed, and the King saw the provision of vernacular Bibles as part of his campaign to unite and pacify the kingdom. He responded by sponsoring two Bible translations: first Coverdale's Bible (whose frontispiece shows the King handing the Bible to his bishops, in imitation of the traditional image of Moses handing the law to the people of Israel), and then the 'Great Bible', a copy of which he ordered to be available for reading in every parish church. The crowds who gathered to read the six copies placed in St Paul's Cathedral were so noisy and enthusiastic that the Bishop of London forbade the reading of them during services. Before long, however, the King began to blame disunity on unguided reading of the Bible, and so an Act of 1543 forbade the reading of Bibles by women, merchants, artificers, journeymen and yeomen.[3] That the King's chief concern was unity becomes clear in his last address to Parliament in December 1545. He extensively quotes First Corinthians 13 about unity before chiding the 'Lords spiritual and temporal' for their lack of charity in religious name-calling, and then going on to bewail the abuse of the Bible 'to dispute and make scripture a railing and taunting stock against priests and preachers. I am very sorry to know and hear how irreverently that most precious jewel the word of God is disputed, rimed, sung and jangled in every ale-house and tavern'.[4]

The Great Bible was soon surpassed in popularity by the Geneva Bible, produced by English Protestant exiles in Geneva and published in 1560. This was illustrated and equipped with an extensive apparatus, not surprisingly heavily Calvinistic in tone, for Calvin's influence in Geneva was paramount. It was the first English Bible to contain not merely chapter divisions but also verse-numbering for ease of reference. The notes did not fit the delicate balance Elizabeth I was intent on achieving between tradition and reform, but attempts to replace it with the 'Bishops' Bible', shorn of the 'bitter' notes (Archbishop Parker), were unsuccessful. The Geneva Bible remained a runaway success and was printed in multiple editions of every size, from folio to sextodecimo; it remains easy and attractive to use today. Its success is perhaps best gauged by its use in the preface to the King James Version, where it is quoted 14 times. It is also the version principally used by Shakespeare. To the Geneva Bible must in the first place be attributed the dominance of biblical influence in early seventeenth-century England, at least until its position was taken over by the King James Version.

The Genesis of the King James Version

One of the first problems confronting King James VI of Scotland as he became King James I of England in 1603 was to maintain the fragile religious unity of his new realm. The Lutheran position – in so far as it had penetrated into Anglicanism – dictated that nothing should be acceptable if it was *contrary to* the Bible, whereas the Puritan attitude was the Calvinistic doctrine that nothing should be accepted unless it was positively *in* the Bible.[5] Elizabeth had with difficulty held the balance between Anglicanism and the Calvinistic Puritanism of Geneva, a balance eventually enshrined in the Act of Uniformity of 1559. An example of the compromise position is the instruction that clergy should wear a surplice for the service – half-way between full vestments and ordinary lay dress. Puritans saw the accession of James as their opportunity, for in Scotland he had been king of a fully Protestant nation, and already on his way south in 1603 he was met by the Millennary Petition, signed by (nearly) a thousand Puritan ministers of the Church of England, begging to be free of 'a common burden of human rites and ceremonies'. To this James responded by the Hampton Court conference in the following year, at which the Puritan John Reynolds suggested a new translation of the Bible. His motives are unclear, but the King seized on this opportunity to get rid of the anti-royal tone of the notes of the Geneva Bible. He was perhaps less aware that the climate was right for a great translation, which would form the English language, capture the imagination and shape the expression of ideas in English for many years to come. It was a great moment in English writing. During the years in which this version was being created, an astonishing constellation of great writers was at work. Poets like John Donne (1572–1631), dramatists like William Shakespeare (1564–1625) and Ben Jonson (1573–1637), essayists like Francis Bacon (1561–1626), and homilists like Launcelot Andrewes (1555–1626) were at the height of their powers, writing with vigour, drama and confidence.

James had long disliked the Geneva Bible, considering it the worst of the translations available. This was no doubt because of its strongly anti-monarchical marginal notes, which he regarded as 'very partiell, untrue, seditious and savouring too much of daungerous and trayterous conceits'. Kings are regularly described as 'tyrants' (a word that would never be used in the King James Version). James considered the note on Exod. 1.19, approving the decision of the Hebrew midwives to disobey Pharaoh, 'seditious'.[6] Nor could he approve such notes as that on 2 Kgs 9.33-37, where Jezebel's death is described as 'a spectacle and example of God's judgement on all tyrants'; or on Isa. 30.33 that 'Tophet [the burning rubbish-dump of Jerusalem, the image of hell] is prepared of old . . . even for the king'. There were also what James regarded as glaring misinterpretations: James regarded kings as the Lord's anointed, and yet the Geneva Bible glossed Ps. 105.15 'Touch not mine anointed' as referring not to the king but to the anointed people of God, 'those whom I have sanctified to be my people'. The notes at Dan. 6.22 and 11.36 even question the authority of the king.

This consistent questioning of the royal authority was to James wholly unpalatable. He had made clear in his deeply religious little tract *Basilikon Doron,* written in 1599 as guidance to his son and would-be successor, that the right of kings is God-given and that this can be proved by the Scriptures. In so saying he clearly alludes to Psalms 8 and 110: 'Ye have a double obligation; first, for that he made you a man; and next, for that he made you a little GOD to sit on his Throne, and rule over other men. Remember, that as in dignitie he hath erected you above others, so ought ye in thankfulnesse towards him, goe as farre beyond all others.'[7] It is no surprise, therefore, that the new translation which was to be used in all churches of England for divine service would leave no opportunity for 'seditious' marginal notes.

James's zeal to replace the Geneva Bible and its notes was well founded. Since the common availability of Bibles in translation, by the end of the sixteenth century 'the Bible was the source of virtually all ideas; it supplied the idiom in which men and women discussed them'.[8] It is estimated that between 1520 and 1640 a million whole Bibles and New Testaments were printed in England. Milton refers to it as 'that book within whose sacred context all wisdom is enfolded'.[9] Thomas Hobbes's work, *Leviathan,*[10] the foundational work of modern political philosophy, published in 1651, has 657 citations of the Bible. The Bible was the source not only for geology, chemistry, astronomy and medicine, but also for heady political discussion.[11] In a world before the invention of the distractions of the novel, it was so well known that subversive ideas could be expressed vividly by allusion. Thus in 1623, when the marriage of Prince Charles to the Spanish Infanta was being discussed, a preacher in St Michael's Church, London, expressed his disapproval by likening her to Jezebel.[12] In 1626 Thomas Hooker, in suggesting that the King should repudiate his French wife, merely needed to allude to the strictures of Malachi (Mal. 2.11-12) on the divorces of mixed marriages in Judaism after the return from exile,[13] and in the following year Thomas Scott MP could refer to Buckingham as Agag (cf. 1 Samuel 15).[14] In the closing years of the reign of Charles I and at his trial in 1649 the King was powerfully excoriated as 'the man of blood' (Num. 35.33), whose blood-guilt was defiling the land.

The Fast Sermons

The apogee of the use of the Bible in political discussion was perhaps the series of Fast Sermons, preached not quickly but on fast days, solemnly so declared by the Houses of Parliament on special occasions of crisis or of desire to show gratitude to God. These were regularly preached on the last Wednesday of each month 1640–1649, and thereafter more intermittently until April 1653. They constituted an encouragement to reflect on the current situation in terms of biblical situations. So the first Fast Sermon, preached by Cornelius Burges on 17 November 1640, took as its text Jer. 50.5 in order to inveigh against Archbishop Laud's high church or even Romanizing tendencies, speaking of the 'deepest lakes of superstition and idolatry' and urging the hearers to 'purge and cast away all idols and idolatry'.

In the following year, when a plot was discovered to rescue Strafford from prison, a sermon urged that the Irish charges against him (which seemed less plausible) be dismissed and the others pursued with all haste, likening Strafford to Achan, the 'troubler of Israel', summarily executed by Joshua (Josh. 7.24). To strengthen his case the preacher also brought in other biblical examples, including Ahitophel, the counsellor of King David, who committed suicide. A speedy execution would give the same joy to the Church as Israel felt when the Egyptians were drowned in the Red Sea, or when Sisera was beheaded (Judg. 4.22), or Haman hanged (Est. 7.10). Strafford was executed within the month.

As the crisis between King and Parliament approached, the biblical precedents became ever more vivid and bloody. The protagonists in this truly 'biblical' contest were Edward Calamy and Stephen Marshall. Calamy proclaimed that the city was as ripe for destruction as Sodom for failing to reform, and Parliament should follow good King Josiah, who 'consulted not with flesh and blood' but simply went ahead with his reforms 'with zeal and fervency'. The most famous of all sermons was that of Stephen Marshall, entitled *Meroz Cursed*,[15] preached some 60 times up and down the country and frequently printed. Now was the time that 'God's blessed servants must come down from mount Gerizim, the mount of blessing, and go up on mount Ebal, the mount of cursing, and there curse, and curse bitterly'. Nor must they withhold their hands from bloodshed, for 'cursed is everyone who withholds his hand from shedding blood'. Baying for the execution of Archbishop Laud (on 22 October 1644), Edmund Staunton whipped up his audience with the precedents of Phinehas, who speared Zimri and the Midianite woman without any legal authority (Num. 25.7-11), of the eunuchs who threw Jezebel down from the window so that 'her blood spattered the walls' (2 Kgs 9.33), and drew the counter-example of Saul, who lost his throne for refraining from killing Agag (1 Sam. 15.21-23). In the run-up to the trial and execution of the King, the examples of Phinehas and Saul were repeated *ad nauseam*.[16]

The importance of the Bible in English writing in the seventeenth century continued unabated in the second half of the century, reaching its zenith in the great works of John Milton (1608–1674), John Dryden (1631–1700), and perhaps especially Bunyan's *Pilgrim's Progress* (1678). Though all three of these may be considered to have used the Bible for political propaganda, none reached the vigour, acrimony and therefore forcefulness of the Fast Sermons.

Further Reading

Hill, C., *The English Bible and the Seventeenth Century Revolution* (London: Allen Lane, 1993).

McGrath, A., *In the Beginning: The Story of the King James Bible* (London: Hodder & Stoughton, 2001).

John and Charles Wesley

Introduction

The hymns and writings of John and Charles Wesley form a treasure that cannot be omitted from this haphazard survey of the use and abuse of the Bible. They show, in a way no other example could, the use of the Bible in popular devotion, its use as an expression and a tool of a religious revival. They are indissolubly linked to the rise of Methodism in England, and so constitute a unique feature in the sociological history of religion. They have also formed the hymnology of the English Church up to the present day. *Hymns Ancient and Modern* contains three hymns (and one translation) of John Wesley, but of Charles Wesley 30 hymns.[1] The nearest rival is the eighteenth-century Puritan Isaac Watts, who is responsible for 17 hymns in the book; no other author has more than a dozen. The secret of the popularity of these hymns is probably their warmth and fervour. But they are also Bible-based in a way that the hymns of no other epoch, even the early Latin hymns, have been. Every line is touched by the stories, the thoughts and the language of the Bible.[2] They bespeak the biblical spirituality of these remarkable brothers, founders of the Methodist movement. We shall consider first the early history of the brothers and their relationship to one another, then their relationship to the Church of England, and finally their conversion experiences and the consequences of these.

The Brothers John and Charles

Because of the vibrant link between the hymns and the religious and missionary experiences of the two brothers, the hymns and their use of the Bible cannot be understood without some knowledge of the story of the two brothers. Their father, Samuel Wesley (1662–1735),[3] was the impoverished rector of Epworth in Lincolnshire. He fathered 19 children, of whom 9 survived. The family regime was strict. The children were roused for prayer at 5 a.m., and received six hours of schooling each day from their mother. Nevertheless, from an early age John's logical way of life was such that his father remarked to his mother, 'I think our Jack would not attend to the most pressing necessities of nature unless he could give a reason for it.' His rigid self-discipline is visible throughout his life in his meticulous diaries, which record every incident, however trivial. From an early age he had a strong sense of purpose, describing himself often as 'a brand snatched from the flames' (Zech. 3.2). This is a reference to a narrow escape in his childhood. The rectory was set on fire. When it was thought that all the children had been rescued, little John, aged five, appeared at an upstairs window. His father could not fight his way back in through the flames, and John was eventually rescued through the window by a human chain of three men on each other's shoulders. The incident clearly left an indelible impression in a firm sense of destiny, a sense that he had work to do for the Lord.

Born in 1703, at the age of ten John was sent to Charterhouse, and then in 1720 to Christ Church, Oxford. There he studied industriously, for he remained somewhat donnish throughout his life, described as 'a little man, neat in dress, precise in habit, in life disciplined to its last moment, from his silver hair to his silver buckles a child of the eighteenth century'.[4] Dr Samuel Johnson complained of him, 'John Wesley's conversation is good, but he is never at leisure. He is always obliged to go at a certain hour. This is very disagreeable to a man who loves to fold his legs and have out his talk, as I do.'[5]

His learning was prodigious. It goes without saying that in his writings he ranges easily throughout the Bible, both the Protestant canon and the so-called Apocrypha. But in addition to these he quotes widely from the classics – Virgil, Horace, Plato, Quintilian, Suetonius and Lucretius – to say nothing of English authors such as Milton.[6] In his exegesis it is clear that he works from the Greek text of the New Testament, and that he has a real feeling for the meaning of the Greek words.

When John had taken his degree, he followed his mother's suggestion to take orders, and was ordained deacon in 1725, becoming a fellow of Lincoln College. He took his MA in 1727, and then went to help his ailing father at Epworth. When he returned to Oxford two years later his younger brother Charles was installed in Christ Church. Charles had already formed a little religious group with a strict way of life to study theology as well as Classics. They also visited prisoners in the Oxford jail and taught them to read. (In later life Charles made visiting condemned prisoners, and even accompanying them to execution, an important part of his mission.) This group became notorious from their custom of taking Communion as often as weekly, and were given various sobriquets, such as 'Bible Moths', the 'Holy Club' or the

'Methodists'. John, as the senior member, took over the leadership of the group.

The relationship between the two brothers is fascinating and multi-faceted. John was the more academic of the two, but Charles the more sensitive and intellectually adventurous. By contrast – or perhaps in consequence – Charles's living habits were the more conventional; he married into a county family, ceased the travelling mission and settled down. He was very conscious of his status, and was found condescending by many of the lay preachers. John cared nothing for reputation, whence his famous saying, 'Brother, when I devoted to God my ease, my time, my life, did I except my reputation? No!'[7] Nevertheless, the two worked closely together, and until 1749 all their hymns are jointly attributed to both of them. John's hymns are more academic, Charles's more passionate and personally involved. Later, when John came to edit Charles's hymns, he tended to remove expressions which he thought too sentimental or affectionate. He changed 'dear Redeemer' to 'great Redeemer', and omitted 'Jesus, Lover of my soul', possibly as too passionate. The difference between the two brothers is perhaps typified by the proportion of their hymns in *Ancient and Modern*, John's three against Charles's 30. While Charles is remembered for his hymns, John is remembered for his vast volume of sermons.

When the brothers both left Oxford they continued to work together. In 1735 they set sail to bring the Gospel to the new province of Georgia in America, where they worked together for nearly three years. The ultimate proof, however, of the closeness of their relationship is that Charles felt able to interfere even in John's marital affairs. When, in 1748, John informed Charles that he meant to marry Grace Murray, Charles posted straight up to John in Newcastle and burst in on him to prevent the marriage, telling him that if he married her the Methodist movement was doomed, for 'all the preachers would leave if he married so mean a woman'.[8] Only an exceptionally strong relationship could brook such brotherly interference, but John accepted the rebuke, and Grace married another man.

The Wesleys and the Church of England

Another factor that bound them together was their loyalty to the Church of England. Being so thoroughly formed by the Fathers of the Church, both retained a strong loyalty to the tradition of the Church. As early as 1739, after preaching strongly, and in a way that was considered to cause offence, the brothers were summoned by the Archbishop of Canterbury (who, as Bishop of Oxford, had ordained both of them), to whom they declared that they were prepared to suffer persecution for the sake of the Church of England. Five years later a group of like-minded friends came together for the first Methodist Conference, but Charles would not contemplate any sort of splinter-group away from the Church of England, writing in his journal[9] of his 'strong resolution to live and die in the communion of the Church of England'. Perhaps the devotion of Charles to the Church of England was the stronger. It was he who declared after his friend Robert Jones's death,

> With pious JONES and ROYAL CHARLES may I
> A martyr for the *Church of England* die.

When John laid hands on three men, authorizing them to serve as pastors for the American mission in 1784, this did lead to a partial break between the two. One of them, Coke, was 'set apart' by the laying on of hands as 'superintendent of the Societies in America', and in fact soon became known as 'Bishop'. If any single event should be considered the moment when Methodism as an entity separate from the Church of England was born, this was it. Writing to a friend, Charles suggests that it amounted to a separation from the Church of England, and excuses John for deserting his avowed proposition that 'he would never separate from the Church without my consent'. He wittily, but somewhat lamely, attributed the ordination to a lapse of memory on the part of his 81-year-old brother. Writing to John himself, however, Charles accuses him that finally, 'Lo, he turns out at last a Presbyterian'.[10] The seriousness of the break is shown by the fact that when Charles died, three years later, he was buried in his local churchyard rather than in the shared tomb that John had prepared for them both.

The churchmanship of both brothers is further shown by their devotion to the Eucharist. It was principally their unusually frequent attendance at the Eucharist during their Oxford career that had earned the brothers and their associates the nickname, 'the Holy Club'. So John wrote the eucharistic hymn, thoroughly biblical:

> Author of life divine
> Who hast a table spread
> Furnished with mystic wine
> And everlasting bread,
> Preserve the life thyself hast given
> And feed and train us up for heaven.

Immediately after his conversion experience Charles attended the Eucharist almost daily.[11] The following year (26 March 1739) he movingly describes his devotion: 'I began the sacrament with fervent prayer and many tears, which almost hindered my reading the service. In the sacrament I was constrained to pray again and again, with strong

cryings and prayers. So it was every day of this great and holy week.'
In 1745 he published his *Hymns on the Lord's Supper*, containing no less
than 166 eucharistic hymns.

He has no doubt about the true presence of Christ in the
sacrament:

> The cup of blessing, blest by Thee,
> Let it Thy blood impart;
> The bread Thy mystic body be,
> And cheer each languid heart.

Impatiently he refutes doubters (in his slightly laughable, popular
dactylic metre):

> Ah, tell us no more
> The Spirit and Power
> Of Jesus our God
> Is not to be found in this Life-giving Food.

> Did Jesus ordain
> His Supper in vain,
> And furnish a Feast
> For none but his earliest servants to taste?

He refused to speculate on the mode of presence of Christ in the
Eucharist, but there was in his mind no doubt about its reality. This he
frequently affirms:

> In rapturous bliss
> He bids us do this.
> The joy it imparts
> Hath witness'd His gracious design in our hearts.

> Receiving the bread
> On Jesus we feed:
> It doth not appear,
> His manner of working; but Jesus is here![12]

In another hymn he similarly brushes the problem aside:

> Who shall say how Bread and Wine
>   God into Man conveys!
> *How* the bread His flesh imparts,
> *How* the wine transmits his Blood.

John is less strong in his language about the real presence in the Eucharist, being quite content to interpret the copula '*is* my body' as '*represents* my body', supporting this interpretation with parallel cases. In his *Explanatory Notes on the New Testament* on Mt. 26.26, he writes, 'This bread is, that is, signifies or represents, my body, according to the style of the sacred writers. Thus Gen xl.12, "The three branches are three days." Thus Gal iv.24, St Paul, speaking of Sarah and Hagar, says "These are two covenants".'[13]

Two other important elements of Charles's eucharistic devotion appear. First, he insists on the presence of the whole Church at the Eucharist, not merely the congregation but also the saints. Naturally he draws on the imagery of Rev. 5.8:

> The church triumphant in thy love
>   Their mighty joys we know.
> They sing the Lamb in hymns above
>   And we in hymns below.
>
> Thee in thy glorious realm they praise
>   And bow before thy throne;
> We in the kingdom of thy grace;
>   The kingdoms are but one.

Second, Charles sees the offering of the sacrifice as continuous now, effectively enriching the 'once and for all' entry of Christ into the sanctuary (Heb. 9.12 and 10.10) with the imagery of the Lamb standing as though slain (drawn from Revelation 5), and blood-stained garments of the conquering Messiah of Isa. 63.2:

> An offering in the Sinner's stead,
> Our everlasting Priest art Thou,
> And plead'st thy Death for Sinners now.
> Thy Offering still continues New,
> Thy Vesture keeps its Bloody Hue,
> Thou stand'st the ever-slaughtered Lamb,
> Thy Priesthood still remains the same.

Conversion: Charles

It is remarkable that the moment that set each of the brothers on his evangelical and revivalist mission was a conversion experience in May 1738, within three days of each other; first Charles and then John. On Whit Sunday Charles was ill with pleurisy and heard a voice say to him, 'In the name of Jesus of Nazareth, arise and believe, and thou shalt be

healed of all thy infirmities.' He then arose and looked at three scriptural passages, including Isa. 40.1, 'Comfort ye, comfort ye, my people,
saith your God.' He wrote in his journal for that day, 'I now found peace
with God and rejoiced in hope of loving Christ.'

A couple of days later he wrote a hymn reflecting on his
conversion:

> Where shall my wondering soul begin?
>   How shall I all to heaven aspire?
> A slave redeem'd from death and sin,
>   A brand plucked from eternal fire,
> How shall I equal triumphs raise
> And sing my great Deliverer's praise?
>
> O, how shall I the goodness tell,
>   Father, which thou to me hast show'd?
>   That I, a child of wrath and hell,
> I should be call'd a child of God!
> Should know, should feel my sins forgiven,
> Blest with this antepast of heaven!

This hymn already shows many of the characteristics that would persist
throughout his great evangelical hymns: the wondering joy and appreciation of the work of God, the conviction of salvation expressed in the
feeling of forgiveness, and the real dependence on – not just allusion
to – scriptural ideas. The clue to each stanza is the third line, the first
being from Rom. 6.16, 'You can be the slave either of sin which leads
to death, or of obedience which leads to saving justice.' The second
centres on Rom. 8.15, 'You received the spirit of adoption to sonship,
enabling us to cry out "Abba, Father!".'[14] It is also a mark of fraternal
closeness that Charles permits himself to adopt the phrase applied to
John, 'a brand plucked from the fire'.

A much greater poem on his conversion followed four years later;
it is a truly biblical statement. It is based on the mysterious struggle
of Jacob with the angel of the Lord at the ford of the River Jabbok
(Gen. 32.23-33), an experience that was the turning point in Jacob's
life, converting him from being a trickster to being the 'man seeing
God' (the meaning of the name 'Israel'), according to verse 29. Charles
meditates on this scene as a model of the encounter of the individual
– and particularly himself – with Christ, and with divine, salvific love in
Christ. He identifies the angel with the crucified Redeemer – characteristically, for he regularly identifies Christ with Old Testament figures.[15]
Elsewhere, using first Jn 5.39 and then Heb. 1.1 and 9.23, he sees Christ
everywhere in Scripture, even throughout the Old Testament:

Chief subject of the sacred book,
Thou fillest all, and thou alone.

Those feeble types and shadows old
Are all in thee, the Truth, foretold.

The excitement mounts to the ninth stanza – this is most clearly presented by the build-up of the insistent refrain – with the characteristic
climax, after the search for the name of the mysterious figure: the
discovery as the morning breaks (compare Gen. 32.31) that 'Thy
name is love, pure UNIVERSAL LOVE'. Here appears Charles's strong
conviction of belief in universal salvation, as opposed to the Calvinist
restriction of salvation to only a few. This is a feature of his hymns:

Thy sovereign grace to all extends
    Immense and unconfined:
From age to age it never ends;
    It reaches all mankind.

Throughout the world its breadth is known
    Wide as infinity,
So wide, it never passes one,
    Or it had passed by me.

Divine grace and salvation extend to all. Again and again Charles rejects
the notions of a punishing God and of eternal damnation:

My soul disowns
    The image of a torturing God
Well pleased with human shrieks and groans.

As well as the underlying biblical foundation in the Jacob story, the
poem is rich in Pauline allusions, such as 'When I am weak then I am
strong' (2 Cor. 12.10); 'see thee face to face' (2 Cor. 3.18); and other
biblical reminiscences, such as 'Healing in his Wings' (Mal. 4.2) and
'a bounding Hart' (Isa. 35.6), all sensitively and appropriately applied.
The poem must be quoted in full.

Come, O Thou Traveller unknown,
    Whom still I hold, but cannot see,
My company before is gone,
    And I am left alone with Thee,
With Thee all Night I mean to stay
And wrestle till the Break of Day.

I need not tell Thee who I am,
   My Misery or Sin declare,
Thyself hast call'd me by my Name
   Look on thy Hands, and read it there,
But who, I ask Thee, who are Thou,
Tell me thy Name, and tell me now?

In vain Thou strugglest to get free,
   I never will unloose my Hold:
Art Thou the Man that died for me?
   The secret of the Love unfold;
Wrestling I will not let Thee go
Till I thy Name, thy Nature know.

Wilt Thou not yet to me reveal
   Thy new, unutterable Name?
Tell me, I still beseech Thee, tell,
   To know it Now resolv'd I am;
Wrestling I will not let Thee go,
Till I thy Name, thy Nature know.

'Tis all in vain to hold thy Tongue,
   Or touch the Hollow of my Thigh:
Though every sinew be unstrung,
   Out of my Arms Thou shalt not fly:
Wrestling I will not let Thee go
Till I thy Name, thy Nature know.

What tho' my shrinking Flesh complain,
   And murmur to contend so long,
I rise superior to my Pain,
   When I am weak then I am strong,
And when my All of Strength shall fail,
I shall with the GOD-man prevail.

My Strength is gone, my Nature dies,
   I sink beneath thy weighty Hand,
Faint to revive, and fall to rise;
   I fall, and yet by Faith I stand,
I stand, and will not let Thee go,
Till I thy Name, thy Nature know.

Yield to me Now – for I am weak;
   But confident in Self-despair:

Speak to my Heart, in Blessings speak,
　　Be conquer'd by my Instant Prayer,
Speak, or Thou never hence shalt move,
And tell me, if thy Name is LOVE.

'Tis Love, 'tis Love! Thou diedst for Me,
　　I hear thy Whisper in my Heart.
The Morning breaks, the Shadows flee:
　　Pure UNIVERSAL LOVE Thou art,
To me, to All thy Bowels move,
Thy Nature and thy Name is LOVE.

My Prayer hath Power with God; the Grace
　　Unspeakable I now receive,
Thro' Faith I see Thee Face to Face,
　　I see Thee Face to Face and live:
In vain I have not wept, and strove,
Thy Nature and thy Name is LOVE.

I know Thee, Saviour, who Thou art,
　　JESUS the feeble Sinner's Friend;
Nor wilt Thou with the Night depart,
　　But stay, and love me to the End;
Thy Mercies never shall remove,
Thy Nature and thy Name is LOVE.

The Sun of Righteousness on Me
　　Hath rose with Healing in his Wings,
Wither'd my Nature's Strength; from Thee
　　My Soul its Life and Succour brings,
My Help is all laid up above;
Thy Nature and thy Name is LOVE.

Contented now upon my Thigh,
　　I halt, till Life's short Journey end;
All Helplessness, all Weakness I,
　　On Thee alone for Strength depend,
Nor have I Power, from Thee, to move;
Thy Nature and thy Name is LOVE.

Lame as I am, I take the Prey,
　　Hell, Earth and Sin with Ease o'ercome;
I leap for Joy, pursue my Way,
　　And as a bounding Hart fly home,

Thro' all eternity to prove
Thy Nature and thy Name is Love.

All the features that characterize Charles's use of Scripture in his immense output of hymns – it is reckoned that he wrote 8,000 pieces – are here present. Below I discuss three major themes.

First are the imaginative word-pictures, as in the splendid satire on the Pharisee and the tax-collector, applied to the present, for the sense of his own unworthiness was never far from Charles's mind:

The modern Pharisee is bold
In boasting to surpass the old:
Triumphant in himself he stands
Conspicuous with extended hands,
With hideous screams and outcries loud
Proclaims his goodness to the crowd,
Glories in his own perfect grace,
And blasphemies presents for praise!
'Again I thank thee, and again,
That I am not as other men,
But holy as thyself, and pure,
And must O God, like thee indure:
Thyself I now to witness call
That I am good and cannot fall,
Thee to exalt, repeat the word,
And thus I glory – in the Lord.'

A penitent indeed
Has nothing good to plead,
Guilt confesses with his eyes,
Dares not to lift them up to heaven,
Not so much in words, as sighs,
Prays and begs to be forgiven.

O'erwhelm'd with conscious fear
He trembles to draw near;
Far from the most holy place,
Far from God his distance keeps,
Feels his whole unworthiness,
Feels – but shame has seal'd his lips.

Labours his struggling soul
With indignation fell,
With unutter'd grief opprest

Grief too big for life to bear
Self-condemn'd he smites his breast,
   Smites his breast – and God is there!

Loos'ed by the power of grace,
Behold at last he prays!
Pleads th'atoning sacrifice
For meer sin and misery,
Humbly in the Spirit cries,
   'God be merciful to me.'

The contrasting attitudes of the two men are vigorously and wittily presented – with some exaggeration for the complacent Pharisee and sympathy for the emotions of the tax-collector.

Second, the biblical text is personalized and applied to the poet, who sees himself in the biblical picture. A number of examples could be adduced, but I choose a famous passion hymn for three reasons: it is intensely biblical, dependent line after line on the Isaian prophecies of the suffering servant; it is an example of Charles's use of popular metres; and it shows a preoccupation with Christ's blood, which often appears, even in a somewhat sickly and mawkish way.[16] These factors (and the clumsy rhymes) contribute to the fact that it is not a particularly good poem, at times almost descending into doggerel, which contrasts sadly with the noble biblical phrases. With such a vast output, Charles could not uniformly achieve the highest standards. Even his loyal and devoted brother wrote of his hymns, 'Some were bad, some mean [i.e., middling good] and some most excellently good'.

All ye that pass by,
To Jesus draw nigh
To you is it nothing that Jesus should die?
Your ransom and peace
Your surety he is;
Come, see if there ever was sorrow like his . . .

His death is my plea;
My advocate see,
And hear the blood speak that hath answered for me.
My ransom he was
When he bled on the cross
And by losing his life he hath carried my cause.

Third, there is the enthusiasm and exaltation that buoyed up both brothers in their mission, as in countless other hymns; for example

one inspired by Isaiah 55. The King James Version text of Isaiah 55 is
here given alongside the hymn:

Ho! Every one that thirsts, draw nigh!	Ho, everyone that thirsteth,
'Tis God invites the fallen race:	come ye to the waters,
Mercy and free salvation buy,	yea, come, buy wine and milk
Buy wine and milk and gospel grace.	without money and without price.
Far as the heavens that earth surpass,	For as the heavens are higher the earth,
Far as my throne those nether skies	so are my ways higher than your ways,
My ways of love and thoughts of grace	and my thoughts than your thoughts.
Beyond your low conceptions rise. . . .	
Nations who knew not thee shall run	Nations that knew thee not shall run
And hail the God that died for all.	unto thee because of the Lord thy God.

The intensely personal nature of the devotion expressed in the hymns is
an attractive and constant feature of their fervour, and it is expressed in
various ways. In a typical hymn Charles Wesley imagines himself before
the Saviour, seeing the Gospel miracles of healing as responding to his
own needy spiritual state:

Jesu, if still thou art today
    As yesterday the same,
Present to heal, in me display
    The virtue of thy name!

If still thou goest about to do
    Thy needy creatures good,
On me, that I thy praise may show,
    Be all thy wonders showed.

Now, Lord, to whom for help I call,
    Thy miracles repeat;
With pitying eyes behold me fall
    A leper at thy feet.

Loathsome and foul and self-abhorred
   I sink beneath my sin;
But if thou wilt, a gracious word
   Of thine can make me clean.

In another hymn (one of the three for which Handel wrote a tune),
Charles movingly puts himself in the position of Peter before the risen
Christ in Jn 21.15-17, neatly reproducing the triple question:

O that with humbled Peter I
Could weep, believe and thrice reply
   My faithfulness to prove,
Thou know'st (for all to thee is known),
Thou know'st, O Lord, and thou alone,
   Thou know'st that thee I love.

The same prayerful application of the Scripture to himself occurs in
Charles's use of the Old Testament. A supreme example is his 'Psalm 23
as a Prayer', a poetic meditation which weaves into the psalm many
elements of Charles's spirituality, especially the warmth of his love, his
devotion to the 'gentle Shepherd' and his sense of his own helplessness
and need of conversion. The early Methodist movement was essentially
a revivalist movement of conversion. I quote only the first four stanzas,
with the Psalm beside, for comparison. The tenderness and emotion
are striking.

O gentle Shepherd, hear my cry,	The Lord is my Shepherd:
And hearken as thou passest by	I shall not want.
To a poor wandering sheep;	
Relieve me with thy tender care	
Behold my want of help; draw near	
And save me from the deep.	
Come, lead me forth to pastures green,	He maketh me lie down
To fertile meads, where all serene	in green pastures:
Invites to peace and rest.	
Near the still waters let me lie,	He leadeth me
To view them gently murmur by,	beside the still waters.
Then bless the Ever-blest.	

O God, thy promis'd aid impart,

Convert my soul and change my heart,	He restoreth my soul,
And make my nature pure.	
Come, change my nature into thine,	leadeth me in the path of
Still lead me in the path divine,	righteousness for his name's sake
And make my footsteps sure.	
When thro' the gloomy shade I roam,	Yes, though I should walk
Pale death's dark vale, to endless home,	through the valley of death
O save me then from fear;	I will fear no evil.
Vouchsafe with love my soul to fill,	
That I in death may fear no ill,	
And only praise declare.	

Conversion: John

At the time of Charles's conversion John was undergoing grievous doubts about faith. On 24 May he went unwillingly to a society where Luther's preface to the Epistle to the Romans was being read. 'While he was describing the change which God works in the heart through faith in Christ, I felt my heart strangely warmed. I felt I did trust in Christ, Christ alone for salvation; and an assurance was given me that He had taken away my sins, even mine, and saved me from the law of sin and death.' John continued to be uneasy because he did not feel 'the transports of joy that usually attend the beginning' of faith, but was gradually reassured.[17]

The importance for Charles of the personal experience of salvation has become clear from its prominence in his hymns. It was one of the most salient points of the whole Wesleyan revival. Despite his intellectualism, for John also Scripture and experience were the two pillars on which religion rested, so that well before his conversion he wrote to his father (10 December 1734) 'for the proof of every one of these weighty truths experience is worth a thousand reasons'. In his journal for 25 May 1737 he refers to 'the strongest of all proofs, experience'. In a later letter (1749) he writes, 'So Christianity tells me, and so I find it. I am now assured that these things are so: I experience them in my own breast. Christianity is holiness and happiness, the image of God impressed on a created spirit, a fountain of peace and love springing up into everlasting life.'[18] This is borne out by his rich and forceful interpretation of Scripture, especially in his *Sermons on the Witness of the Spirit*, where he sees the important New Testament concept of witness (*martyria*) to be fulfilled in this experience. One of the passages of Scripture to which he frequently refers – 26 times, according to Scott J. Jones[19] – with characteristic grasp of and emphasis on the Greek words, is Heb. 11.1. His emphasis is on the probative force of the experience of faith, its 'evidence and conviction': 'Faith in general is defined by the Apostle *elengchos pragmaton ou blepomenon* – "an evidence", a divine "evidence and conviction" [the word means both], "of things not seen" – not visible, not perceivable either by sight or by any other of the external senses. It implies both a supernatural *evidence* of God and of the things of God, a kind of spiritual *light* exhibited to the soul, and a supernatural *sight* or perception thereof.'

On the other hand, it is important that he remain cautious about excess of feeling in such matters. He writes[20] of examining his followers about their experience: 'Thus far I approved of their experience (because agreeable to the written Word) as to their feeling the working of the Spirit of God, in peace and joy and love. But as to what some of them said farther concerning feeling the blood of Christ running upon their arms, or going down their throat, or poured like warm water upon their breast or heart, I plainly told them . . . that *some* of these circumstances might be from God (though I could not affirm that they were), working in an unusual manner, no way essential either to justification or sanctification, but that all the rest I must believe to be the mere, empty dreams of an heated imagination.'

The Mission of Revival

After these experiences of conversion the single aim of the two brothers was to convert England. Both brothers redoubled their missionary efforts. From now on they were tireless, enduring mockery and mobbing, travelling ceaselessly to stir a supine nation. As a recent writer caustically put it, 'Wesley and his followers might feel themselves driven by some inner compulsion to travel towards the celestial city,

> And nightly pitch their moving tents
> A day's march nearer home.

But in the 1740s most Englishmen asked nothing better than to be allowed to sleep quietly in their beds.'[21] The unremitting travelling recorded in John's journal is truly staggering. John's zeal and eagerness took precedence even over the ties of the married state, so that he wrote, 'I cannot understand how a Methodist preacher can answer to God to preach one sermon or travel one day less in a married state than in a single state'. When he eventually married, adherence to this motto was the ruin of his unhappy marriage. On his missionary journeys he read and wrote on horseback. He finished Book 10 of the *Iliad* on horseback, and had time to comment on it appreciatively in his journal (12 August 1748). He wrote his sermons on horseback. He would preach to a large crowd at 5 a.m. and continue all day. 'Some gentlemen of Yarm earnestly desired that I would preach there in the afternoon. I refused for some time, being weak and tired; so that I thought preaching thrice in the day and riding upwards of fifty miles would be work enough. But they took no denial' (16 August 1748). He had ridden from Newcastle to Stockton; eventually he preached again at Yarm and Osmotherly (where it rained continuously), and rode on at 5 in the afternoon, reaching Leeds the next afternoon.

He was not always welcomed. Two journal entries are typical:

> To attempt speaking was vain; for the noise on every side was like the roaring of the sea. So they dragged me along till we came to the town, where, seeing the door of a large house open, I attempted to go in; but a man, catching me by the hair, pulled me back into the middle of the mob. They made no more stop till they had carried me through the main street, from one end of the town to the other. I continued speaking all the time to those within hearing, feeling no pain or weariness. Many cried out, 'Knock his brains out; down with him; kill him at once.' Others said, 'Nay, but we will hear him first.' I began asking, 'What evil have I done?' And continued speaking for above a quarter of an hour, till my voice suddenly failed. (*Journal*, 20 October 1743)

> At one I went to the Cross in Bolton. There was a vast number of people, but many of them utterly wild. As soon as I began speaking, they began thrusting to and fro, endeavouring to throw me down from the steps on which I stood. They did so once or twice; but I went up again, and continued my discourse. They then began to throw stones; at the same time some got upon the Cross behind me to push me down; on which I could not but observe how God overrules even the minutest circumstances. One man was bawling just at my ear, when a stone struck him on the cheek and he was still. A second was forcing his way down to me, till another stone hit him on the forehead: it bounded back, the blood ran down, and he came no further. The third, being got close to me, stretched out his hand, and in the instant a sharp stone came upon the joints of his fingers. He shook his hand, and was very quiet till I concluded my discourse and went away. (*Journal*, 28 August 1748)

Such heroic scenes can be replicated many times in John Wesley's accounts of his missionary endeavours given in his journal.

Conclusion

The value of this chapter has been to show how inspiring and effective a serious study of the Bible can be, and was in the case of these two brothers. However, the modality of their biblical zeal was different. The younger brother passed on his enthusiasm chiefly by his hymns, which have remained vehicles of fervent prayer over the centuries. The elder, more academic, brother, perhaps less ebullient, his heart less worn on his sleeve, has left a fuller memorial of his tireless missionary activity, his determination to pass on the biblical message in all quarters of the British Isles and beyond. As he never tired of saying, 'The world is my parish'. Between them, they have left a memorial in the Methodist movement and its intense devotion.

Further Reading

Hattersley, R., *A Brand from the Burning* (New York: Little, Brown, 2002).

Jones, S. J., *John Wesley's Conception and Use of Scripture* (Nashville, TN: Kingswood Books, 1995).

Kimbrough, S. T. (ed.), *Charles Wesley: Poet and Theologian* (Nashville, TN: Kingswood Books, 1992).

Tomkins, S., *John Wesley: A Biography* (Oxford: Lion Publishing, 2003).

Waller, R., *John Wesley: A Personal Portrait* (London: Continuum, 2003).

CHAPTER 11

Newman

Introduction

The reasons for including John Henry Newman as the last historical figure in this survey of the way the Bible has been understood are overwhelming. Two reasons predominate. First, Newman sowed the seed for overcoming the awkward dichotomy of two sources of doctrine: Scripture and tradition. The seed sown by Newman reached its flowering in the Constitution on Revelation, *Dei Verbum*, of Vatican II. Newman's great work, *An Essay on the Development of Christian Doctrine* (1845), is the culmination of his long struggle to come to terms between his affectionate loyalty towards the Church of England and the importance of a teaching authority in the Church. To a Catholic it seems to solve the problems posed by the brilliant but uncontrolled exegesis of Martin Luther and the shattering of Church unity that followed. Newman's second great contribution to biblical studies was his confrontation with the new archaeological and literary discoveries that were beginning to convulse the Church during the nineteenth century. Far from recoiling and reacting in horror to these challenges, Newman saw them in terms of the problem of inspiration and inerrancy: if the Bible is the inspired Word of God, how can it be historically mistaken, as the scholars and archaeologists seemed to be showing? In his work *On the Inspiration of Scripture* (1884), he did not himself reach the ultimate answer, but his questioning and the controversy that ensued were instrumental in moving the discussion to a satisfying solution – again at Vatican II.

Newman's Path to Rome

The life story of John Henry Newman is so rich and varied, so full of important endeavours and disastrous disappointments, that it would be impossible to chronicle it here. It has also been so fully described, both by Newman himself (the first half, up to 1845, in his incomparable autobiographical *Apologia pro Vita Sua*[1]), and by biographers such as Meriol Trevor, Ian Ker, Sheridan Gilley and Avery Dulles, that a further biography would be superfluous. However, some biographical background is essential to the understanding of the two moments we wish to examine.

The *Apologia* was written in reply to Charles Kingsley's gibe, 'Truth, for its own sake, had never been a virtue with the Roman clergy. Father Newman informs us that it need not, and on the whole ought not to be'.[2] Newman's purpose, therefore, was to demonstrate that in his gradual and often agonizing journey towards Roman Catholicism he had been scrupulously truthful, honest with himself and with others, and that he had no alternative to the painful decision to turn his back on his friends and his influential position in Oxford by committing himself to the Roman Catholic Church. Though not the initiator of the Tractarian Movement – that honour must go to John Keble, at his assize sermon – he was the principal author of the tracts that established his concept of the *via media*, a middle way between the Roman Catholic and the Protestant positions. It tells us much about Newman's character that he proclaimed, 'I was not the person to take the lead of a party; I never was, from first to last, more than a leading author of a school'. Whether he was the leader of a party or not, it was his firm stance and his relentless pursuance of a train of reasoning that made him the predominant influence. Even he has to admit in the *Apologia* that 'Of late years I have read and heard that [young men] even imitated me in various ways.' The evolution of Newman's point of view, as outlined in the *Apologia*, is fascinating to follow.

His position in 1833 was founded on three principles:

1. **The principle of dogma, 'the fundamental principle of my religion' since he was 15 years old**: this he opposed to the principle of liberalism, which he regarded as 'a mere sentiment', 'a dream and a mockery'.
2. **That there was 'a visible Church, with sacraments and rites which are the channels of invisible grace'**: this he regarded as the doctrine of Scripture, of the early Church and of the Anglican Church. For the sacraments and sacramental rites he appealed to the Book of Common Prayer. In particular, for the Episcopal system he appealed to the letters of Ignatius of Antioch.[3] 'My own Bishop was my Pope;' he says, 'I knew no other; the successor of the Apostles, the Vicar of Christ'.
3. **An antipathy to the Church of Rome, and particularly to its veneration of the saints**: this third was the principle from which he gradually retreated, partly under the influence of his friend Hurrell Froude, partly from his experience, in his foreign travels, of the

noble churches and the prayerful practices of the Roman Church. 'Thus I learned to have tender feelings toward her; but still my reason was not affected at all.'

An important step was taken in 1838, in Tract 85, a series of eight lectures on the scriptural proofs of the Catholic Creed. Here Newman argues that the Bible is not a dogmatic textbook, in which a system of all Christian teachings is clearly and methodically expounded. The differences between different branches of Christianity are sufficient to show that 'No system is on the surface of Scripture'. Hence 'we have a choice of three conclusions. Either there is no definite religious information given us by Christianity at all, or it is given in Scripture in an *indirect and covert way* [my italics], or it is indeed given, but not in Scripture.'[4] He rejects the first position as Latitudinarian. He sees the third as the Roman Catholic position, which could – until Vatican II – validly be interpreted as holding that some truths are drawn from Scripture and some only from tradition. Newman therefore accepts the position that doctrines are 'hidden under the text of Scripture from the view of the chance reader', and must be drawn out of it under the guidance of the tradition of the Church. The Bible is a haphazard collection of books, in which one should not expect a systematic exposition. Newman likens it to a collection of papers: 'It is as if you were to seize the papers or correspondence of leading men in any school of philosophy or science, which were never designed for publication, and bring them out in one volume. . . . You would have many repetitions, many hiatuses, many things which looked like contradictions; you would have to work your way through heterogeneous materials, and after your best efforts, there would be much hopelessly obscure; and, on the other hand, you might look in vain in such a casual collection for some particular opinions which the writers were known nevertheless to have held, nay to have insisted on.'[5] The Scripture must therefore be interpreted by the tradition.

The second, and decisive, step was taken in 1841 with Newman's famous Tract 90. He had now reached the more exact stage of distinguishing between Roman dogmas and the popular understanding of them, and between some dogmas and others. Purgatory seemed to be one of the chief difficulties, for he could accept neither the dogma that it existed nor the popular understanding of the fires of purgatory. On the other side, it was normally thought that the 39 Articles of the Church of England were deliberately framed against the Roman Catholic position as enunciated in the anti-Protestant decrees of the Council of Trent. Historically, Newman saw this to be incorrect, for they were formed before the work of Trent was finished and promulgated. They were also framed deliberately with such elasticity that they could bear several interpretations. The purpose of Tract 90 was to try out whether they were 'tolerant of a Catholic or even a Roman interpretation'.

Furthermore, for a dozen years he had been fascinated by the history of the early Church and the development of the understanding of the faith in the first four centuries of the Church. Now he noted that the Convocation of the Church of England in 1571, which imposed the 39 Articles, had laid down that no teaching should diverge from 'the doctrine of the Old and New Testaments and which the Catholic Fathers and ancient Bishops have collected from that very doctrine'. This is the crucial factor that sets Newman's reading of the Scripture apart from that of Luther. It constituted the return to the rule of faith which had been enunciated in the second century by Irenaeus, that the Scripture is the book of the Church and may be read only as it has always been understood in the Church. It was the abuses that had crept into the Church and the abusive treatment he had received from the Church authorities which, for all his scintillating powers of exegesis, blinded Luther to this fact.

The storm of indignation at Newman's attempt to stretch the 39 Articles to a Catholic sense set off the final move. This would not be the last time Newman stood his ground while a storm howled around him. Newman's heroism consisted precisely in this: that, though he might lose the confidence of his associates and dearest friends, he never lost his integrity, never wavered in his search for truth. He was, however, left with a dilemma. With regard to Rome this is well illustrated by the issue of purgatory. He saw that 'sensible pain' in purgatory is not part of the Roman dogma, and yet was confronted by the popular conception, luridly illustrated in Italian art, of souls burning in flames. The wider issue, and the ultimate dilemma to which this led, was this: the Churches were divided over the two notes of authenticity. The Roman Church seemed corrupted, and thereby seemed to have lost the note of antiquity or apostolicity. On the other hand the Church of England was not in communion with the other Churches, and so had lost the note of catholicity or universality.

A further, external, blow to Newman's equilibrium was struck by the affair of the Jerusalem bishopric. In 1841 an agreement was made between the Archbishop of Canterbury and Prussia that there should be a bishopric in Jerusalem (held alternatively by an English and a Prussian bishop), which would have jurisdiction over the Anglicans, Lutherans and Calvinists in Jerusalem. To Newman this constituted connivance in heresy. He withdrew to the tranquil solitude he had built for himself at Littlemore, on the edge of Oxford, to review his position. There his historical studies did nothing to quiet him, for he saw in his own *via media* the weakness of a position that tried to bridge a gap between two opposing schools. The mediating positions in the Arian controversy of the fourth century, and again in the Monophysite controversy of the fifth century, had both failed to win through. The problem still remained of the Roman popular accretions which he found to distort the purity of the ancient faith. Chief among these were the place held in popular devotion by purgatory as a place of torment, and by exaggerated veneration of Mary and the saints. So he set about discovering the marks of a true Church, and where these were to be found. This was the impetus behind the questions asked by his *Essay on the Development of Christian Doctrine*, which he now began (1844).

Essay on the Development of Christian Doctrine[6]

For us, today, the idea of development and progress is taken for granted in every sphere. The staggering novelty of this work is that, when Newman wrote, the concept of fixed species was still dominant: things were as they always had been and always would be. Similarly, in doctrine and faith the paradigm criterion of dogmatic truth was the dictum of Vincent of Lerins: *quod semper, quod ubique, quod ab omnibus creditur*, 'what is believed always, everywhere and by all'. Newman moved from this static model to search out not the content of belief so much as the true principles of development; not so much content as continuity. Darwin's work *On the Origin of Species*, the spark for all evolutionary notions, was still not to burst on the world for a dozen years. Granted the striking originality of his approach, Newman's task was to discern the criteria for genuine development as opposed to distortion. First he enunciates the thesis that great ideas take time to develop and come to their full fruition. Then, in a wonderful passage of deep insight, he explains how such an idea develops:[7]

> When an idea is of a nature to interest and possess the mind, it is said to have life, that is, to live in the mind which is the recipient of it. . . . New lights will be brought to bear upon the original idea, aspects will multiply, and judgements will accumulate. There will be a time of confusion, when conceptions and misconceptions are in conflict; and it is uncertain whether anything is to come of the idea at all, or which view of it is to get the start of the others. After a while some definite form of doctrine emerges; and, as time proceeds, one view of it will be modified or expanded by another, and then, combined with a third, till the idea in which they centre will be to each mind separately what at first it was only to all together. It will be surveyed, too, in its relation to other doctrines or facts, to other natural laws or established rules, to the varying circumstances of times and places, to other religions, polities, philosophies, as the case may be. How it stands affected towards other systems, how it

affects them, how far it coalesces with them, how far it tolerates, when it interferes with them, will be gradually wrought out.

The seven 'tests' or criteria for true development which Newman formulated are preservation of idea, continuity of principles, power of assimilation, early anticipation, logical sequence, preservative additions and lasting vigour.[8] Some of these are more convincing than others,[9] but together they form a family that at least roughly delineates a true development.

1. **Preservation of idea**: 'a popular leader may court parties and break with them, he may contradict himself in words, and undo his own measures, yet there may be a steady fulfilment of certain objects, or adherence to certain plain doctrines.'

2. **Continuity of principles**: 'The true policy of the American Union, or the law of its prosperity, is not the enlargement of its territory, but the cultivation of its internal resources.' 'The political principles of Christianity are laid down for us in the Sermon on the Mount. Contrariwise to other empires, Christians conquer by yielding; they possess the earth by renouncing it.'

3. **Power of assimilation**: 'As strong frames exult in their agility, and healthy constitutions throw off ailments, so parties or schools that live can afford to be rash, and will sometimes be betrayed into extravagances, yet are brought right by their inherent vigour.'

4. **Early anticipation**: 'The child Cyrus mimics a despot's power, and St Athanasius is elected Bishop by his playfellows.' The phenomenon of the learned Benedictine, despite Benedict's emphasis on manual labour, is anticipated by his insistence that monks should also read.

5. **Logical sequence**: 'An idea grows in the mind by remaining there; it becomes familiar and distinct, and is viewed in its relations; it suggests other ideas, and these again others; and thus a body of thought is gradually formed.' 'St Justin or St Irenaeus might be without any digested ideas of Purgatory or original Sin, yet have an intense feeling, which they had not defined or located, both of the fault of our first nature and of the liabilities of our nature regenerate.'

6. **Preservative additions**: 'A true development is conservative of the course of development which went before; it is an addition which illustrates, not obscures, corroborates, not corrects, the body of thought from which it proceeds.'

7. **Duration**: 'While ideas live in men's minds, they are ever enlarging into fuller development; they will not be stationary in their corruption any more than before it. Corruption cannot, therefore, be of long standing.'

152 *The Use and Abuse of the Bible*

These criteria are illustrated from a wide range of history – philosophical, political and ecclesiastical. No idealized picture is painted, but rather the Church is seen in all its faults and failures. Consonant with Newman's unrivalled command of the sources then available for classical and early Christian history, his concentration is on the development during the early centuries of the Church, the first centuries and the fourth century,[10] the fifth and sixth centuries.[11] Each chapter ends with a conclusion in Newman's limpid rhetorical style, of which a portion of the finale of Chapter V may serve as an example:

> If then there is now a form of Christianity such that it extends throughout the world, though with varying measures of prominence or prosperity in separate places; – that it has lost whole churches by schism, and is now opposed by powerful communions once part of itself; – that it has been altogether or almost driven from some countries; – that in others its line of teachers is overlaid, its flocks oppressed, its churches occupied; that heresies are rife and bishops negligent within its own pale; – and that amid its disorders and fears there is but one Voice for whose decisions its people wait with trust, one Name and one See to which they look with hope, and that name Peter, and that See Rome; – such a religion is not unlike the Christianity of the fifth and sixth centuries.

Two Scriptural Emphases

As with all Newman's writing, the discussion is spattered with gems. One of these is his stress on development within the Scripture, another his stalwart championship of the 'mystical' sense of Scripture. Of particular relevance here is the fact of development from the Old Testament to the New. The failure of Judaism consisted in its failure to accept such development:

> One cause of corruption in religion is the refusal to follow the course of doctrine as it moves on, and an obstinacy in the notions of the past. Certainly: as we see conspicuously in the history of the chosen race. The Samaritans who refused to add the Prophets to the Law, and the Sadducees who denied what lay hid in the Book of Exodus, were in appearance but faithful adherents to the primitive doctrine. Our Lord found His people precisians in their obedience to their letter; He condemned them for not being led on to its spirit, that is, to its developments. The Gospel is the development of the Law; yet what difference can seem wider more than that which separates the unbending rule of Moses from the 'grace and truth' which 'came by Jesus Christ'?

Despite the somewhat harsh judgement on the Jews, this conception of development between the Old and the New Testaments is taken up fully by recent documents of the Pontifical Biblical Commission.[12] There is direct continuity of many themes between the Old and New Testaments; many figures and images in the New Testament remain unintelligible if they are considered without reference to the Old, and conversely such figures and images in the Old Testament achieve a new depth and new dimension in the New. It is particularly clear in the development of the moral teaching of the Bible; whereas in the Old Testament limited revenge was permitted ('an eye for an eye'), in the Sermon on the Mount it is altogether forbidden; whereas divorce is permitted in the Old Testament (Deut. 24.1), in the New it is entirely ruled out.

Another emphasis of Newman here is on the continuity within the Church not only of doctrine founded on Scripture, but of what he calls – somewhat vaguely – the 'mystical interpretation' of Scripture. Though more definition would have been enlightening, it is not necessary for Newman's purpose to define in detail what this means. It suffices that the non-literal use of Scripture has been a constant element in the tradition of the Church. Newman sides definitely with the Alexandrian rather than the Antiochene school of exegesis. The 'mystical' usage is one of the marks of continuous and therefore true development in the Church. It dates back to the very earliest apologists (such as Trypho and Justin in the second century) in the Church. Newman cites the use of the psalm-verse 'My heart has burst forth with a good Word' as a proof of the divinity of Jesus, as well as such standard texts from the wisdom literature as Prov. 8.22, 30-31. In supporting the Alexandrian school of allegorical interpretation, stemming from Origen, he goes so far as to condemn their opponents, the Antiochene school, as 'the very metropolis of heresy', the breeding ground of Arius and Nestorius. He will have no truck with John Hales's[13] insistence on 'the literal, plain, and incontroversable meaning of Scripture'. Hales followed Luther (particularly Luther's *Babylonian Captivity of the Church*) in objecting to the use of the applied sense of Scripture. He quotes Hales: 'When we receded from the Church of Rome, one motive was, because she added unto Scripture her glosses as Canonical, to supply what the plain text of Scripture could not yield.' Newman dryly leaves uncommented Hales's further observation that 'if we absolutely condemn these inter-pretations, then must we condemn a great part of Antiquity, who are very much conversant in this kind of interpreting'. His point is proved: if you condemn the 'mystical' sense at all, you must condemn its use throughout the tradition of the Church.

On the Inspiration of Scripture

Before he had finished writing *The Development of Christian Doctrine*, Newman had made his submission to the Roman Catholic Church. It is not to our purpose to relate what followed: his studies in Rome, his ordination as a priest there (1847), his foundation of the two English oratories (in Birmingham and London), the unsuccessful attempt to found a Catholic university in Dublin (1854–1858). We may not delay even on Newman's editorship of *The Rambler* magazine and his own brilliant article 'On Consulting the Faithful in Matters of Doctrine' (1859), whose frank criticism of bishops did so much both to sour his relationships with the hierarchy and to open Catholic eyes to the importance of the laity. This would be one of the major emphases of Vatican II.

In the matter of Scripture, Newman's second contribution was in the area of the inspiration and inerrancy of Scripture. The nineteenth century was a period of a great opening onto ancient history and literature, and especially that of the Bible. Major archaeological work and discoveries in the Near East were constantly raising new questions about the factual accuracy of the Bible. Despite his own limitations in foreign languages, Newman was sufficiently in touch with currents in Oxford to be well aware of these, as is shown particularly in Tract 85, which devoted two chapters to historical difficulties in the Bible. In those lectures, delivered in the university in 1838, he uses as an illustration – seemingly familiar to his hearers – the difference between the two Creation narratives in Genesis, distinguishing them by the name used for the deity, 'God' or 'Lord God', or as modern exegesis would say, the Elohist and the Yahwist.

However, 20 years later the less well-informed educated world was thrown into confusion by the publication of Darwin's *On the Origin of Species*. Within two years (March 1860) appeared the volume *Essays and Reviews*, consisting of essays by seven well-known churchmen,[14] whose objective was to 'encourage free and open discussion of biblical topics' (said the editor, William Temple, then headmaster of Rugby, later Archbishop of Canterbury) in view of the new discoveries. The public reaction to their frankness was shock and horror. The consequent upset boiled over into the famous Oxford meeting of the British Association for the Advancement of Science (June 1860), at which Bishop Wilberforce insultingly asked Thomas Huxley whether he claimed descent from an ape on his grandfather's or his grandmother's side. To Newman all this came as no surprise. One of the authors, Mark Pattison, describes a chance meeting with Newman: 'Happening to come down from town in the train with Father, since Cardinal, Newman, whom I had not seen for a long time, I was in terror as to how he would regard me in consequence of what I had written. My fears were quickly relieved. He blamed severely the throwing of such speculations broadcast upon the general public. It was, he said, unsettling their faith without offering them anything else to rest upon. But he had no word of censure for the latitude of theological speculation assumed by the essay, provided it had been addressed *ad clerum*, or put out, not as a public appeal, but as a scholastic dissertation addressed to learned theologians.'[15]

Newman duly wrote a friendly letter of congratulation the following year, when Pattison was elected Rector of Lincoln College. The controversy, however, turned Newman's own thoughts again to the question of the inerrancy, and therefore the inspiration, of Scripture. The chief problem arises first from the obvious inaccuracy of many of the statements of Scripture; how can it then be God's revelatory word? Another problem had been raised already by Origen, who held that the real, inspired sense of Scripture is not necessarily the literal sense. Indeed he held that some statements of Scripture have no literal sense but only a mystical sense. Did he mean by this that the inspired meaning of such statements is not their obvious, literal meaning? He does, after all, complain that it is of no interest to him that Abraham was standing under a tree, before he sets about elucidating the meaning of the tree under which Abraham stood, thus opening the way to his allegorical interpretations (cf. p. 40).

The first problem is the extent of inspiration of Scripture. Newman's answer was that inerrancy does not touch the *obiter dicta* of Scripture. On this he frequently quotes[16] the example of the casual time-marker, when Nabuchodonosor was King of Nineveh (Jdt 1.1), though in fact he was King of Babylon. This was certainly a 'throw-away remark', an *obiter dictum*, by the biblical writer, by which he was not enunciating a deep truth of revelation but merely locating (incorrectly, as it turns out) a particular character. Could it therefore be dismissed as incorrect? On occasion Newman also asks whether Paul could have been wrong in saying that he left his cloak with Carpus (2 Tim. 4.13). If in fact he had left it with Eutychus, would we have to admit that the Scripture was not inspired?[17] The problem then becomes how far these *obiter dicta* are to be held to extend.

In his final writings on inspiration, essays written in 1884, Newman first simply alludes to the opinion that in the early Church God, being *auctor utriusque testamenti* (author of both testaments), was for long understood to mean principally that God is the author of both dispensations, the old and the new, so the originator, founder, primary cause.[18] The Greek word for 'testament' or 'dispensation' is the same, *diatheke*. This would say nothing about the literary authorship of the books of the Bible.

On the matter of inerrancy, instead of using his former argument, excluding *obiter dicta* from inerrancy, Newman goes on to deal with the problem of historical inaccuracies by working in the other direction, attaching inerrancy to faith and morals, though not limiting it to these matters. He explains that the Councils both of Trent and of the Vatican 'specify "faith and moral conduct" as the drift of that teaching which has the guarantee of inspiration', and that they say nothing about the records of historical fact: 'it is remarkable that they do not say a word directly as to its inspiration in matters of fact. Yet are we therefore to conclude that the record of facts in Scripture does not come under the guarantee of its inspiration? We are not so to conclude'.[19] In his second essay he again insists that 'the Scriptures are inspired, and inspired throughout . . . they are inspired in all matters of faith and morals, meaning thereby, not only theological doctrine, but also the historical and prophetical narratives which they contain'.[20] He continues, 'I am not here affirming or denying that Scripture is inspired in matters of astronomy and chronology as well as in faith and morals; but I certainly do not see that because Inspiration is given for the latter subjects, therefore it extends to the former'.[21] He is not, therefore, liable to the criticism made later, after his death, in the encyclical *Providentissimus Deus* (1893), against those who confine inspiration to matters of faith and morals. These criticisms were made directly against the theories of Salvatore di Bartolo, published in 1888. He continues, however, to be worried about questions of historical accuracy in biblical matters, as appears from several letters he wrote to Bishop William Clifford. On 7 January 1883 he asks whether it is necessary to hold that Solomon wrote Ecclesiastes. A month later he is worried ('I have no confidence in myself', he writes) by a book presenting the book of Judith as a drama. On 18 March he is still worrying about Nabuchodonosor as King of Nineveh.[22]

Conclusion

The importance of Newman's work on the Bible is twofold. First, it shows the balance in revelation between Scripture and tradition, and the path on which this led him to the Roman Catholic Church. Second, it shows the struggle of a theologian to come to terms with the new archaeological, historical and literary studies of the nineteenth century on the Bible.

In conclusion, it must be said that Newman did not succeed in fully solving the problem of the historical inaccuracies in the Bible. He merely left it open, insisting that the whole Bible is inspired. The solution is finally given in the Constitution on Revelation of Vatican II, *Dei Verbum* section 12, which puts the focus on the intention of the writers and on the variety of literary forms employed: 'Therefore the interpreter must carefully investigate what meaning the sacred writers intended, and especially the literary form used, since truth is expressed differently in history, prophecy, poetry and other forms of speech. Due attention must be paid to contemporary conventions of writing and expression. At the same time, however, attention must be given to the unity of Scripture and to the living tradition of the Church.

It is, however, remarkable that Newman did at least approach this solution as early as 1834, when he comes near to expressing the difference between the different literary genres of philosophers (i.e., natural philosophers or scientists) and the revelatory purpose of Scripture: 'Thus we are led on to consider, how different are the character and effect of the Scripture notices of the structure of the physical world, from those which philosophers deliver. I am not deciding whether or not the one and the other are reconcilable; I merely say their respective effect is different.'[23]

The difference consists in the purpose and form of the writing. Similarly, Newman approaches the same solution in his discussion of the purpose of the two creation narratives in Genesis 1–3.[24] Perhaps the nearest he came to it was his congratulatory letter in response to Bishop Clifford's article in the *Dublin Review* for 1881, in which Clifford treated the first Creation narrative as a sort of hymn, 'a consecration of *the days of the week* to the memory of the creation, and not a history of *the days of creation*'. Clifford explicitly stated that the expectation of historical accuracy 'does not apply to similar statements when they occur in liturgies, hymns, or other writings of a ritual nature'.[25] Newman wrote to him, 'We need not seek to shake ourselves free from science any longer, since you have suggested an interpretation which ignores science altogether'.[26] The way was open to take the final step.

Further Reading

Dulles, A., *John Henry Newman* (London: Continuum, 2009).
Ker, I., *John Henry Newman: A Biography* (Oxford: Clarendon Press, 1988).
Trevor, M., *Newman: The Pillar of the Cloud* (London: Macmillan, 1962).
—*Newman: Light in Winter* (London: Macmillan, 1962).

CHAPTER 12

The Bible and the State of Israel

The Balfour Declaration

In November 1917, under the pressures of the First World War, the British government issued the Balfour Declaration, which began, 'His Majesty's Government view with favour the establishment in Palestine of a national home for the Jewish people, and will use their best endeavours to facilitate the achievement of this object'. This represented the fulfilment of the slogan floated by the Zionist movement for the previous two decades, 'A country without a people for a people without a country'. The beginning of the Zionist movement may conveniently be dated from the first Zionist Conference in 1897. From the beginning, therefore, the slogan had presupposed that the 'country' was uninhabited, whereas the area that was eventually designated for the Zionists, though admittedly not overpopulated, had for centuries been the stable homeland of a considerable population, administered as part of the Ottoman Empire.

In fact the British government had first offered the Zionists the territory of Uganda, which was considered to be largely uninhabited. This offer had been refused on the grounds that they wanted a biblical land. In refusing the offer of Uganda, Chaim Weizmann (1874–1952), the distinguished scientist who was later to become the first president of Israel, added that 'if Moses had come into the 6th Zionist Conference when it was adopting the resolution in favour of the Commission for Uganda, he would surely have broken the tablets once again'.[1] Next, the peninsula of Sinai was offered, but an exploratory expedition pronounced this territory to be uninhabitable. In fact, Palestine was once again, as so often in ancient times, the political plaything of the Great Powers. By the end of the First World War the Asiatic elements of the defeated Ottoman Empire were entirely – with the exception of northern Syria – under the practical control of Britain. The strategic factor was that Britain had no intention of relinquishing control of

Palestine, which provided the 'strategic buffer'[2] to Egypt and the Suez Canal, the vital link to India, the 'jewel in the crown' of the British Empire. But the biblical warrant provided the vital propaganda that made its administration on behalf of the Jews morally acceptable to the world. The arrangement proposed by the Balfour Declaration was duly confirmed at the Versailles Peace Talks and in 1922 was ratified by the League of Nations, with some recognition of the historical connection of the Jewish people with Palestine. Menahem Ushishkin – himself an unbeliever – there argued explicitly for 'the restoration to the Jews of the land that was promised to them four thousand years ago by the Power Above'.[3]

Persistent Difficulties

There remained some considerable difficulties. First, what was Palestine? Several definitions of the country were available. All of these were dependent on the Bible, but several different texts might be, and are, invoked as a basis of claims for the territory of the modern State of Israel.

The biblical account of the partition of land by Joshua (Josh. 13–19) to the 12 tribes included (as any biblical atlas will show) a large area east of the Jordan, now more or less coterminous with the Hashemite Kingdom of Jordan. A second possible definition was the standard biblical expression 'from Dan to Beersheba' (e.g., Judg. 20.1; 1 Kgs 4.25). This was the definition favoured by the British Prime Minister, David Lloyd George. However, Lloyd George, a staunch Welsh Nonconformist, who had great sympathy for this little underprivileged hilly country so like his own, thought that this area included Damascus. Damascus had, in any case, been designated as the capital of the Arab kingdom promised to the Arab peoples in the name of the British government by T. E. Lawrence. It had to be pointed out to Lloyd George on a school atlas that Damascus was some 50 miles north of Dan. Another standard biblical definition would extend the territory as far as the Euphrates, 'from the Great River to the torrent of Egypt', the Wadi Arish, just to the south of the modern Gaza Strip. This is the extent of the land promised to Abraham in Gen. 15.18, and again to Moses in Exod. 23.31.

The standard work by the distinguished Israeli archaeologist Y. Aharoni, *The Archaeology of the Land of Israel*,[4] considers the land of Israel – primarily from the scientific archaeological point of view rather than for the sake of politics – to cover 'the total area inhabited by the Israelite people, corresponding most closely to the territory governed by David and Solomon'. This could be considered to include the greater part of the modern kingdom of Jordan and territory well up into the modern country of Lebanon, as far as the entry to the pass of

Hamath, over 100 miles north of Damascus (1 Kgs 8.65). This is the extent of the territory restored to Israel in Ezekiel's vision (Ezek. 47.16, 20). There are, however, as we shall see, difficulties about this as a historical claim. Some hold that the 'empire' of David and Solomon is a fictitious creation, a biblical myth, and that David was no more than a tribal leader, whose sphere of influence was much more limited. The claims of 'empire', on this view, originated several centuries after David and Solomon in a reconstruction and aggrandisement of the history in the post-exilic period.

A second difficulty was to establish exactly what the connection was between this land and Judaism. While some Jews claim vociferously that the homeland of every Jew is in Jerusalem, others contend that Zionism and Judaism are not to be equated. The one Jewish member of the British government, Edwin Montagu, protested three months before the publication of the Balfour Declaration that it was positively anti-Semitic, on the grounds that it would justify the expulsion of Jews from European countries. His was no lone voice.

Still more pressingly, what right had Jews to claim the land as their own, since Jews had been expelled from Judaea by the Romans in the early second century, and few had lived there in the intervening time? After the expulsion of the Jews the territory had been part of the Byzantine Empire until the Muslim invasions. At various times since then it had been fought over vigorously during the Crusades, finally settling into being part of the vast Ottoman Empire. How long does a particular ethnic group need to be resident in a territory to generate a right to this land? How long does this right last after their expulsion? Do the Britons, squashed by the Saxon invaders into Wales, still have a right to claim England as their own? Do rights of residence override the promises to Abraham?

A third problem, no longer theoretical but deeply practical, was the claim of the Palestinian population. The Balfour Declaration had added a proviso about safeguarding the rights of the non-Jewish population, but it was already publicly proclaimed by the American Supreme Court Judge Louis Brandeis at Versailles that the policies of the British Mandate for Palestine could not be put into practice without bloodshed. Soon after the Balfour Declaration, Chaim Weizmann admitted that 'The British told us that there are some hundred thousand negroes [the Hebrew word was *kushim*, used in the Bible of black Africans] and for those there is no value'.[5] This difficulty was only increased, not created, by the pressures of Jewish immigration in the attempt to escape Hitler's genocide. However, by 1941 David Ben Gurion writes to his son about the removal of the Palestinian population: 'It is impossible to imagine general evacuation without compulsion and brutal compulsion.'[6]

The Biblical Justification

Faced with these problems, the modern State of Israel has made every effort to support its right to the territory by an appeal to the Bible. Perhaps the master document is the Declaration of the State of Israel in May 1948: 'Eretz-Israel was the birthplace of the Jewish people. Here their spiritual, religious and political identity was shaped. Here they first attained to statehood, created cultural values of national and universal significance,' etc. This is, of course, historically tendentious. To begin with, the name Eretz-Israel occurs only once in the Bible (1 Sam. 13.19), referring to a territory far smaller than the modern state, the central spine of the hill-country, invaded by the Philistines in the days of Saul.

The most important point in the persuasive use of the Bible has been to draw a comparison between modern Jewish occupation and the entry of the Israelites under Joshua. Three myths are combined.

1. **The myth of the lightning campaign:** the Israelites, under Joshua, conducted a blitzkrieg, sweeping all before them. This may not, by modern standards, have been entirely justified, but it does create a precedent for the modern conquest of Palestine. Furthermore, if there was any brutality in the modern conquest, it was far less violent than that practised by Joshua. It was also far less brutal than Joshua's *herem*, or 'ban of destruction', pronounced in Deut. 7.2: 'The Lord your God will put them at your mercy and you will conquer them. You must put them under the curse of destruction. You must not make any treaty with them or show them any pity.' A standard 1960 biblical history proclaims, 'There is no reason to doubt that this conquest was, as The Book of Joshua depicts it, a bloody and brutal business.'[7]

However, the impression given by the book of Joshua of a lightning campaign of conquest is not confirmed by archaeology. For one thing, the great stories of the capture of Jericho and Ai, and the other memorable stories about the crossing of the Jordan, and of Gilgal and the Gibeonites, all refer to the territory of one tribe, and the smallest one at that, Benjamin (Joshua 2–9). For example, there is evidence only at one city (Hazor) of violent destruction at about the time usually postulated for Joshua. Jericho and Ai were destroyed long before the date responsibly postulated for the entry into Canaan (1206 BC). The stories are overwhelmingly considered to be aetiological myths, explaining features of the landscape. The conquest theory is also qualified by other accounts in the Bible itself (Judges 1–2). Three other theories of the entry of Israel into Canaan currently compete for scholarly support: infiltration, a peasants' revolt and changes in settlement patterns.

According to the infiltration theory, the Hebrews simply infiltrated gradually from the desert, possibly against some armed resistance. The peasants' revolt theory holds that the inhabitants of Canaan themselves rebelled against their Egyptian overlords and threw them out, perhaps with the aid of infiltrating Hebrews. The chief protagonist of this view is Norman Gottwald, inspired by the protest movements of the 1970s and by Communist ideals.[8] A further possible explanation is that improvements in water storage and improvements in agriculture made new settlement patterns possible.

The *herem*, or curse of destruction, which is used to show that violence is endemic, and as a precedent for violence and brutality on the part of modern Israelis, is seldom nowadays considered to be historical. Many responsible scholars consider it a retrojection from early post-exilic times. The books of Ezra-Nehemiah show a similar xenophobia among the early-returned exiles. In Babylon they had retained their identity by developing a rigorous rule of life, centred on Sabbath, circumcision and clean food, which they were terrified of losing by contamination with the 'people of the land'. This was the cause of the forcible prohibition and dissolution of marriages between the returning Jews and women from among the 'people of the land' (Ezra 9–10) and the emphasis on strict observance in the other literature of the period. It may even have been the cause of the rigorous centralization of the cult on Jerusalem, a regulation easier for a small community huddled round Jerusalem than for a community spread several days' journey from Jerusalem.

2. **The myth of empty territory**: this myth takes two forms, not altogether reconcilable with each other. It is supposed that there were virtually no inhabitants of Canaan – or at most isolated pockets of dwellers – when Joshua entered it, and that the same situation obtained when the Jews returned in the twentieth century. Alternatively, the culture of the inhabitants, Canaanites/Arabs, was so low on each occasion that the entry of the Israelites/Jews brought fertility and fulfilment to the land. This view is well expressed by G. E. Wright, who wrote, 'Canaanite civilization and religion was one of the weakest, most decadent, and most immoral cultures of the civilized world at that time'.[9] He also speaks of the 'terrible iniquity of Canaan'.[10] So in modern times the Zionists 'made the deserts bloom . . . and brought the blessings of progress to all the country's inhabitants' (Israeli Declaration of Independence). The cultural level of the few Arabs was so low that it negated any rights they might have had.

It is, however, more than difficult (without any written records) to distinguish between the excavated products of the new settlers and those of the older inhabitants, or to know which archaeological sites belong to the Canaanites and which to the Hebrews/Israelites. The argument is circular. The depravity of Canaanite culture is based largely on evidence of fertility cults, which continued to flourish beside the Yahwistic religion until the Babylonian exile in 586 BC. The theory was pressed by the great archaeologist W. F. Albright, who was working in Israel during the 1930s, and was clearly affected by the Zionist ethos of those days. 'His construction of an imagined past has been one of the most influential in the history of the discipline, and still retains wide popular support and considerable influence particularly among Israeli scholars. As such, it is an influential reconstruction of the past which has laid claim to Palestine for Israel, thereby denying any such claim by the indigenous population whether ancient or modern.'[11]

3. **The myth of continuity, or the denial of exile**: the intervening history of the country in Roman, Byzantine, Persian, Muslim, Crusader and Ottoman hands is forgotten, and the impression is given that the country remained always in the hands of the Children of Abraham. An oversimplified version of this timelessness in a children's school-book is given by Masalha: 'Joseph and some of his men thus crossed the land on foot, until they reached Galilee. They climbed mountains, beautiful but empty, mountains, where nobody lived. . . . Joseph said, 'We want to establish this Kibbutz and conquer this emptiness. We shall call this place Tell Hai [Hill of Life]. The land is empty; its children have deserted it. They are dispersed and no longer tend it. No one protects or tends the land now.'

The same attitude is shown in the constant emphasis in Israeli archaeology and restoration of sites. 'In modern Israel archaeology plays an important role in affirming the links between an intrusive population and its own ancient past, and by doing so asserts the right of that population to the land'.[12] Objects and sites that can be linked to biblical and Jewish history are made much of, and carefully exhibited, while those from other periods of the country's history have often been neglected or passed over. With the same purpose in view, ancient biblical place-names, such as Efraim, Teqoa, or – the largest and most notorious of all the settlements – Ma'aleh Adummim, are chosen for new settlements as justification of these thorns in the side of the Palestinian population. It would, however, only be fair to say that in very recent years, as the country has settled down, this monocular vision of the archaeology and history of Israel has become a little less exclusive.

The Empire of David and Solomon

The boldest of all pieces of biblical propaganda is also currently the most controverted; namely, the empire of David and Solomon, seen as the moment of greatest expansion of the biblical state, a magnificent cultural achievement, unparalleled for many centuries in the ancient world. This empire was taken as the model for the expansion into 'Greater Israel' in 1956, with the inclusion of Sinai and parts of Lebanon and Syria. Ben Gurion announced to the *knesset* (the Israeli parliament) that the purpose of the invasion of Sinai was 'the restoration of the kingdom of David and Solomon'. Not only was it the model for expansion; it was used as a model for peaceful, or at least defensive, expansion. It should not, of course, be thought that this Davidic empire was aggressive, any more than the Israeli expansion was: 'The Davidic expansion clearly can be classified among the empires arising from the defensive or accidental sort of empire-building.'[13] It was merely that Saul set up the kingdom, to be followed by David, who took advantage of the temporary weakness of Egypt and Mesopotamia to form an empire, which was 'one of the ranking powers of the contemporary world'.[14]

The literary record has caught the imagination of generations. The contest of David and Goliath has become proverbial, although it is one of the least proven elements in the David story; 2 Sam. 21.19 attributes the killing of Goliath to Elhanan, one of David's champions. The main story of David's reign (2 Sam. 9–20) is a literary masterpiece unsurpassed for nearly three thousand years. Its origin in an age when the only writings we possess are primitive scratchings on mug-handles remains a mystery. The archaeological confirmation for this 'empire' remains, however, slim. Albright discovered Saul's 'palace' at Tel el-Ful. It has now been re-excavated and dubbed 'a typical Palestinian watchtower with a few outlying buildings'.[15] The foundation of a dynasty by David has been established by the chance discovery of an inscription at Tel Dan in 1992, completed by another piece found in 1994. The inscription shows that the 'House of David' was important enough to be remembered nearly three centuries after David's death. David was, therefore, no transitory, petty tribal chieftain. But did he found an empire? There is very little hard evidence for the control over a large territory which David and Solomon are said to have exercised, and some suspicious silences (e.g., no mention in Egyptian records of the marriage of the daughter of a Pharaoh to Solomon, claimed in 1 Kgs 9.17).

Conclusion

At every stage, therefore, of the development of Zionism and the State of Israel, appeal has been made to the Bible as a precedent and justification for Israeli claims to the territory and for the neglect of the claims of the indigenous inhabitants. Not only has the Bible been used as a political tool, but some of the most influential writings on the interpretation of biblical history have, in consequence of swallowing the political interpretation, been shaped in a way that supported this use.

If this, then, is an abuse of the Bible, what would be the correct use? The Bible is not primarily a history book, but a series of books showing God's way of acting or interacting with human beings whom he created in his image to complete his work, but to whom he gave the freedom and ability to turn away from this task and to abuse his gifts. David may be taken as an example. The greatness of David does not consist in his conquests or in his prowess; he has, not unjustifiably, been described as an oversexed bandit. Perhaps two factors stand out.

1. **David's sin and repentance**: David's sin was his adultery with Bathsheba and his subsequent murder of her husband in an attempt to cover up his sin. His repentance shows his heartfelt acceptance of the divine rebuke delivered to him by Nathan. He is the great sinner, presented in all his extraordinary charisma, charm, leadership, unscrupulous political ambition, love, weakness towards his family and pathetic senility.

2. **His development of the concept of the divine sovereignty**: he made Jerusalem his capital, but also God's capital and place of residence. Although he did not build the Temple or establish the Temple liturgy, he prepared the ground for it. Without David's preparation for this expression of the kingship of God, the message of Jesus about the divine sovereignty and its expression in human history and relationships could not have been built on this foundation.

In the same way, the greatness of Solomon lies not in his wealth and commercial or imperial success, but in his request to the Lord for the gift of divine wisdom at the beginning of his reign. God's response is expressed in terms understood in the culture of the times, in which wealth was seen as a sign of divine blessing: 'Since you have asked for a discerning judgment for yourself, here and now I do what you ask. I give you a heart wise and shrewd as no one has had before and no one will have after you. What you have not asked I shall give you too: such riches and glory as no other king can match' (1 Kgs 3.11-14).

The abuse of the Bible lies in its use as justification for a purely secular state of affairs, taking the promises made to Abraham in a fundamentalist way as the promise of a secular possession of land. Taking a longer-term view of the history of Abraham's descendants, we may see the promise fulfilled not in possession of a land but in being the chosen servant of the Lord. As Christians we must, with Paul, see this vocation as a servant of the Lord fulfilled in Abraham's 'seed', Jesus, the suffering servant of the Lord (Gal. 3.16). In a wider sense, we may also see the promise fulfilled in the vocation and mission of the Jewish people, the suffering servant of the Lord, in the sense that Israel continues to bear witness to the mission entrusted to it by God, still bearing witness to the divine promise through its fidelity in suffering. In this sense Israel, the people of God, but decisively not the state of Israel, continues to witness by its steadfastness in suffering over the centuries. This witness before the world continues to be the vocation of the faithful people of God, trusting in God, even in the horrors of the Holocaust. Not without justification is it argued that the establishment of the purely secular state of Israel is a falling away, a diversion from this vocation.

Further Reading

Masalha, N., *The Bible and Zionism* (London: Zed Books, 2007).
Tuchman, B. W., *Bible and Sword* (London: Macmillan, 1957).

Lectio Divina

Introduction

The private reading of the Bible for personal spiritual nourishment has, of course, always been practised throughout the varied traditions of the Christian Church. It is associated particularly with the monastic tradition, as we have seen in the writings of Jerome and Bernard of Clairvaux. Two early and striking stories are of the conversion of Antony of the Desert and of Augustine of Hippo, in which each of them understands the Bible as the Word of God addressed directly to himself to revolutionize and direct his life.

> Less than six months after the death of his parents, Antony was on his way as usual towards the house of the Lord, reflecting on how the apostles left all and followed the Saviour, and how in the Acts they sold their possessions and brought them and laid them at the feet of the apostles for distribution to the poor. He was pondering these things when he entered the church. It happened that the gospel was being read, and he heard the Lord saying to the rich man, 'If you would be perfect, go and sell what you have and give it to the poor. Come follow me and you will have treasure in heaven.' Antony, as though the passage had been read on his account, went out immediately from the church and gave his ancestral possessions to the villagers, so that they should no more weigh upon himself and his sister. And all the rest that was movable he sold, and gathering a large sum of money together, he gave it to the poor, reserving only a little for his sister's sake.[1]

No less moving is the story of the conversion of Augustine from his dissolute life-style.

> I was asking myself these questions, weeping all the while with the most bitter sorrow in my heart, when all at once I heard the singing voice of a

child in a nearby house. Whether it was the voice of a boy or a girl I cannot say, but again and again it repeated the refrain, 'Take and read, take and read'. At this I looked up, thinking hard whether there was any kind of game in which children used to chant words like these, but I could not remember ever hearing them before. I stemmed my flood of tears and stood up, telling myself that this could only be a divine command to open my book of scripture and read the first passage on which my eyes should fall. For I had heard the story of Antony, and I remembered how he had happened to go into a church while the gospel was being read and had taken it as a counsel addressed to himself when he heard the words, 'Go and sell, etc'. By this divine pronouncement he had at once been converted to you. So I hurried back to the place where Alypius was sitting, for when I stood up to move away I had put down the book containing Paul's Epistles. I seized it and opened it, and in silence I read the first passage on which my eye fell, 'Not in revelling and drunkenness, not in lust and wantonness, not in quarrels and rivalries. Rather arm yourselves with the Lord Jesus Christ. Spend no more thought on nature and nature's appetites.' I had no wish to read more and no need to do so, for in an instant as I came to the end of the sentence, it was as though the light of confidence flooded into my heart and all the darkness of doubt was dispelled.[2]

Less dramatic is a whole host of monastic writers,[3] right up to such twentieth-century writers as Columba Marmion and Anscar Vonier. Such a reading is founded on the conviction that the Word of God, addressed to a particular group of the people of God at a particular time and now enshrined in the Bible, has permanent validity; and that it is also addressed, secondarily but directly, to every individual of the people of God in every age. It is, of course, a dramatic error to suppose that:

- the strictures of Amos 4.1 against the luxurious, fat cows of Bashan are addressed to me directly, or
- the affectionate appeal of Paul to Philemon on behalf of Onesimus is addressed personally to me, or
- I sit at the feet of Jesus like the healed demoniac of Gerasa in Mk 5.15, or that I stand in the crowds on the mountain for the sermon in Matthew 5–7.

Nevertheless, the conviction that the Word of God is addressed to believers in every age, and has been preserved for this purpose, implies that each of these passages teaches the ways of God to every believer, and that every believer may enter into fruitful dialogue with God through these passages. To penetrate this message and achieve this dialogue it may even be helpful to imagine oneself personally addressed on these occasions.

A renewed evaluation of the prayerful reading of Scripture was, however, marked in 1965 by the Dogmatic Constitution on Divine Revelation of Vatican II, entitled *Dei Verbum*. This Constitution made several important points about the reading of Scripture by all the faithful.

Dei Verbum

A Deepening Insight

In speaking of the tradition of the Church, and mindful of the prophetic role of the whole people of God (not merely the hierarchy) in preserving and developing the tradition of the Church, the Constitution emphasizes that 'There is a growth in insight into the realities and words that are being passed on. This comes about in various ways. It comes through the contemplation and study of believers who ponder these things in their hearts',[4] citing Lk. 2.19 and 51, which describe Mary doing just that. In the document this comes in the chapter on the transmission of revelation, stressing the part that thoughtful and prayerful reading of the Scriptures plays in maintaining and deepening the understanding of revelation. Such reading has, then, a strictly ecclesial part to play. It is not merely a private activity, but contributes to the role that each individual has as a member of the Church. It takes place both in the public reading of the Scripture in the liturgy, especially the readings of the Eucharist and the psalms and readings of the Prayer of the Church; that is, the Liturgy of the Hours. Even the believer who reads and prays the Scriptures alone ('pondering these things in their hearts') does so as a member of the Church, the Body of Christ, personalizing and responding to the public revelation of Christ in the Word of God to the community. By such inevitably personal commitment the individual comes to know Christ better, is guided and directed, and is knitted more closely into Christ's body, the Church.

The Whole of Scripture

A further point is that this meditative reading of Scripture needs to embrace the whole of Scripture, not just one part of it. 'No less attention must be devoted to the content and unity of the whole of scripture, taking into account the tradition of the entire Church and the analogy of faith, if we are to derive their true meaning from the sacred texts.'[5] This may envisage the danger of concentrating too much on particular angles of some emphases in Scripture, as occurs in some movements, such as Liberation Theology, concentrating on Christ as the liberator, to the neglect of other important Christological emphases. It also avoids the fundamentalist trap, which consists in taking one particular teaching on its own, out of context. A point that is surely intended is that there is a development of understanding in the course of the Bible; for instance, on the matter of life after death, of Jesus's teaching on divorce and on forgiveness. The earlier teaching on the desolate situation of Sheol is to be understood as a partial revelation, preparing for the later revelation of the resurrection of the dead. The biblical acceptance of divorce under certain circumstances (Deut. 24.1-4) is removed by Jesus. The acceptance of a limited revenge ('an eye for an eye, a tooth for a tooth') is perfected by Jesus's prohibition of all revenge. The full meaning of many prophetic messianic texts may be perceived only in the light of their fulfilment in Christ. The Bible must be read as a whole, each part throwing light on all others, Old Testament as well as New.

This point is often focused on the Christological prognosis of the Old Testament, with stress on such sayings as 'Ignorance of scripture is ignorance of Christ', or 'The economy of the Old Testament was deliberately so orientated that it should prepare for and declare in prophecy the coming of Christ and of the messianic kingdom'.[6] The reading of the Bible as a whole has, however, further lessons than this, as is richly illustrated by the 2001 document from the Pontifical Biblical Commission, *The Jewish People and Their Sacred Writings in the Christian Bible*. The central section of this document shows how principal themes of the Old Testament, such as creation (and new creation), election, covenant (and new covenant), prayer and the consummation of the world, are already, in the Old Testament, rich revelations of God's loving approach to humanity, reaching their completion and fullness in the New Testament. The study of the development of these themes enables the student to appreciate how the whole Bible is one continuous story of God's self-giving to human beings, to which believers cannot but respond in faith and love. Every incident and every passage of the Bible has its part to play in contributing to understanding the ways of God with his people, as he gradually forms and shapes them. It is tempting to say that only by reading the whole of the Bible does the believer get to know God in all his moods! More accurate would it be to say that only in this way can the believer assimilate before God the diverse lessons of human life and apply them personally.

A Nourishment for the Christian Life

It is also a matter of intimate and loving communication of the Trinity, Father, Word and Spirit with the individual believer: 'The scriptures

make the voice of the Holy Spirit sound again and again in the words
of the prophets and apostles. It follows that all the preaching of the
Church, as indeed the entire Christian religion, should be nourished
and ruled by sacred scripture. In the sacred books the Father who is
in heaven comes lovingly to meet his children and talks with them.
Such is the force and power of the Word of God that it can serve the
Church as her support and vigour, and the children of the Church as
strength for their faith, food for the soul and a pure and lasting fount
of spiritual life.'[7]

This passage is carefully phrased to show that in this engagement
with the Scriptures, all three persons of the Trinity have their part to
play: the Father as the source of revelation, coming lovingly to meet
his children; the Word, supplying the force and vigour; and the voice
of the Spirit, sounding throughout the Scriptures. It is also presented
as an intimate conversation, which invigorates the believer, as does
any conversation with a truly loving father, and as any supportive word
in ordinary human converse confirms. In a following section there is
again stress that through the Scriptures the Holy Spirit teaches the
Church in a way that intimately affects the individual: 'This nourishment enlightens the mind, strengthens the will and fires human hearts
with the love of God.'[8]

A Privilege of Every Individual Believer

Such reading is the right, privilege and source of nourishment not
merely of clergy and religious, but of every individual. 'All clerics,
particularly priests of Christ and others who, as deacons or catechists,
are officially engaged in the ministry of the Word, should immerse
themselves in the scriptures by constant sacred reading and diligent
study.'[9] Both reading and study, not merely one or the other, are
required. The reading is not the same as the study, but the study – as
has been made clear in previous sections of the document – will clarify
and bring out the meaning and the appeal of the reading. The authors
of the document are well aware that the world of the Bible is alien to
the modern reader, that to enter into the world of the Bible involves
entry into a whole set of unfamiliar symbols and conventions. These
demand study; that is, explanation from outside themselves, but above
all familiarity and sympathy, which can be gained only from committed
and prolonged reading.

There follows a vigorous concluding passage:

> The sacred Synod forcefully and specifically exhorts all the Christian
> faithful, especially those who live the religious life, to learn 'the surpassing
> knowledge of Jesus Christ' (Phil. 3.8) by frequent reading of the divine

scriptures. 'Ignorance of the scriptures is ignorance of Christ' (Jerome). Let them therefore go gladly to the sacred text itself, whether in the sacred liturgy, which is full of the divine words, or in devout reading, or in such suitable exercises and various other helps which are happily spreading everywhere in our day, Let them remember, however, that prayer should accompany the reading of sacred scripture, so that a dialogue takes place between God and the believer.[10]

The reading of Scripture, therefore, whether in public as an ecclesial activity or in solitude, is the indispensable means to knowledge of Christ. It is an essentially prayerful activity, introducing a dialogue with God, in which the believer first listens and then speaks to God. It is enjoined not only on those whose task it is to spread the Word of God to others, but also on all those devoted to deepening their personal understanding of and union with Christ.

Guigo II, Prior of the Grande Chartreuse

For a description of the method of this prayerful reading, the standard treatments of the subject turn to the Letter *Scala Claustralium*[11] of Guigo II to his friend Gervase.[12] Guigo II was prior in about 1180, and is not to be confused with his great predecessor of the same name, organizer and disseminator of the Carthusian Order half a century earlier. He outlines the method – which he calls rungs of the ladder – in four stages: *lectio, meditatio, oratio, contemplatio. Lectio* is the careful study of the Scripture, concentrating all one's powers on it. *Meditatio* is the busy application of the mind to seek with the help of one's own reason for knowledge of the hidden truth. *Oratio* is the heart's devoted turning to God to drive away evil and obtain the good. *Contemplatio* is the raising of the mind to God and holding it above itself, so that it tastes the joys of everlasting sweetness.

Lectio

Guigo takes as his example 'Blessed are the pure in heart, for they shall see God'. The starting point is *hearing*, not reading, these words, presumably in the liturgy or at least in public reading. Perhaps Guigo's monks did not all read fluently themselves. This phrase Guigo likens to a grape put in the mouth and savoured. The reader or listener realizes that there is something good, precious and promising here, and determines to examine it more closely: 'the soul begins to bite and chew on this grape, as though putting it in a wine press'.

Meditatio

This is not meditation in the popular sense of the word, nor in the Ignatian sense of the word: composition of place, and so on. Guigo calls it hammering the phrase out on the anvil of meditation. This is really a preliminary study of the text; it is not yet prayer, and can be done by the good and the wicked alike and even by pagan philosophers, though the motivation will be different. It is first an analysis of the words 'pure in heart' rather than 'pure in body': what is the difference in significance between them? When attention is turned to the reward, the analysis concerns what can be meant by 'seeing God'. Also pertinent to this stage is the association with other passages of Scripture where the same phrases and thoughts occur; for instance, a psalm that reflects on the conditions of purity of heart, or Job's declaration of purity of conscience, then – for the apodosis of the phrase – the appearance of the divine glory in the risen Lord: what can be meant by being filled with this glory? In modern circumstances this may be helped by lexicographical aids and such adjuncts as the notes and marginal references of a study Bible in order to understand what is meant by the words and the biblical images.

This is all preliminary and propaedeutic, inexorably leading the believer (as opposed to the philosopher or disinterested scholar, who do not appreciate that the material is the Word of God) on to the next stage. Guigo continues: 'The soul is set alight by this kindling . . . it is consumed with longing, yet can find no means of its own to have what it desires. The more it searches, the more it thirsts. As long as it is meditating, so long is it suffering, because it does not feel that sweetness which, as the meditation shows, belongs to purity of heart, but which meditation does not give.'

Oratio

The inevitable consequence of this meditation is to bring the believer to the realization of personal insufficiency and humility before God, who alone can satisfy the longings of the heart. So 'the soul betakes itself to prayer, saying, "Lord, you are not seen except by the pure of heart"'. In his description Guigo then gives a series of four more invocations, each begging the Lord to respond to the unworthiness of the one who prays. It is at this stage, therefore, that the believer is really cast before God in humility, prayer and devotion. Here the dialogue with God really begins. 'Give me, O Lord, at least one drop of heavenly rain with which to refresh my thirst, for I am on fire with love,' prays Guigo.

Contemplatio

This stage involves the enjoyment of the divine company. Guigo says that the Lord comes to meet the one praying, 'does not wait until the longing soul has said all its say, but breaks in upon the middle of its prayer, runs to meet it in all haste'. The meeting is described in terms drawn from the Song of Songs, and the ensuing ecstasy is likened to the sexual rapture: 'Just as in the performance of some bodily functions the soul is so conquered by carnal desire that it loses all use of reason, and man becomes as it were wholly carnal, so by contrast in this exalted contemplation all carnal motives are so conquered and drawn out of the soul that in no way is the flesh opposed to the spirit, and man becomes, as it were, wholly spiritual.'

This consolation, weeping sweet tears of joy, cannot be counted upon, for 'the Spouse bestows what he pleases and to whom he pleases; it is not possessed as though by lawful title'. It is a mere taste of the glory that is to come. Guigo concludes his letter by stressing that all these rungs of the ladder are interlinked, that each has its own function in terms of the whole. The one who prays has a personal part to play, and ought to play this part continually. However, 'the eye of the human heart has not the power to bear for long the shining of the true light', and will rest now on one rung, now on another, as the circumstances of time and place, and as the divine choice, suggest.

A Lived Experience

The purpose of this book is to describe the use and interpretation of the Scriptures in Christianity rather than to exhort, still less to provide a handbook of instruction. *Dei Verbum* speaks of 'devout reading or such suitable exercises and various other helps which are happily spreading everywhere in our day'.[13] The devout and prayerful reading of the Scriptures has, of course, never been a rarity in the Church. But since *Dei Verbum* was written in 1965 there has been a growing emphasis on the nourishment for personal spiritual union with the Lord provided by *lectio divina*. This has manifested itself in various ways.

a. **Prayerful reading**: there has been an insistence that every community activity among Christians should begin with a prayerful reading, which will alert the participants to the presence of the Spirit of Christ at the meeting and provide guidance for that meeting.

b. **Bible study meetings, among both clergy and laity**: sometimes the discussion of a meeting may be led by a professional student of the Bible, but more often not. The prayerful insights of the individuals into the biblical text are shared, and often witness may be given to the way in which passages of the Bible have guided particular members of the group at particular times. Such meetings are not dependent on clergy participation, for the Word of God speaks directly to each. They are common practice, as is a Sunday service in far-flung communities (for example, in Australia or Africa), where priests or ministers can visit only rarely. Such Bible studies also have the advantage of uniting the different traditions within Christianity from which participants are drawn, transcending difficulties raised by sacramental and authoritarian differences.

c. **Communities solidly built on the practice of** *lectio divina*: for these communities, such shared readings have become a staple source of nourishment, a regular family meal, taken as much for granted as any other regular square meal. The process of preparation for the meal is undertaken with similar care, and the training in conventions of good table manners gives a stability and solidity which enables the food to be savoured at its best. African friends in West, East and Southern Africa tell me that a regular evening shared reading in the family is common practice among Christian families in Africa, each family member sharing and speaking of what he or she has found particularly touching to the heart.

d. **Prayerful formation of clergy, religious and laity alike**: this includes the development of such skills by various courses and training in methods of *lectio divina*, introduced, tried, amalgamated, rejected, and varied according to the needs and temperaments of individuals. Some find it more helpful to engage in shared *lectio* always, regularly or at specific intervals; others prefer silent privacy. Some find that they meet God more easily through the liturgical cycle of readings proposed by the Church's lectionaries; others through the continuous or semi-continuous reading of a particular book of Scripture. Some stress the element of study outlined above in *meditatio*; others find it a learned distraction from heartfelt dialogue with the Lord.

In the eyes of the Church such ways of prayer form a preparation for the Eucharist and reach their consummation in it, for the Church is most fully realized in the Eucharist. However, without any deliberate intention, it sometimes happens that these paths to God become more important to individuals than the practice of the sacraments, and even of the Eucharist.

A Reflection on the Lord's Prayer

A short example of the prayerful reading and meditation on Scripture may here be offered.

'OUR FATHER IN HEAVEN', but in Luke's version Jesus calls you simply 'Father', a straightforward address which reminds me of Jesus in the Garden, asking you to deliver him from the agony of the approaching Passion. He calls on you in a way that shows that intimate union with you which he has transmitted to us, as his brothers and your adopted sons. It was the union that sustained him always, and for which he went off to spend his nights in prayer. How much in that agony did he know of what was going to happen to him? At least he knew that you would never desert him. At least he had the confidence shown by Psalm 22, that through suffering and contempt he would win glory for God and would be vindicated by you. How much do I know of what is to happen to me? What do you have in store for me, to test my faith and my fidelity to your promises? I may be sure that, whatever cross it is, this will be just the trial I most dread. I may be sure that it will bring me purified to you, with just some of the dross that clogs my love removed.

'HALLOWED BE YOUR NAME' takes us back to Ezekiel's sad reflection that Israel had defiled your name, besmirched your reputation by being so unfaithful that you had no alternative to allowing Israel to be taken into exile, and so giving the neighbouring nations cause to say that the LORD was powerless even to defend his own people. In the restoration after the exile your name and reputation would be restored. But did that restoration happen? We are still awaiting the coming of your kingship, when all creation recognizes that you are sovereign. It began with Jesus's proclamation of your Kingdom, but how much have I done to promote the realization of your Kingdom? How much have I done to delay and obscure it?

'YOUR KINGDOM COME' is surely the central petition of all those whom Jesus your Son puts before us. Your kingship filled his whole horizon. It forms the middle petition of the three petitions about your glory which come in Jesus's own prayer, which he taught to the disciples. Matthew was inspired to put that prayer at the very centre of his Sermon on the Mount, the abstract of your requirements – or Jesus's requirements – for being members of your chosen people. Jesus set out from his baptism (and your voice of recognition there) to establish your sovereignty. He was aware that he was fulfilling your plan when he healed the sick, when he brought back lepers from their disastrous situation of loneliness and alienation, when he called back sinners into your love and even unexpectedly and spontaneously forgave them the sins that kept them from you. How he must have been frustrated by the failure of the representatives of his own people (and yours) to see what he was trying to do, at their screen of petty observances which kept them from seeing the breadth and depth of your longing for their direct response. Of course he knew that all could not be solved in a day, but that the Kingdom would take time to form. At what stage did he realize that it would involve his death? Whenever it was, he went straight ahead, unflinching. He knew that he would have to declare your kingship by showing the emptiness of the Temple cult, the meagre grapes produced by your choice vineyard, on which you had lavished such love over the centuries. They would not let him get away with this – or perhaps even, if they did, his gesture would be pointless and insufficient. So he knew that he must undergo utter rejection.

'YOUR WILL BE DONE'. Why does Luke omit this petition? Or does Matthew include it? To do your will is so central for his Gospel. It is not those who cry 'Lord! Lord! Who will enter the kingdom of heaven, but those who do the will of the Father'? Again in the agony in the garden Jesus uses this exact formula, as though Matthew wants us to see that, at this central moment of his mission, when he is about to reach the climax, he is following the example of praying the prayer he taught his Disciples. In his obedience on the Cross, the obedience of the Second Adam, which undid the disobedience of Adam, our model in failure and disintegration, he was at perfect union with you, the wills of Father and Son utterly united in one act of love. We can conceive this unitive love only in the sort of act of love a son might perform for his sick or dying father, some supremely difficult act, painful and hurtful, yet illuminated and transformed into joy by love. The union of Father and Son is also expressed by the centurion, 'Truly, this man was son of God', saying more than he knew, but perhaps divining that, in the Son's love for his Father, the Father's love for all people too could be seen. As the Son reaches up to the Father, so the Father bends down to the Son.

Conclusion

The Scriptures are, as we have seen throughout this book, God's gift of himself in love, evoking a response in faith and friendship. The renewal and dissemination in the Church of the ancient monastic practice of *lectio divina* is an enrichment which cannot but further these objectives.

Further Reading

Bianchi, E., *Praying the Word: An Introduction to Lectio Divina* (Kalamazoo, MI: Cistercian Publications, 1998).
Foster, D., *Reading with God* (London: Continuum, 2005).
Magrassi, M., *Praying the Bible* (Collegeville, MN: Liturgical Press, 1998).

CHAPTER 14

General Conclusion

By means of a dozen probes we have seen various human reactions to the Word of God, a scarlet thread that runs through Christian history. The New Testament is itself the foundation document, or, better still, the foundation documents, of the Church, the attempts of those who knew Jesus or were close to those who had known Jesus to explain how he had fulfilled the promises of God and the destiny of Israel. This understanding of the meaning of Jesus remains authoritative for Christians, but must itself be understood and assimilated in the terms of each succeeding age.

First we saw two attempts in the succeeding century, both to a certain extent polemical. In his poetic prayer Melito expresses his love of Christ in a hymn of mixed triumph and mourning against the background of the Jewish rejection of Jesus. After another half-century marked by the influx of Graeco-Roman culture into Christianity and the attempts to understand events in terms of Graeco-Roman culture and myths, Irenaeus sets out to bring together the scattered strands of understanding into the first system of orthodoxy. Formed in the East but living in the West, he is guided by the Roman community, which he considers to represent the Rule of Faith.

Next we have the great scholar, Origen, as the last persecutions by the Roman Empire wane, attempting to recover the true text of the Bible and to understand it in the light of the Platonism of Alexandria. A couple of generations later the brilliant and pugnacious Jerome, formed in the West but working in the East, translates the Christian wisdom of the East into a message understandable in terms of the language and culture of the dying Western Roman Empire.

A new era is seen in the life of the Bible in Christian Europe, where the Bible is the only book that matters. It is interpreted from various angles by the loving monastic scholarship of the Venerable Bede, the graceful chivalry of Bernard of Clairvaux and the intellectual systematization of Thomas Aquinas. This era is seen at its height in the two ladies of Norwich and their passionate and all-consuming attachment to Christ.

Within a century this world comes to an end with the protests of Martin Luther against the dominance of a monolithic ecclesiastical system, as his original and scintillating exegesis throws off the traditional guidance of the Roman Church. Contrasting consequences of the principle of *sola scriptura* are seen in the manipulation of Scripture to present utilitarian political decisions under the mask of biblical propriety, and in the revival of religious enthusiasm by the Wesley brothers.

After a gap while the railways are built and Christianity spreads across the globe, the convulsions of world wars and a peculiarly virulent strain of anti-Semitism result in the use of the Bible to explain and justify the foundation of the State of Israel. Finally, we have seen how the meditative reading of the Bible is again being used by Christians to seek the message of God for the problems and opportunities of daily life, how the Word of God to his chosen people may still guide us in the twenty-first century of Christianity.

Time Line

30	The Resurrection of Christ
40–62	Paul, his mission and writings
65–95	Writing of the Gospels
70	Jerusalem sacked by the Romans
fl. 150	Marcion
fl. 170	Melito of Sardis
fl. 180	Irenaeus of Lyons
c. 185–254	Origen of Caesarea
c. 345–420	Jerome
354–430	Augustine of Hippo
c. 675–735	The Venerable Bede
1079–1142	Peter Abelard
1090–1153	Bernard of Clairvaux
fl. 1180	Guigo II of the Grande Chartreuse
c. 1225–1274	Thomas Aquinas
1330–1384	John Wycliffe
1343–1416	Julian of Norwich
1373–1440	Margery Kempe
1483–1546	Martin Luther
1494–1536	William Tyndale
1509–1564	John Calvin
1611	The King James Version of the Bible
1640–1653	The Fast Sermons
1703–1791	John Wesley
1707–1788	Charles Wesley
1801–1890	John Henry Newman
1870	First Vatican Council
1917	The Balfour Declaration
1948	Foundation of the State of Israel
1952–1958	Kenyon's excavations at Jericho
1962–1965	Second Vatican Council

Notes

Foreword

1 *Lumen Gentium*, Section 12 (see Tanner, Vol. 2, pp. 849–98).

Chapter 1: The Interpretation of the Old Testament in the New

1 In this chapter the expression 'the Bible' refers to the Bible as it was accepted by Jews and Christians at the time of the composition of the writings of the New Testament. These writings themselves had not yet achieved the status and authority of the inspired scriptural Word of God.
2 So R. Bultmann, *The History of the Synoptic Tradition* (Oxford: Blackwell, 1963), p. 136. Barrett, in *The Gospel According to St Mark*, and Dunn, in *Unity and Diversity in the New Testament*, both tentatively opt for its origin with the historical Jesus.
3 For more detail see Wansbrough, pp. 219–44.
4 This is interesting as an example of the different interpretations of the law espoused by different rabbis: a second-century ruling exists that on the Sabbath such an animal may not be hauled out of the pit, but it may be fed. The precedent quoted by Jesus assumes that it is legitimate to haul the animal out on the Sabbath.
5 It is perhaps interesting that the most recent document of the Pontifical Biblical Commission, *The Bible and Morality* (2008), section 50, gives preference to biblical moral norms with a theological basis over other biblical norms. In the first of these cases the norm would be the creation of human beings as a couple; in the second case, the honour due to parents.
6 On this is built the strange view found in some Christian theology that Christ was somehow accursed and 'subject to the pains of the damned', that the Father exacted from his sinless Son the punishment due to sinners: the Son paid the price which should have been paid by sinners. To others this theory, built on a misunderstanding of the Latin translation of 1 Cor. 6.20; 7.23 ('you have been bought at a price!' instead of 'you have been dearly bought!'), seems a paradigm case of hideous injustice.

181

7   For further examples, see the cases quoted in *The Jewish People and its Holy Scriptures in the Christian Bible* (Vatican: Libreria Editrice Vaticana, 2001), section 14.

8   Most easily available in Sparks, *The Apocryphal Old Testament.*

9   Other similar apocalyptic works also abound at Qumran (see Vermes, *The Dead Sea Scrolls in English*); e.g., 'The Testament of Amram' (4Q544 and 545) and an important fragment on the new and heavenly Jerusalem. The community at Qumran was dedicatedly eschatological, waiting for the coming of the messiah and the final war between the sons of light and the sons of darkness.

10 Biblical scholars divide the book of Isaiah into three major portions: Isaiah of Jerusalem (prophesying 740–700 BC), Deutero-Isaiah (during the Babylonian exile, c. 550 BC), and Trito-Isaiah (after the return from exile in 538 BC). The 'Apocalypse of Isaiah' may be even later than this.

11 Paul's language here differs in small details from Paul's own mode of expression, and he introduces it with the formula 'The tradition I *handed on* to you in the first place, a tradition which I had myself *received*', using the technical terms of rabbinic tradition, 'handed on' and 'received'.

12 Fitzmyer, p. 300.

13 A targum is a commented translation. The Aramaic targums were produced when Hebrew was no longer the normal language of the eastern Jews.

14 This is in the Greek form of the text. The Greek translation – and the Greek form of the Old Testament, rather than the Hebrew, which is that normally used in the New Testament – has 'virgin', whereas the Hebrew has the less apt 'young woman'.

15 See the extended discussion in Gerhardsson, pp. 234–45.

16 Crossan, p. 375.

17 Both are expressed by the characteristic Markan style of the double negative (literally, 'Jesus did not answer nothing'), and the former also by a Markan double-expression ('Jesus was silent and did not answer nothing'). The narrative was surely composed by Mark, on the basis of oral tradition.

18 I was greatly helped to the understanding of this sense by an (unscripted) lecture of R. T. France in March 2008, and by his commentary, *The Gospel of Matthew.*

19 For fuller treatments, see A. T. Hanson, *New Testament Interpretation of Scripture*; C. K. Barrett, 'Interpretation of the Old Testament in the New Testament'; S. Porter, *The Scrolls and the Scriptures*; M. Black, 'Christological Use of the Old Testament in the New Testament'.

Chapter 2: The Second Century

1   Eusebius, 4.26.

2   *Ibid.*, 5.24.

3   Section 10, 45, 65, 105.

4 Section 2–4.
5 Section 72.
6 Section 19.
7 Section 97.
8 Section 32.
9 Sections 73–93.
10 Section 50.
11 Section 103.
12 Section 8.
13 Sections 57–58.
14 Section 66.
15 Section 96.
16 Section 72–99.
17 E.g., Sections 83–85.
18 Section 70.
19 Sections 72–105.
20 Section 72.
21 Literally, 'something pricked out beforehand'.
22 Sections 36–37.
23 Sections 41–45.
24 Section 49.
25 Sections 47–64.
26 Section 80.
27 Sections 83–84, 87–88.
28 On the Quartodeciman controversy, see above, p. 18. The Bishops of Smyrna and Rome reached an amicable stalemate, each keeping their own custom but remaining in communion.
29 *Hist. Eccl.*, 5.4.2.
30 *Adv. Haer.* 3.3.3. Henceforth all references to Irenaeus's work (in the form 0.0.0) are to *Adversus Haereses* unless otherwise stated.
31 3.6.4.
32 Another striking piece of evidence of how cut-off Irenaeus is from the roots of the Scripture is an extraordinary vagueness about the history of the period. He thinks (*Demonstration*, 74) Pilate was procurator under the Emperor Claudius (AD 41–54). In fact Pilate ruled Judaea for the ten years AD 26–36. Arguing from Jn 8.57, 'You are not yet fifty!' Irenaeus held that Jesus was 49 years old at the time of his death.
33 2.35.3.
34 3.21.2. Nevertheless, his scholarly approach is clear from the fact that he points out (3.21.1) that the first-century Jewish translators Symmachus and Aquila at Isa. 7.14 translate as 'young woman' the Hebrew word rendered by the Septuagint as 'virgin'. Their translation would make it unusable by Matthew, who regards it as proof of the virginal conception of Jesus. Modern (Christian) scholars agree that the Hebrew literally means 'young woman',

and regard the Septuagint translation, 'virgin', as one of the evidences of the inspiration of the Septuagint translation. Irenaeus also correctly points out that the Septuagint translation was made long before the birth of Jesus, and so was a true prophecy (3.21.2).

35 What exactly are 'aeons'? Basically the word means 'age, era, epoch', but is used for these mythical beings. K. F. Johansen writes: 'To us the various Aeons are a mythical garb, but to the Gnostics it was probably the other way around: the world of man is a reflection of the cosmic drama' (p. 528).

36 1.1.2.

37 Irenaeus's work is preserved in its entirety only in Latin. Most of it exists in an Armenian translation, and some (including this passage) is quoted in the original Greek by Eusebius and others.

38 2.13.3.

39 1.6.1.

40 1.15.1.

41 1.1.3.

42 1.28.3.

43 2.14.2.

44 Nor is he beyond the occasional burst of lavatory humour, best left in Latin (1.4.3)!

45 1.8.1.

46 1.9.4.

47 1.11.4.

48 5.13.2.

49 And their mumbo-jumbo 'sacraments' (1.21.3–4).

50 1.10.2; cf. 4.26.2.

51 3.3.2.

52 3.3.3–4.2.

53 The expression *kanon tes aletheias* comes in 1.9.4.

54 1.10.1; 1.22.1; 3.4.1; 4.33.8; 5.20.1; *Demonstration*, 6.

55 R. M. Grant (p. 50) calls Irenaeus 'the father of authoritative exegesis in the church'.

56 Cf. MacCullough, e.g., pp. 248–53.

57 Nos 7, 16, 18, 25.

58 Sagnard, p. 29.

59 A lovely example of Irenaeus's modern-style exegesis is his little study of the hour of Jesus in the Gospel of John (3.16.8).

60 Since Irenaeus uses the Septuagint exclusively, where the numbering of the Hebrew differs from the Greek, I give only the Greek reference.

61 In his *Apology* Justin touches on it only twice, using Jn 1.23; 3.3, neither of them in strong Christological argument. For Irenaeus, this Gospel is the basis of his strong Christology.

62 3.9.3.

63 3.17.3.

64 3.14.3.
65 Quoted 3.11.8.
66 3.11.3.
67 3.16.6.
68 3.22.2.
69 3.11.9.
70 3.18.1; cf. 3.16.6.
71 3.21.10-22.2.
72 3.18.2.
73 Cf. also 5.19.1.
74 5.23.2.
75 3.22.4.
76 3.23.3.
77 3.23.5.

Chapter 3: Origen

1 The English official translation 'irreversible turning-point' is of course a nonsense. The Italian was *una svolta irreversibile.*
2 Audience, 25 April 2007.
3 *Commentary on John,* 6.204–12) The difficulty about the texts supported by the manuscript tradition is that Gerasa is 30 kilometres from the Lake of Galilee, and Gadara a good 10 kilometres. Even this shorter distance is a very long run for a pig, whereas Gergesa plops them nicely into the lake.
4 The columns gave the biblical text in Hebrew, in a transliteration of the Hebrew into Greek letters, in the Septuagint Greek, and in three other first-century Greek versions (Aquila, Symmachus and Theodotion) – and sometimes other versions too. It was a unique bibliographical achievement, taking some 15 years to complete and running to over 6,000 pages. It was lodged at Caesarea, where it was consulted by such scholars as St Jerome, but no full copy was ever made. It is presumed to have been destroyed in the Persian invasion of the early seventh century. The remaining fragments are most conveniently available in Field, *Origenis Hexaplorum Quae Supersunt.*
5 E.g., on Jer. 15.10 in *Homily on Jeremiah,* 14.2.
6 An excellent example of his method occurs in the homily on Exodus 12–13: the Israelites departed from 'Remesse'. This name Origen interprets as 'the motion of a moth' (perhaps deriving it from the Hebrew *remes* = creeping things). He then links this to the 'moth' of the Sermon on the Mount (Mt. 6.20), which destroys the things of this world, and sees leaving Remesse to be the same as leaving behind the things of this world, and thus following Christ. In his homily on the Good Samaritan he makes play on the (false) etymology of 'Samaria' as 'guardian' to explain that Christ is the guardian, leading the wounded traveller to the Church (*Homily on Luke,* 34). In *Homily*

on 1 Samuel, 1, he interprets the name 'Samuel' as 'God is there' (literally sam-hu-el).

7 *De Principiis*, 4.3.14.
8 Bardy, pp. 217–52.
9 *Ibid.*, p. 251.
10 *Ibid.*, p. 221.
11 *Letter to Gregory*, 4, *PG* 11, col. 92.
12 For instance, legends about the childhood of a saint are particularly prone to fantasy. Eusebius relates how Origen's father used to kiss the chest of the sleeping child, as a shrine of the Holy Spirit.
13 In view of this, it is surprising that in discussing Mt. 5.28 he comments only that the command to pluck out the right eye cannot be understood literally, on the grounds that the right eye is not solely responsible (*De Principiis*, 4.3.3). If he really did castrate himself, he would surely have insisted on the literal meaning of Mt. 5.28. However, this alleged self-castration may well be part of the reason why he was never canonized by the Church as an example of sanctity.
14 Origen is clearly indebted to both of them. He frequently acknowledges his debt to Philo, but not to Clement, though Clement (c. AD 150–AD 215) was teaching at Alexandria in Origen's youth. Is this because Clement moved away to Cappadocia at the time of the persecutions in which Origen's father was martyred?
15 Origen's writing fills seven volumes of Migne's *Patrologia Graeca*, more than half the length of all the Greek patristic writers before him.
16 *Homily 5 on 1 Samuel.*
17 *Homily 7 on Joshua.*
18 *Homily 11 on Genesis.*
19 Gregory Thaumaturgus, *Address of Thanksgiving to Origen*, 6–7).
20 *De Legum Allegoria*, 1–2).
21 *Quaestiones in Gen.*, I.6).
22 *De Specialibus Legibus*, I.207).
23 *Philocalia*, 2.4.
24 *De Principiis*, 4.1.7.
25 *Homily 2 on Genesis.*
26 *De Principiis*, 4.3.2.
27 *Homily 35 on Luke*, no. 7.
28 *De Principiis*, 4.2.1.
29 *Anthropika, Homilies on Jeremiah*, 18.6.
30 *De Principiis*, 4.3.1.
31 *Homily on Genesis*, 4.3.
32 *Homily on Numbers*, 27.
33 We cannot check this extraordinary assertion, for this work of Melito is now lost. It is, however, worth remarking that while Origen calls the work 'About God being corporeal', Eusebius calls the work 'About the incarnate God' and

Rufinus (c. AD 345–411) 'About God assuming a body'. Was it a book about the Incarnation?

34 *Fragments on Genesis, Patrologia Graeca*, 12, col. 93. It is, of course, absurd to hold that Copernicus and Galileo were the first to discover that the earth was round and that it moved round the sun. This was well known to the ancient Greeks. Eratosthenes, the Librarian at Alexandria in 200 BC, calculated the circumference of the earth to 39,690 km, which is correct to within a few hundred kilometres. The slight miscalculation was the result of unawareness that it flattened at the poles.

35 *Commentary on John*, Book 10.2.

36 Book 10.19.

37 He instances the multiple wives and concubines of the patriarchs.

38 *De Principiis*, 4.2.8.

39 *De Principiis*, 4.2.9.

40 In the New Testament, *soma* (body) does not suggest any sense of inferiority. If anything, there can be a dichotomy between *pneuma* (spirit/Spirit) and *sarx* (flesh). But *sarx* represents primarily that which is human, available to be transformed and elevated by the Spirit, rather than that which is opposed to the Spirit. The 'works of the flesh' (Gal. 5.18-21) are not all bodily works. *Soma* and *sarx* must, then, be carefully differentiated.

41 *De Principiis*, 4.2.6.

42 This is unfortunate, since here the LXX is a haphazard translation of a corrupt Hebrew text. The modern understanding of the Hebrew text refers it to the 'thirty' chapters of an Egyptian Book of Wisdom, avoiding any hint of three senses.

43 Wrong again! Paul is using the Jewish argument from the analogy of a precedent. The primary meaning of the text of Deuteronomy is the rights of oxen!

44 *Homilies on the Book of Numbers*, 9, 7. Quoted by Pope Benedict XVI, Audience, 25 April 2007.

45 *Homily 4 on Joshua.*

46 *Homily 11 on Joshua.*

47 *Adv. Haer*, 4.36.7.

48 *Commentary on Matthew*, 36.

49 Jeremias, pp. 35, 37.

50 *Commentary on John*, Book 10.152.

51 The furthest he goes on historicity is to say, 'The historical meaning in our passage, if indeed it even occurred, indicates that a miracle was executed' (10.148).

52 E.g., in Justin, *Dialogue*, 81; Irenaeus, 5.34.4.

53 *De Principiis*, 2.11.2.

54 He held she was always sinless, but not that she was conceived without sin. According to Bernard, she was cleansed of sin in the womb, like the prophet Jeremiah.

55   Originally published in 1959, republished in 2002.
56   Hanson, p. 364.
57   *Ibid.*
58   Hanson, p. 371.

Chapter 4: Jerome

1   And often carelessly. To the charge that he omitted words, he cites a parallel in the insertion of words into the LXX version of Psalm 22, and replies airily to his critics, 'Let me tell them that even if I did omit a couple of words in the speed of dictation, the standing of the Churches is not affected' (Letter 77.10, *PL* 22, col. 577).
2   *PL* 29, col. 39.
3   Letter 22, *PL* 22, cols 416–17.
4   This is a perfectly fair judgement. Especially in the poetic parts of the Bible the LXX is far too respectful of the Hebrew word order and constructions to yield a coherent and intelligible rendering.
5   This was whether it was permissible to use the term *hypostasis* of the three persons of the Trinity, according to the eastern usage, or whether this was tantamount to acknowledging three separate beings or substances in the Trinity. Trinitarian terminology was still somewhat fluid, but since the West had already accepted this formula in the Synod of Alexandria (to which Jerome refers in the first letter), it is difficult to see why he wrote – unless it was to draw himself to the Pope's attention.
6   This accounts for his anachronistic depiction in Renaissance art as a cardinal.
7   Letter 20, *PL* 22, cols 375–79.
8   Letter 21, *PL* 22, cols 379–94.
9   Section 39.
10 Letter 71, *PL* 22, col. 671.
11 This is clear because in his later commentaries on the rest of the New Testament he criticizes the text he uses. It is obviously not his own translation. In the Vulgate, therefore, the Latin translation that was standard in the West until vernacular languages took over, the only part of the New Testament attributed to Jerome should be the four Gospels. The text used in the Vulgate for the Pauline epistles closely resembles that used by Pelagius in his commentary, written in the first decade of the fifth century.
12 Letter 22, 30. *PL* 22, col. 416.
13 Letter 49, 4, *PL* 22, col. 512.
14 *PL* 29, col. 525.
15 Letter 27, *PL* 22, col. 431.
16 *Ibid.*
17 Letter 45, *PL* 22, col. 481.
18 *PL* 23, col. 105.
19 Letter 22, *PL* 22, col. 412.

20 Letter 33, 4, *PL* 22, col. 447.

21 *PL* 23, 665.

22 He does indeed say this in *De Principiis* 1.1 and 2.4, but he is making a point about anthropomorphic language: God cannot be *seen*, being immaterial, but he can be *known*. The editor of the *Sources Chrétiennes*, not surprisingly, calls this a 'scandale peu explicable de Epiphane et de Jérôme'.

23 Jerome's translation of Epiphanius's letter is included among Jerome's letters, *PL* 22, cols 517–27.

24 He nicknames Vigilantius 'Dormitantius' (not 'vigilant' but 'sleepy'), suggests that his tongue should be cut out, and finally jokes that his only chance of being saved is if Origen is right that the devil himself will eventually be saved. In a later pamphlet against him, Jerome makes much of the fact that while he was staying with Jerome in Bethlehem the unfortunate Vigilantius came bursting out during a nocturnal earthquake with no clothes on (*PL* 23, 349).

25 Letter 61, *PL* 22, col. 603.

26 *PL* 23, col. 360.

27 Letter 84, *PL* 22, col. 746.

28 *Apologia against Rufinus*, 1.16.

29 Lecturing at an American university in the 1990s, I found the students surprised to find that their familiar English version was not the Bible as it came from the hand of God.

30 Letter 7, *PL* 22, col. 339.

31 Letter 125, *PL* 22, col. 1079.

32 Letter 26, *PL* 22, col. 430.

33 Letter 36, *PL* 22, col. 452.

34 *PL* 28, col. 1126.

35 The legend of the LXX translation, attaching it to Ptolemy's sponsorship, in fact applies only to the first five books of the Bible. Perhaps the translation was begun at that time, but in fact the work of translation of the various books was spread over at least a century. Even so, it reflected a Hebrew text half a millennium older and more accurate than the Hebrew texts of AD 390. The standard Hebrew text we now use is based on the Aleppo Codex, another half-millennium later than that. One important thing about the discoveries at Qumran was to reveal a Hebrew text one thousand years older than the Aleppo Codex. It is, of course, very fragmentary, Isaiah being the only complete book discovered.

36 *Hebrew Questions on the Book of Genesis*, preface, *PL* 23, cols 936–37.

37 *PL* 22, col. 573.

38 There is a difference of a single letter between this Hebrew text and the presumed Hebrew underlying the LXX.

39 See Melvin Peters's important article 'Septuagint' in *Anchor Bible Dictionary* (ed. D. N. Freedman; New York: Doubleday, 1992).

40 Letter 129.6, *PL* 22, col. 1105.

41 So his special recommendation of the book of Daniel is 'None of the prophets has spoken so clearly concerning Christ as did this prophet Daniel' (*Preface*).

42 It is not particularly helpful that a subsequent letter to Paulinus, no. 58, section 10, puts forward a succession of possible teachers and systematically rejects each of them: Tertullian, Cyprian, Victorinus, Lactantius, Arnobius and Hilary. Paulinus is left with Jerome himself 'and while I refuse to act as a master, I pledge myself to be a fellow-student' (*PL* 22, col. 549).

43 *PL* 22, col. 544.

44 He describes in exultant detail the fulfilment of the prophecies of Zephaniah about the destruction of Jerusalem, dwelling on the miseries of the Jews who come to commemorate the Fall of the Temple on its anniversary, *PL* 25, col. 1354).

45 *PL* 25, col. 1335.

46 *PL* 25, cols 1117, 1129.

47 *PL* 25, col. 349.

48 Letter 77, 11, *PL* 22, col. 577.

49 *PL* 23, col. 456.

50 Various Hebrew fragments of Ecclesiasticus (Ben Sira) have lately been discovered, so that now some two-thirds of the book is known in Hebrew.

51 Preface, *PL* 28, col. 1241.

52 *PL* 28, col. 1433.

53 *PL* 29, cols 26 and 39.

54 *PL* 28, cols 772–73.

55 *De Civitate Dei*, 18.44.

56 The fuss was about the plant that God produced to shade Jonah in Jn 4.6. In his *Commentary on Jonah*, Jerome suggests that the best translation of the Hebrew *kikiyon* was 'ivy'. *Kikiyon* apparently grows quickly in Palestine, becoming a bush (*arbusculum*), claims Jerome, in a few days (*PL* 25, 1148). The LXX translation was *cucurbita*, a sort of gourd-type plant. Jerome points out that this runs along the ground and provides no shade, but he wants to avoid introducing an outlandish new word for this plant. My guess is that he chose *kissos* (ivy) for the initial similarity of sound in Greek. Modern translations have settled for a castor-oil plant, which grows in that area, has wide leaves and can reach a height of 3 metres in a year.

57 Augustine, Letter 71, p. 327.

58 Jerome was nine years older than Augustine. In 404 Jerome was 59 years old; he was to live another 16 years.

59 Among Augustine's letters, Letter 72, *PL* 33, col. 261.

60 A paradigm case of the opposite is Ronald Knox's brilliant and scintillating translation of the Bible, produced at the request of the English hierarchy during the 1940s. For all its richness and cleverness, it is redolent of the Oxford common rooms of the period. It is a translator's translation, a joy to scholars, but too opaque to be accessible to ordinary listeners.

Chapter 5: St Bede

1 Dawson, pp. 210–11.
2 Tangl, 63. References are to the text in Tangl, *Die Briefe des Heiligen Bonifatius* – my translation.
3 Tangl, 75 and 76.
4 Tangl, 116.
5 Tangl, 91.
6 Ecclesiastical History of the English People.
7 'Kinsmen' not 'parents'. Was Bede an orphan, cared for by relations?
8 *Vita Ceolfridi*, 14.
9 Bede, Homily 1.13 on the feast of Benet Biscop, *CCSL* 122, pp. 92–93.
10 *PL* 91.454.
11 Additional Codex 37777, Additional Codex 45025 and Loan 81.
12 Meyvaert, 1995 and 1996.
13 Letter of Cuthbert to Cuthwin.
14 See Ward, Preface to *Bede: A Biblical Miscellany*, pp. xx–xxiv.
15 It does not, of course, mean 'retractation', but 're-handling'. He did not take back what he had formerly written.
16 *PL* 92, col. 997.
17 Col. 1012.
18 Col. 998.
19 *CCSL* 123A.3.5–9. Alcuin of York (AD 740–804) was a favourite pupil of Bishop Egbert, who had himself studied under Bede.
20 *PL* 90.208.
21 *PL* 93.48, on 1 Pet. 2.5.
22 Quoted by Blair, p. 204.
23 On Tob. 6.1-2. They had obviously never seen that broad and placid river.
24 The liver (Latin *iecur*) is named from fire (*ignis*), because its heat is responsible for the digestion of food. The worm (*teredo*) is so named because it eats away wood by wearing it down (*terendo*). Bede uses these gems from Isidore (AD 560–636) to throw light on Tob. 6.4 and on 2 Sam. 23.8, respectively (*PL* 91, cols 928 and 721).
25 *CCSL* 120, p. 7.
26 Augustine (AV), Ambrose (AM), Jerome (HR) and Gregory (GR). See Laistner, 'Source Marks in Bede Manuscripts'. They are indeed transcribed in several early manuscripts of the commentaries on Mark and Luke.
27 Col. 999.
28 A work most instructive to one who knows the holy places only as they are today.
29 Col. 1006.
30 Col. 1014.
31 Smalley, p. 35.
32 I am grateful to Dr Lesley Smith for this and other information about the *glossa ordinaria*.

33 *PL* 92, col. 658.
34 *PL* 92, col. 686.
35 *PL* 92, col. 690.
36 *PL* 92, cols 925–26.
37 *De Genesi ad Litteram*, 1.1.1 (*CSEL* 28.1).
38 de Lubac, p. 37, attributes the elaboration of the doctrine to Bede and his contemporary, Aldhelm of Sherborne. In Bede the passage is *PL* 91, col. 410.
39 The classic case is 'The virgin shall conceive and bear a son' (Isa. 7.14, according to the Greek version). Following the Gospel of Matthew this is understood to mean Mary's virginal conception of Jesus, but it is dangerous to invoke this *sensus plenior* without such clear biblical warrant.
40 *PL* 91, col. 425.
41 *PL* 91. cols 499–500.
42 *PL* 91, cols 923–38.
43 Jenkins, p. 180.

Chapter 6: The High Middle Ages – Bernard of Clairvaux and Thomas Aquinas

1 As Bruno Scott James humorously remarks, 'He refers to his humble profession and then, immediately, to his professions of humility. It would be impossible for him to speak of patient zeal without promptly mentioning zealous patience' (p. xv).
2 Examples are given below.
3 Bernard's use and development of this style is brilliantly analysed by Christine Mohrmann in '*Observations sur la Langue et le Style de Saint Bernard*'.
4 Abbots like to think that they are far more steadily resident in their monasteries than they in fact are.
5 It is clear that Bernard's letters were freely copied and circulated, even in their draft form (*PL* 182, 213).
6 *PL* 182, 67–79.
7 My clumsy English does not capture the delicate balance of the Latin: *Mutatus mutatum invenies, et quem ante metuebas magistrum, comitem amplectere securus.*
8 *Fugisti saevum, revertere ad mansuetum.*
9 He later writes that he would rather live at Bernard's side than be Abbot of Cluny (*PL* 189, 443).
10 *PL* 182, 901.
11 *PL* 182, 910–14.
12 *PL* 182, 535.
13 *PL* 182, 357.
14 Some 68 manuscripts from the twelfth century and early thirteenth survive, showing how widely it was used (Leclercq, p. 29).
15 The doctors of the Church were, in medieval times, each given a sobriquet.

Bernard's was *Doctor Mellifluus*. The image of flowing honey is frequent in his discussions of scripture-reading.

16 E.g., *PL* 183.45.
17 *Sermon 16 on the Song of Songs*, 1.
18 *SC* 39.3.
19 *SC* 37, 3.
20 *SC* 16, 2 (I.90).
21 *PL* 183, 718a.
22 *PL* 75, 615.
23 *SC* 22, 2 (I.130).
24 *Sermon 16 on the Song of Songs*, 1.
25 *Sermon 7 on Song of Songs*, 5.
26 *Sermon 12 on the Song of Songs*, 5.8.
27 To us this pressure is surprising, since he seems to have travelled extensively on such missions.
28 Leclerq, pp. vii–xxx. Their composition seems to have begun in 1135 and to have been unfinished at Bernard's death in 1153.
29 *Sermon 9*, 5.7.
30 *Sermon 10*, 2.2.
31 *PL* 183, 438.
32 *Opuscula I.* Marietti edition, 1954, pp. 442–43.
33 Parma edition, p. 2.
34 Letter 93, 8 (*PL* 33, 334).
35 *Quodlibet*, 17, 14 ad 3.
36 *Summa*, 1a, Q1, art 10 ad 1 um.
37 Spicq, col. 736.
38 *Summa*, I, Q1, art 1 ad 2 um.
39 Spicq complains of Thomas's '*ignorance à peine excusable*' of Greek and reproaches him '*plus vivement encore*' for his lack of Hebrew, since knowledge of Hebrew had been widespread among theologians since 1150 (cols 705–6). This is strong language for one so generous and affectionate as Père Spicq. Thomas certainly knew the Hebrew alphabet and had some idea of Hebrew tense structure, but most of his attempts at etymology of Hebrew names are faulty.

Chapter 7: Two Norfolk Ladies

1 Colledge and Walsh, pp. 41, 43.
2 *The Revelations of Julian of Norwich*, Section 4.
3 *Ibid.*, Section 9.
4 *Ibid.*, Section 51.
5 *Ibid.*, Section 5.
6 *Ibid.*, Section 7.
7 E.g., Section 17.

8   *Ibid.*, Section 26.
9   *Ibid.*, Section 2.
10   *Ibid.*, Section 3.
11   *Ibid.*, Section 8.
12   *Ibid.*, Section 4; cf. Section 25.
13   *Ibid.*, Section 15.
14   *Ibid.*, Section 6.
15   *Ibid.*, Sections 45, 46, 49.
16   *Ibid.*, Section 50.
17   Julian does not, of course, intend a complete equality between Adam's culpable fall into sin and the *kenosis* of God's Son, the second person of the Trinity, by which he 'fell' from heaven to earth.
18   Section 57.
19   Extracts from the text were published by one of the first English printers, Wynkyn de Worde, in 1501, but the full manuscript, a fifteenth-century copy of the original, was made known only in 1934. For generations it had been in the possession of an old Catholic family, the Butler-Bowdens. In the late medieval period this manuscript had been in the library of Mount Grace Priory; it carries some annotations made there.
20   Chapter 72. All references are to Book 1 unless explicitly to Book 2.
21   Chapter 4.
22   Chapter 11.
23   Book 2, chapter 4.
24   Bhattacharji, p. 4, argues that he may be the original scribe, who wrote in a mixture of German and English. She does indeed say that 'she opened her heart to him, showing and informing him how our Lord had drawn her through his mercy and by what means' (Book 2, chapter 2).
25   Book 2, chapter 2.
26   Chapter 1.
27   Chapter 2.
28   Chapter 57.
29   Chapter 61.
30   Chapter 62.
31   Bhattacharji, p. 51.
32   Chapter 14.
33   Chapters 6 and 7.
34   In his letter to his sister on prayer, *De Institutione*, ch. 14, 17–22.
35   Chapter 28.
36   Chapter 44.
37   Chapters 34 and 35.
38   Owing to the difficulty or impossibility of obtaining pure drinking-water, wine was no luxury but a necessity.
39   Quoted in Beauchesne, col. 329.
40   Chapter 36.

41 Chapter 38.
42 Chapter 54.
43 Chapter 47.
44 Chapter 52.
45 Knowles, p. 48.
46 Bhattacharji, p. 139.

Chapter 8: Martin Luther

1 The standard German edition, the Weimar Ausgabe, stretches to 105 volumes, including Luther's letters and his table talk.
2 Pelagius (fl. AD 418) is commonly thought of as the archetype of the Englishman, 'the self-made man who worships his maker'.
3 Perhaps more important was the 'semi-Pelagian' view that if a person plays their own part (*quantum in se est*), God will respond with the gift of grace. The usual analogy was a coin made of base metal: such a coin will be rewarded with goods to the full face value of the coin, far exceeding the value of the metal itself, see below, p. 116.
4 The 50th of Luther's famous 95 theses was, 'The whole of Aristotle is to theology as darkness is to light'. It is important to realize, as is clear in this instance, that the theses were not calmly considered views, but were deliberately provocative propositions for debate.
5 *Works*, vol. 31, p. 281.
6 *Ibid.*, p. 322. See also Eck's account of the debate in Bettenson, pp. 192–93.
7 Naphy, p. 18.
8 Bettenson, p. 197.
9 In fact Isidoro Isolani.
10 *Works*, vol. 36, p. 18.
11 For example, Beasley-Murray, p. 87.
12 For example, Brown, p. 272.
13 Works, vol. 36 (Philadelphia: Fortress Press), p. 21.
14 p. 26.
15 p. 31.
16 p. 32.
17 p. 34.
18 Bettenson, p. 197.
19 *WA* 26, 462.
20 Bettenson, p. 201.
21 See below, p. 115.
22 p. 345.
23 *Works*, 37 (1961), p. 231.
24 *WA* 18, 166; 26, 487.
25 *WA* 26, 483.
26 *WA* 26, 317.

27 *WA* 30.2, 687.
28 *Appeal to the German Nobility.* See Bettenson, p. 195.
29 *WA* 40.1, 458.
30 *WA* DB 6, 10.
31 *WA* DB 404.
32 *WA* DB 8, 12.
33 *WA* 8.87.
34 *WA* 40.1, 132.
35 *WA* 17.1, 232.
36 *WA* 39.1, 189.
37 *WA* 7, 323.
38 *Works,* vol 36 (Philadelphia: Fortress Press, p. 40).
39 *Ibid.,* p. 41.
40 *Ibid.,* p. 54.
41 *Ibid.,* p. 55.
42 *Works,* vol. 34, pp. 336–37.
43 The Greek in Genesis 15 and Romans 4 is *elogisthe,* a word used in the language of accountancy.
44 Quoted in Althaus, p. 228.
45 *WA* 7, 24.
46 Quoted in Althaus, p. 240.
47 *WA* 39.1, 46 and 114.
48 *WA* 10.3, 225.
49 'Preface to Romans', *WA* DB 7, 10–11.
50 *Diatribe* does not, of course mean 'diatribe' in the modern sense. In the modern sense the word suggests an intemperate harangue. To Erasmus it was a classical technical term for a certain kind of rhetorical argument.
51 Luther, M., *Freewill and Salvation,* ed. E. G. Rupp and P. S. Watson (Philadelphia: Westminster Press).
52 *Ibid.,* p. 39.
53 He uses the unusual term *conglutinatio,* 'sticking together', which must surely be a gentle joke.
54 *Ibid.,* p. 42.
55 I assume that the 'Gregory', penultimate in the chronological list, is Gregory of Rimini (AD 1300–1358), who wrote much on this subject, not Pope Gregory the Great.
56 There exists an amusing letter of Erasmus, terribly put out because in 1499 Thomas More took him on a walk to visit the royal children. The eight-year-old future King Henry VIII presented him with a Latin poem to which he, the greatest scholar in Christendom, had no reply ready.
57 *Ibid.,* p. 113.
58 *Ibid.,* p. 26.
59 *Ibid.,* p. 293.

Chapter 9: The Bible in the Politics of Early Seventeenth-century England

1 Cf. Rowland, *Radical Christianity*.
2 The same prohibition was made by the Archbishop of Mainz in 1485 on the grounds that 'the lack of the German language does not permit the rendering of the highest ideas of the Christian religion without distortion and falsification' (Raeder, p. 396).
3 Cf. Duffy, p. 422.
4 Henry VIII, p. 421.
5 Cf. Norman Sykes in Greenslade, p. 176.
6 James I, *Works*, p. 530.
7 http://www.stoics.com/basilikon_doron.html (accessed 4 April 2008).
8 Hill, p. 34.
9 Milton, vol I, p. 747.
10 It is, of course, significant that the names of both of Hobbes's major works, *Leviathan* and *Behemoth*, were biblical, drawn from the Book of Job, chapters 40–41.
11 James I, gauche, frank and uncouth as he was, had no hesitation in justifying his relationship with George Villiers, Earl of Buckingham, to the Lords of the Council in the same way: 'I, James, am neither God nor an angel, but a man like any other. Therefore I act like a man, and confess to loving those dear to me more than other men. You may be sure that I love the Earl of Buckingham more than anyone else, and more than you who are here assembled. I wish to speak in my own behalf, and not to have it thought to be a defect, for Jesus Christ did the same, and therefore I cannot be blamed. Christ had his John, and I have my George' (quoted in Kenyon, p. 59).
12 *Calendar of State Papers, Domestic, 1619–23*, p. 551.
13 Hunt, p. 201.
14 J. Morrill in Schochet, p. 95.
15 '"Curse Meroz", said the angel of the Lord, "curse, curse the people living there for not having come to the Lord's help, to the Lord's help as warriors"' (Judg. 5.23).
16 Trevor-Roper, p. 47.

Chapter 10: John and Charles Wesley

1 Including such memorable favourites as 'Lo, He Comes with Clouds Descending'; 'Come Thou Long-expected Jesus'; 'Hark, the Herald Angels Sing'; 'O for a Thousand Tongues to Sing'; 'Love Divine, All Loves Excelling'; 'Gentle Jesus, Meek and Mild'. But everyone has their own favourites.
2 John Lawson, in his analysis of the Wesleys' hymns, *A Thousand Tongues*, gives a scriptural reference for almost every line of the hymns.
3 Not to be confused with his eldest son, Samuel, who was 13 years older than John, and to some extent his mentor, nor with his more famous grandson,

Samuel (1766–1837), Charles's son, a musical prodigy (at the age of 16 he presented the score of his oratorio *Ruth* to Dr Boyce) and much-loved organist and composer of church music.

4 Rattenbury, p. 16.
5 Shepard, *Everybody's Johnson*, p. 290.
6 Listed by Jones, p. 250, footnote 47.
7 Quoted by Rattenbury, p. 260.
8 *Journal*, 3.431.
9 *Journal*, 2.135.
10 Both quoted by Leaver, p. 163.
11 *Journal*, 1–8 June, 1738.
12 Charles experimented boldly with metre. In the first half of the eighteenth century the hugely predominant metre (considered by Dr Johnson to be the only true English metre) was the heroic couplet beloved of Pope and Dryden. Wesley courageously uses the metres of popular song, which would immediately appeal to his audiences.
13 Jones points out (p. 207) that John's argument is weak, in that neither of the two cases quoted is really parallel to the words of Jesus. The first refers to the interpretation of a dream, the second to the interpretation of an allegory.
14 I would hazard that Charles is thinking of the Greek text rather than the King James Version (KJV), for the allusion is less clear in the KJV than in the Greek. Similarly, the Greek underlying 'the antepast (foretaste) of heaven', referring to the pledge of the Spirit (2 Cor. 1.22), is never so translated in the KJV. In another hymn, he 'emptied himself [of all but love]' translates literally the Greek less accurately rendered by the KJV 'made himself of no reputation'.
15 This, too, accords with the rich patristic tradition. Compare St Ambrose: 'In the Book of the Psalms not only is Jesus born for us; he accepts too his saving passion, he dies, he rises from the dead and ascends into heaven and sits at the Father's right hand' (*In Psalmos* 1, 4.7–8).
16 Compare: My Jesus to know, / And feel his blood flow / 'Tis life everlasting / 'Tis heaven below.
17 The whole experience is minutely and movingly described in his journal entry for 24 May 1738.
18 Quoted by Jones, p. 97.
19 *Ibid.*, p. 190.
20 *Journal*, 6 September 1742.
21 Sutherland, p. 13.

Chapter 11: Newman

1 Fontana Books, 1959, from which edition the quotations given here are taken.
2 Review of Froude's *History of England* in *Macmillan's Magazine*, January 1864.

3   Ignatius, Bishop of Antioch, was one of the earliest Church writers. Martyred in Rome, c. 115, on his way there he wrote letters to seven different churches. These letters are the first evidence for the triple structure of bishop, presbyter and deacon. In each letter he stresses that the bishop is the shepherd of his flock, and stresses the importance of loyalty to the bishop.

4   Tract 85 is most conveniently available in Newman, *Discussions and Arguments on Various Subjects*, pp. 109–253. The quotations are from pp. 126–27.

5   *Ibid.*, pp. 146–47.

6   Quotations are taken from the Penguin edition.

7   Chapter 1, Section 1.

8   *Ibid.*, Section III.

9   Dulles stresses that 'In the midst of the chapter on the seventh note, Newman abruptly ended his book. Having written enough to answer his own question, he made his profession of faith' (p. 76). Hence 'The book should not be treated as though it aimed to present a finished theory' (p. 79).

10 Chapter 4.

11 Chapter 5.

12 See below, Chapter 12, p. 170.

13 An Oxford theologian, also fellow of Eton, prominent in the early seventeenth century. He veered between Calvinism and Arminianism.

14 Soon to be known as the 'Seven against Christ', a neat classical allusion to the play of Aechylus, 'The Seven against Thebes'.

15 Quoted in Newman, *The Letters and Diaries of John Henry Newman*, vol. xix, p. 477.

16 E.g., Newman, *On the Inspiration of Scripture*, p. 126.

17 *Ibid.*, p. 143.

18 Newman, *On the Inspiration of Scripture*, pp. 107–8.

19 *Ibid.*, pp. 108–10.

20 *Ibid.*, p. 133.

21 *Ibid.*, p. 136.

22 Newman, *Letters and Diaries*, vol. XXX.

23 Newman, *Parochial and Plain Sermons II*, p. 208.

24 Newman, *Discussions and Arguments on Various Subjects*, pp. 154–56.

25 Clifford, p. 319.

26 *Letters and Diaries of John Henry Newman*, vol. XXX, p. 176.

Chapter 12: The Bible and the State of Israel

1   Quoted by Tuchman, p. 314.

2   The words of Lord Curzon to the British Cabinet.

3   Schindler, vol. 3, p. 97.

4   Aharoni, p. xiii.

5   Heller, p. 140.

6   Letter of 15.10.1941, quoted by Masalha, p. 49.

7   Wright, p. 126.
8   See Gottwald, *The Tribes of Yahweh*. He writes also of 'this stress-torn Canaanite society, which was in still further decline' (p. 214).
9   Wright, p. 109.
10 *Ibid.*, p. 110.
11 Whitelam, p. 90.
12 Trigger, p. 358.
13 Meyers, p. 184.
14 Bright, p. 179.
15 Arnold, p. 52.

Chapter 13: *Lectio Divina*

1   Athanasius, *Life of Antony*, c. 2.
2   Augustine, *Confessions*, Book 8.
3   Amply attested in Magrassi, *Praying the Bible*, which is a sort of paean of praise for the monastic tradition of *lectio divina*.
4   *Dei Verbum*, Section 8.
5   *Ibid.*, Section 12.
6   *Ibid.*, Section 15.
7   *Ibid.*, Section 21.
8   *Ibid.*, Section 23.
9   *Ibid.*, Section 25.
10 *Ibid.*
11 *PL* 184, col. 476.
12 For instance, Bianchi, pp. 100–14; Foster, p. 3; Magrassi, pp. 103–19. It is striking that the earliest reference to Guigo II I have found in standard reference works is in the *Catechism of the Catholic Church* (1994), section 2654. He is listed only in the third edition of the *Oxford Companion to the Christian Church*.
13 *Dei Verbum*, Section 25.

Bibliography

Abbreviations

CCSL   *Corpus Christianorum Series Latina* (Turnholt: Brepols, 1953–)
CSEL   *Corpus Scriptorum Ecclesiasticorum Latinorum* (Vienna: Libraria
          Academica Wagneriana, 1886–)
PG   *Patrologia Graeca* (ed. J-P Migne, Paris)
PL   *Patrologia Latina* (ed. J-P Migne, Paris)
SC   *Sources Chrétiennes* (Paris Editions du Cerf, 1946–)
WA   *Martin Luthers Werke Kritische Gesamtausgabe* (Weimar, 1883–)

Other Books

Ackroyd, P. R., and C. E. Evans (eds), *The Cambridge History of the Bible,* vol. 1
    (Cambridge: Cambridge University Press, 1970).
Aharoni, Y., *The Archaeology of the Land of Israel* (London: SCM, ²1982).
Althaus, P., *The Theology of Martin Luther* (Philadelphia: Fortress Press,
    1966).
Arnold, P. M., *Gibeah: The Search for a Biblical City* (Sheffield: Sheffield
    Academic Press, 1990).
Bardy, G., 'Les traditions juives dans l'oeuvre d'Origène', *Revue biblique* 34
    (1925), pp. 217–52.
Barrett, C. K., 'Interpretation of the Old Testament in the New Testament',
    Cambridge History of the Bible (vol. 1; Cambridge: Cambridge University
    Press, 1970).
—*The Gospel According to Saint Mark* (Cambridge: Cambridge University
    Press, 1955).
Beasley-Murray, G. R., *John* (Dallas, TX: Word Inc., 1987).
Bernard of Clairvaux, *A la louange de la vierge mère* (Sources Chrétiennes,
    390; Paris: Le Cerf, 1993).
—*Cistercians and Cluniacs: St Bernard's Apologia to Abbot William* (trans.
    M Casey; Kalamazoo, MI: Cistercian Publications, 1970).

202 *Bibliography*

—*Selected Works* (New York: Paulist Press, 1987).

—*The Works of Bernard of Clairvaux* (*On the Song of Songs*, vols 2–5; trans. K. Walsh and I. Edmonds; Kalamazoo, MI: Cistercian Publications, 1971, 1983, 1979, 1980).

Bettenson, H., *Documents of the Christian Church* (Oxford: Oxford University Press, 1967).

Bhattacharji, S., *God is an Earthquake* (London: Darton, Longman & Todd, 1997).

Bianchi, E., *Praying the Word: An Introduction to Lectio Divina* (Kalamazoo, MI: Cistercian Publications, 1998).

Bible and Morality, The (Vatican: Libreria Editrice Vaticana, 2008).

Black, M., 'Christological Use of the Old Testament in the New Testament' *New Testament Studies* 18 (1971/72), pp. 1–14.

Bright, J., *History of Israel* (London: SCM Canterbury Press, ²1972).

Brown, R. E., *The Gospel According to John* (New York: Doubleday, 1966).

Bultmann, R., *The History of the Synoptic Tradition* (Oxford; Blackwell, 1963).

Burtchaell, J. T., *Catholic Theories of Biblical Inspiration Since 1810* (Cambridge: Cambridge University Press, 1969).

Chadwick, O., *The Early Reformation on the Continent* (Oxford: Oxford University Press, 2001).

Clifford, W., 'The Days of the Week and the Works of Creation', *Dublin Review* 5 (1881), pp. 311–32.

Colledge, E. (ed.), *The Medieval Mystics of England* (London: John Murray, 1962).

Colledge, E., and Walsh, J. (ed.), *A Book of Showings to the Anchoress Julian of Norwich* (Toronto: Pontifical Institute of Medieval Studies, 1978).

Crossan, J. D., *The Historical Jesus* (San Francisco: HarperSanFrancisco, 1991).

Daniélou, J., *Origen* (London and New York: Sheed & Ward, 1955).

Darwin, C., *The Origin of Species* (London: Everyman, 1911).

Davies, B., *The Thought of Thomas Aquinas* (Oxford: Clarendon Press, 1992).

Dawson, C., *The Making of Europe* (New York: Sheed & Ward, 1939).

de Lubac, H., *Medieval Exegesis* (vol. 2; London: T&T Clark, 2000).

Dictionnaire de spiritualité, ed. Ch. Baumgartner, vol. 2 (Paris: Letouzey, 1953).

Duffy, E., *The Stripping of the Altars* (New Haven, CT: Yale University Press, 1992).

Dulles, A., *John Henry Newman* (London: Continuum, 2009).

Dunn, J., *Jesus Remembered* (Grand Rapids, MI: Eerdmans, 2003).

—*Unity and Diversity in the New Testament* (London: SCM Canterbury Press, 1977).

Evans, G. R., *Bernard of Clairvaux* (Oxford: Oxford University Press, 2000).

Farkasfalvy, D., 'The Role of the Bible in St Bernard's Spirituality', *Analecta Cisterciensia* 25 (1969), pp. 3–13.

Field, F., *Origenis Hexaplorum Quae Supersunt* (Oxford: Oxford University Press, 1875).

Fitzmyer, J., 'The Use of Explicit Old Testament Quotations in the Qumran Literature', *New Testament Studies* 7 (1961), pp. 1–14.

Foster, D., *Reading with God* (London: Continuum, 2005).

France, R. T., *The Gospel of Matthew* (Grand Rapids, MI: Eerdmans, 2007).

Geisler, N. L., *Thomas Aquinas* (Grand Rapids, MI: Baker Book House, 1991).

Gerhardsson, B., *Memory and Manuscript* (Uppsala, Sweden: Gleerup, 1961).

Gilson, E., *The Mystical Theology of St Bernard* (Kalamazoo, MI: Cistercian Publications, 1990).

Goodman, A., *Margery Kempe and Her World* (Harlow, Essex: Pearson Education Ltd, 2002).

Gottwald, N., *The Tribes of Yahweh: A Sociology of the Religion of Liberated Israel, 1250–1050 BCE* (London: SCM Canterbury Press, 1979).

Grant, R. M., *Irenaeus of Lyons* (London: Routledge, 1997).

Grant, R. M., and D. Tracy, *A Short History of the Interpretation of the Bible* (London: SCM Canterbury Press, [2]1994).

Greenslade, S. L. (ed.), *Cambridge History of the Bible* (Cambridge: Cambridge University Press, 1963).

Hanson, A. T., *New Testament Interpretation of Scripture* (London: SPCK, 1980).

Hanson, R. P. C., *Allegory and Event* (Westminster: John Knox Press, 2002).

Hattersley, R., *A Brand from the Burning* (New York: Little, Brown, 2002).

Hayward, C. T. R., *Jerome's Hebrew Questions on Genesis* (Oxford: Clarendon, 1995).

Heller, Y., *Bamavak Lemedinah* (in Hebrew; Jerusalem, 1984).

Henry VIII, *Letters of Henry VIII* (ed. M. St. Clare Byrne; London: Cassell, 1968).

Hill, C., *The English Bible and the Seventeenth Century Revolution* (London: Allen Lane, 1993).

Hunt, W., *The Puritan Movement* (Cambridge, MA: Harvard University Press, 1983).

Hunter Blair, P., *Northumbria in the Days of Bede* (London: Gollancz, 1976).

James I, *Works*.

Jenkins, C., 'Bede as Exegete and Theologian', *Bede, His Life, Times and Writings* (ed. A. Hamilton Thompson; Oxford: Clarendon Press, 1935).

Jeremias, J., *The Parables of Jesus* (London: SCM Canterbury Press, 1975).

Jewish People and Its Holy Scriptures in the Christian Bible, The (Vatican: Libreria Editrice Vaticana, 2001).

Johansen, K. F., *A History of Ancient Philosophy* (London: Routledge, 1998).

Jones, S. J., *John Wesley's Conception and Use of Scripture* (Nashville, TN: Kingswood Press, 1995).

Julian of Norwich, *The Revelations of Julian of Norwich* (ed. and trans. Father John-Julian, Order of Julian of Norwich; London: Darton: Longman & Todd, 1988).

Kelly, J. N. D., *Jerome* (London: Duckworth, 1975).

Kempe, Margery, *The Book of Margery Kempe* (trans. B. A. Windeatt; Harmondsworth: Penguin, 1985).

Kenny, A., *Aquinas* (Oxford: Oxford University Press, 1980).

Kenyon, J. P., *The Stuarts* (London: Batsford, 1958).

Ker, I., *John Henry Newman: A Biography* (Oxford: Clarendon Press, 1988).

Knowles, D., *The English Mystical Tradition* (London: Burns & Oates, 1964).

Küng, H., *Great Christian Thinkers* (London: SCM Canterbury Press, 1994).

Laistner, M. L. W., 'Source-marks in Bede Manuscripts', *Journal of Theological Studies* 34 (1933), pp. 350–54.

Lawson, J., *A Thousand Tongues* (Exeter, UK: Paternoster Press, 1987).

Leaver, R. A., 'Charles Wesley and Anglicanism', *Charles Wesley, Poet and Theologian* (ed. S. T. Kimbrough; Nashville, TN: Kingswood Books, 1992).

Leclercq, J., *Bernard of Clairvaux and the Cistercian Spirit* (Kalamazoo, MI: Cistercian Publications, 1976).

—*Receuil d'études sur Saint Bernard et ses ecrits* (Roma: Edizioni di Storia e Letteratura).

—vol. 1 (1962) 'Aux sources des sermons sur les cantiques', pp. 275–320.

—vol. 3 (1969) 'De quelques procédés du style biblique de S. Bernard', pp. 249–66.

—vol. 4 (1987) 'Le cheminement biblique de la pensée de S. Bernard', pp. 11–34.

Luther, M., *Luther and Erasmus: Free Will and Salvation* (ed. E. Gordon Rupp and Philip S. Watson; Philadelphia: Westminster Press, 1969).

McCabe, H., *On Aquinas* (London: Continuum, 2008).

MacCullough, D., *The Reformation: Europe's House Divided 1490–1700* (Harmondsworth: Penguin Books, 2003).

McGrath, A., *In the Beginning: The Story of the King James Bible* (London: Hodder & Stoughton, 2001).

—*Reformation Thought: An Introduction* (Oxford and New York: Blackwell, 1988).

McKim, D. (ed.), *Historical Handbook of Major Biblical Interpreters* (Westmont, IL: InterVarsity Press, 1998).

Magrassi, M., *Praying the Bible* (Collegeville, MN: Liturgical Press, 1998).

Masalha, N., *The Bible and Zionism* (London: Zed Books, 2007).

Meyers, C., 'The Israelite Empire: In Defense of King Solomon', *Backgrounds for the Bible* (ed. M. P. O'Connor and D. N. Freedman; Winona Lake: Eisenbrauns, 1987).

Meyvaert, P., 'Bede, Cassiodorus and the Codex Amiatinus', *Speculum* 71 (1996), pp. 827–84.

Meyvaert, P., 'Bede's Capitula Lectionum for the Old and New Testaments', *Revue Benedictine* 105 (1995).

Milton, J., *Milton's Complete Prose Works* (New Haven, NY: Yale University Press, 1953–1982).

Minns, D., *Irenaeus* (London: Geoffrey Chapman, 1994).

Mohrmann, C., 'Observations sur la langue et le style de Saint Bernard', *Sancti Bernardi opera* (vol. 2 ; Rome: Editiones Cistercienses, 1958).

Naphy, W. R. (ed.), *Documents on the Continental Reformation* (Basingstoke: Macmillan, 1996).

Newman, J. H., *Apologia pro Vita Sua* (London: Fontana Books, 1959).

—*Discussion and Arguments on Various Subjects* (London: Longmans, 1924).

—*Essay on the Development of Christian Doctrine* (Harmondsworth: Penguin Books, 1973).

—*The Letters and Diaries of John Henry Newman* (ed. Stephen Dessain; vols. xix and xxx; London: Nelson, 1969).

—*On the Inspiration of Scripture* (ed. J. Derek Holmes and Robert Murray; London: Geoffrey Chapman, 1969).

—*Opera Omnia* (ed. J. P. Migne) [*Patrologia Latina*, pp. 182–5].

—*Parochial and Plain Sermons* (vol. II; London: Rivingtons, 1873).

Philo, *Works* (trans. C. D. Yonge; Peabody, MA: Hendrickson, 1993).

Pieper, J., *Introduction to Thomas Aquinas* (London: Faber & Faber, 1963).

Porter, S. (ed.), *The Scrolls and the Scriptures* (ed. S. Porter, Sheffield: Sheffield Academic Press, 1997).

Raeder, S., *Hebrew Bible Old Testament II* (ed. M Saebo; Göttingen: Vandenhoeck & Ruprecht, 2008).

Rattenbury, J. E., *Wesley's Legacy to the World* (London: Epworth Press, 1928).

Rebenich, S., *Jerome* (London: Routledge, 2002).

Rowland, C., *Radical Christianity* (Cambridge, UK: Polity Press, 1988).

Sagnard, F., *Irénée de Lyon contre les hérésies* (vol. 3; Paris: Editions du Cerf, 1952).

Schindler, C., *Israel: The First Hundred Years* (ed. E. Karsh; London: Frank Cass, 2002).

Schochet, G. J. (ed.), *Religion, Resistance and Civil War* (Washington DC: The Folger Institute, 1990).

Scott James, B., *The Letters of St Bernard of Clairvaux* (London: Burns & Oates, 1953).

Shepard, E. H. (ed.), *Everybody's Johnson* (London: Bell, 1930).

Simonetti, M., *Biblical Interpretation in the Early Church* (London: T&T Clark, 1994).

Smalley, B., *The Study of the Bible in the Middle Ages* (Oxford: Blackwell, 1952).

Sparks, H. F. D. (ed.), *The Apocryphal Old Testament* (Oxford: Clarendon Press, 1984).

Spicq, C., 'S. Thomas exégète', *Dictionnaire de théologie Catholique* 15.1
    (Paris : Letouzey, 1946).
Steinmann, J., *St Jerome* (London: Geoffrey Chapman, 1959).
Sutherland, J. (ed.), *A Preface to Eighteenth Century Poetry* (Oxford:
    Clarendon Press, 1948).
Tangl, M. (ed.), *Die Briefe des Heiligen Bonifatius* (Berlin: Weidmannsche
    Buchhandlung, 1916).
Tanner, Norman P. (ed.) *Decrees of the Ecumenical Councils* (London, Sheed
    and Ward, and Georgetown University Press, 1990).
Todd, J. M., *Luther* (London: Hamish Hamilton, 1982).
Tomkins, S., *John Wesley: A Biography* (Oxford: Lion Publishing, 2003).
Trevor, M., *Newman: The Pillar of the Cloud* (London: Macmillan, 1962).
—*Newman: Light in Winter* (London: Macmillan, 1962).
Trevor-Roper, H., *The Crisis of the Seventeenth Century: Religion, the Reformation
    and Social Change* (reprinted; Indianapolis: Liberty Fund, 2001).
Trigg, J. W., *Origen* (London: Routledge, 1998).
Trigger, B., 'Alternative Archaeologies: Nationalist, Colonialist, Imperialist',
    Man 19 (1984), pp. 355–70.
Tuchman, B. W., *Bible and Sword* (London: Macmillan, 1957).
Vermes, G., *The Dead Sea Scrolls in English* (Harmondsworth: Penguin,
    ⁴1995).
Von Balthasar, H. U., *Origen: Spirit and Fire* (Washington, DC: Catholic
    University of America, 1984).
Waller, R., *John Wesley: A Personal Portrait* (London: Continuum, 2003).
Wansbrough, H., 'Jewish Methods of Exegesis in the New Testament',
    Studien zum Neuen Testament und Seiner Umwelt 25 (2000), pp. 219–44.
Ward, B., 'Preface', *Bede: A Biblical Miscellany* (ed. W. T. Foley and A. G.
    Holder; Liverpool: Liverpool University Press, 1999).
—*The Venerable Bede* (London: Geoffrey Chapman, 1980).
Whitelam, K. W., *The Invention of Ancient Israel* (London: Routledge, 1996).
—*Works* (Philadelphia: Fortress Press, 1955–1975).
Wright, G. E., *The Book of the Acts of God: Christian Scholarship Interprets the
    Bible* (London: Duckworth, 1960).
Young, F., *The Art of Performance* (London: Darton, Longman & Todd,
    1990).

Index

207

208 *Index*